158

WHEN AM I
GOING TO
BE HAPPY?

Also by Penelope Russianoff, Ph.D.

Why Do I Think I Am Nothing Without a Man?

WHEN AM I GOING TO BE HAPPY?

How to Break the Emotional Bad Habits
That Make You Miserable

Dr PENELOPE RUSSIANOFF

CEDAR

An Imprint of William Heinemann Limited

Published by Cedar Books
an imprint of William Heinemann Limited
Michelin House, 81 Fulham Road, London SW3 6RB

LONDON MELBOURNE AUCKLAND

0 434 11163 5

First published 1988 in the U.S.A. and Canada by
Bantam Books, New York
First published in Great Britain 1989

Printed in Finland by
Werner Söderström Osakeyhtiö

Dedication . . . to my mentors

—To my father, Raymond Pearl, Ph.D., who taught me to live life with curiosity.

—Count Alfred Korzybsky, who taught me the discipline of General Semantics, in which I learned to be aware of what I say and not to confuse words with things or fantasies with realities.

—Leslie White, Ph.D., who taught me to be aware of cultural evolution and not to be caught up unwittingly in its force.

—Albert Ellis, Ph.D., who taught me that it is not so much what happens that causes emotional misery but what you tell yourself about what happened.

—Lionel Ovesey, M.D., who has helped me see the best in myself.

Acknowledgments

———————————————●———————————————

This book came into being because of the faith, encouragement, and help of many of my friends and colleagues. Among them, I want to thank first Linda Grey, president and publisher of Bantam Books, for her immediate belief in the project. Likewise, I am grateful to my editors at Bantam, Peter Guzzardi and Barbara Alpert, for their confidence in the book's message and their superb editorial guidance.

The book is an outgrowth of a course I taught at the New School for Social Research, and there I thank Carla Stevens and Allen Austill for the freedom they have given me to explore new course themes.

Among my colleagues, Sandi Mendelsohn helped me to clarify my thoughts from the jigsaw puzzle of ideas I wanted to express in the book. Letty Cottin Pogrebin also convinced me that I had a useful concept to deliver. While many years my junior, Letty remains a model for me. My other model is Sonya Friedman, who, in the midst of her busy life, always manages to find time to be my confidante, and to advise me, as she did on this project. I am especially grateful to my friend Janet Wolfe, who critiques my work with total honesty and invaluable suggestions. My good friends Mark and Maressa Gershowitz both read the manuscript in progress with enthusiasm and offered sound advice.

Next, I want to express my gratitude to my friend, lawyer, and literary agent, Richard Levy, for his indispensable role.

There are many other friends who may not be aware that, through their closeness to me, the example of their own lives validated many of my convictions as expressed here. Among them, I particularly want to thank Phyllis Haynes, Lillian Gilden, Lawrence Balter, Ph.D., Karen Adams, Karen Chanow-Gruen, Ph.D., Peter Gruen, M.D., and Malvine Cole. Special thanks to Louise Graves, who gave up part of her vacation to review the manuscript with me.

I owe a special debt of gratitude to Harry Holtzman, a caring friend for over forty years, who forced me to stretch my thinking in directions I would never have imagined possible. I also thank Michael Mattioli, a cherished friend who encouraged me all along to promote my ideas through books and in other directions that my career has taken.

Confidentiality is, of course, essential in my practice. Consequently, I have altered the names and certain other details in the cited case histories to provide my students and clients with anonymity while preserving the essential message and lesson of each case.

I am grateful to my children, Sylvia and Charlie, who held up a mirror before me, thus helping me to understand myself as I learned to understand them. And to Leon, my beloved husband, my thanks for encouraging me to apply to myself the principles I urge on others and for his unfailing love and unstinting support through this as well as all my other endeavors.

Finally, I wish to acknowledge my gratitude and admiration for the talents of my valued friend Joseph E. Persico, who wrote this book with me.

Contents

———■———

CONTENTS

WHEN AM I
GOING TO BE
HAPPY?

INTRODUCTION

In the fall of 1986, I gave a course at the New School in New York City entitled "Handling The Negative Emotions: Your Own and Others'." I had developed the course after observing something very disturbing to me in my clinical practice: many of my patients were psychologically crippled by their chronic negative emotional habits. They faced life feeling habitually guilty, rejected, depressed, inferior, or any of a dozen other negative emotions that virtually guaranteed their unhappiness.

How ironic, I thought. Here we are a nation that has elevated the pursuit of happiness to a constitutional right, yet millions of us are going around stuck in self-destructive behavior. I have patients, students, and friends who "know" that they are worthless; who live in a constant state of depression; who feel helpless; who are crushed by reverses that most of us would shrug off; who assume that everything in their lives must go wrong. They look at the world through gray-colored glasses. Worst of all, they are convinced that their negativism is a fixed part of their character. That is the way they are. They "cannot change."

More than thirty years of clinical practice have convinced me of just the opposite. Emotional bad habits are just that—habits that we form. And because we formed them, we can break them. People who are guilt-ridden, depressed, hysterical, phobic, or self-flagellating are not doomed by their genes. They are not predestined to be miserable and frustrated forever. They have simply practiced their bad habits for so long that they have come to think of them as immutable parts of themselves. Not true. Their negative behavior is a learned reflex. And just as it was learned, it can be unlearned.

Of course, habitual negative behavior may have and often does have understandable root causes—for example, a child deserted by a parent, who then goes through life expecting to be rejected. But much of our habitual negativity can be explained by cultural clichés that surround us and that we unthinkingly swallow. This negativism is *imposed* on us by society. We are hemmed in by *Supposed-tos, Supposed-not-tos, Ought-tos, Ought-not-tos, Musts,* and *Must-nots.* We are cowed by cultural claptrap that tells us how we are expected to feel and think, whether these clichés fit our lives or not. And just as we can break emotional bad habits, we can escape the cultural clichés that they feed on.

Because I see so many lives blighted by negative emotional habits, and because I know that these habits can be conquered, I began to develop a course for the New School designed to:

- Help students recognize habitual negative behavior in themselves

- Help them become aware of the cultural clichés that encourage their negative thinking

- Convince them that these bad habits can be broken and replaced by healthy responses to life

2

We were frankly astonished by the response to the course. So many students signed up that the administration closed off enrollment. Those who were shut out kicked up such a fuss that the school reopened enrollment. We finally had to hold the course in an auditorium.

I have never taught a course in which students—students of all ages and both sexes—reacted so intensely. I felt that I had touched a universal nerve. If I could sum up the students' reaction in a sentence, it was this: "Yes, that's me. I am hung up on my negative emotional habits. And they *are* ruining my life. Thank God, this woman thinks I can change."

A few years before, I had given another course, entitled "Why Do I Think I Am Nothing Without a Man?" That course also found an eager audience. Later, my students and colleagues persuaded me to write a book on the subject, with the same title: *Why Do I Think I Am Nothing Without a Man?* The book became a best-seller. After I completed the course on negative emotional habits, my publisher persuaded me to give its message far wider circulation. The result is *When Am I Going to Be Happy?: How to Break the Emotional Bad Habits That Make You Miserable.*

In this book, as in the course, I will explain what our negative emotions are and how we got them in the first place. Far more important, the book deals with answers—how you can throw off the addiction of habitual negative behavior. How you can stop being a slave to guilt, hysteria, anxiety, low self-esteem, depression, perfectionism, and the other negative emotions that are blocking your path to happiness. You will be introduced to techniques that have worked for literally hundreds of my patients and students—people who have overcome the selfsame negative emotions that are plaguing you. You will become familiar with Talk Tenderly To Yourself; The Three Windows of Perception; Replaying The Tape; Broken Record; Send It To The Front Office; To You-ness To Me-ness; and other effective therapies for breaking emotional bad habits and replacing them with constructive emotional responses. These are all practical techniques that, once mastered, you can apply yourself.

Naturally, not everyone will find the answer to every emotional problem in this or any other book. There are serious emotional disorders that people suffer requiring treatment by mental-health professionals. But most of us, addicted to negative emotional habits, can help ourselves. We will see how in the pages that follow.

Chapter 1

EMOTIONAL BAD HABITS: OUR INSECURITY BLANKETS

The young woman sitting before me was attractive, a green-eyed brunette, obviously intelligent but with the distracting habit of holding her fingers over her mouth when she spoke. I will call her Laura S. "I just assume things will go wrong, and they usually do," Laura told me. "Wrongness. That's my theme song. And I know it's all my fault. Even when I can't make a kitchen appliance work, I know somehow I failed. When things do go right, it makes me uneasy. I think I'm riding for a fall. I feel that my life has been singled out for failure. In a way, I have come to terms with it. I accept it. By accepting failure, I can't be disappointed. It's my destiny."

I recognized that I was in the presence of a classic negative personality. I was listening to someone so steeped in emotional bad habits that she saw no other possible response to life. Laura S. *was* her negativity. What I learned further at this first session, not surprisingly, was that Laura was mired in a low-level editorial job far beneath her talents.

Laura's outlook is not at all rare. It is, unfortunately, all too common. Increasingly, I hear this kind of talk from my patients and students:

GERALD L., a lab technician: "There's no point in figuring out what I want since I don't deserve it anyway. And even if I deserve it, I won't get it."

HELEN S., an actuary: "I am going through life with a chip on my shoulder. I'm always angry."

ARNOLD P., a civil servant: "Anything I tackle has got to fail."

LINDA M., a financial analyst: "I run everything through my negative filter."

ANNETTE G., a housewife: "I always feel guilty, no matter what I do."

LOUIS D.: "Nothing ventured, nothing lost. That's my motto. I'm afraid to try for failing."

JERRY A., a music student: "What I don't like is me."

VICKI P., a student: "What's wrong with me! I'm never content. When am I going to be happy?"

These people are hardly alone. Millions of us go through life wallowing in negative emotions that stick to us like psychological napalm. So attached do people become to these bad habits that the habits become, in effect, their insecurity blankets. They cling to the habits ferociously, as though their very identity is bound up in their negativity. If they gave up the bad habit, it would be like giving up a part of themselves.

The most common negative emotional habits that I encounter in my practice are depression, guilt, rejection, anxiety, low self-esteem, anger, helplessness, self-flagellation, hysteria, and various phobias. But there are at least a dozen others that imprison people in permanent pessimism and despair. Shyness can be charming—to a point. But I have had patients whose lives were stunted by pathological shyness. I have had patients who were emotionally crippled by abnormal secretiveness—or constant catastrophizing. Rene F., a mother of three: "If I get on a boat, the boat will sink and I'll drown. If I get on a plane, it'll crash and I'll die. If I hear an ambulance, one of my children must be hurt."

What is a negative emotional habit? Like any habit, it is a learned reflex. It is a response that becomes unthinking and automatic through constant repetition. The drug addict is hooked on heroin or some other dangerous substance. But others of us become guilt addicts, or anxiety addicts, or rejection addicts, or fall into any of a dozen other negative emotional obsessions. Such people reach for their emotional "fix" the way a drug addict reaches for a needle or a pill. And, like drug addiction, emotional addiction rules and ruins our lives. Victoria B., a lab assistant: "I'm afraid of not being perfect. So I just give up." Emotional bad habits are losing games, like playing against an opponent with loaded dice. As long as you keep playing with them, you will keep on losing.

Strange—while negative emotions stick to us like tar, our positive, healthy, happy feelings are often fleeting and fragile. Good moods are shattered by the mildest reversals and instantly replaced by bad moods. A Gresham's Law of emotions seems to be at work here. Bad feelings drive out good feelings. The habit of looking at things negatively is so ingrained in some of my patients that they dismiss even past happy experiences as no longer valid. They create what I call "retroactive misery." A distraught patient tells me: "If my husband can go to bed with another woman, then all those wonderful years we spent together are meaningless."

I can go to my files and pull out instance after instance

7

of patients and students who habitually accentuate the negative:

"I'm in bed with a migraine attack because my friend insulted me."

"I wasn't invited to a party and I'm devastated."

"After all I've done for him, he didn't even thank me. I can't stop thinking about it."

"My father and I haven't spoken for years. He owes me an apology. Every family holiday is a nightmare because of this."

I sometimes suspect that people cling to their emotional bad habits because negativism seems somehow more chic these days. It is fashionable to be cynical and pessimistic. It is cornball to be positive and upbeat. It is Mary Poppins to look for the silver lining. It is sophisticated to find the dark clouds. Gina D., a social worker: "I've always been drawn to the negativism of others."

Why should this be? Why this obsession with accentuating the negative? Why, in a society that has declared the pursuit of happiness as an inalienable right, are so many of us addicted to habits of thinking that virtually ensure our unhappiness? Why do we resolutely see the world through dark lenses?

One major reason is that our culture teaches us to feel that way.

- If I displease my parents, no matter what the circumstances, I'm *supposed* to feel guilty.

- If my husband takes up with another woman, I must be unattractive—or unsexy, or unworthy; whatever, it was my fault.

- If I don't earn as much as my brother-in-law, I'm a failure.

- If I'm not invited to a party, I'm a reject.

- If I let on that I'm intelligent, men will think I'm a pushy bitch.

- If I'm not half of a couple, I'm not a whole person.

In my experience, people are not usually addicted to a single negative habit. More often the habits come in clusters. Yvette D. is an example. Yvette came to me with what I call an umbrella complaint—just a vague dissatisfaction with her life: "I just don't feel good about myself." I asked her to try to sort out what did not feel good, and she told me the following story.

"In the beginning, they said I was the most promising student in my dance school. The first thing I thought was, Oh boy, now they'll be gunning for me. I felt so much pressure that my dancing started to go downhill. In the end, I didn't even get invited to join the dance company. On top of that, I had the guilty feeling that the teachers thought I'd failed deliberately ... just to prove ... I don't know what. All I know is, all my life I've felt worthless. My mother made me feel I was the cause of her divorce. I had a stepfather who abused me verbally. He didn't want me around. Now I find myself fearing success and fearing failure. I don't know any peace of mind."

Yvette's "cluster" of negative habits is composed of low self-esteem, rejection, and the Impostor Syndrome. At heart, she thinks she is unworthy and that her ability is fraudulent. She is addicted to failure. And if others don't impose it, she inflicts it on herself. The result is a talented and attractive young woman committing piecemeal suicide, allowing her emotional bad habits to kill off her talent and her capacity for making something of her life.

I looked at this lithe, lovely young woman and suddenly a vision flashed into my brain. I said to Yvette: "You're a dancer. And a dancer is grace in motion. But suppose a dancer—even the most talented on earth—had a great albatross slung around her neck. How graceful would she be then? Her dancing would be distorted into clumsy stumbling. That's what you've allowed to happen. You're lugging around these emotional bad habits—your certainty of rejection, for example. You're trying to dance with an albatross. And it just can't be done. But the critical point is that you don't have to be saddled like that. You can get rid of the albatross. You can set yourself free of your emotional bad habits. And then you can begin the dance of life."

Notice, I refer to Yvette's cluster of negative emotions as "habits." I deliberately do not use the words *trait, quality,* or *character.* This distinction is critical. Our various addictions to guilt, anger, self-loathing, or pessimism must be seen for what they are. If they were bred in the bone, encoded into our genes, then there would be no hope for us. But, *if* they are habits, then there is hope, since habits can be broken. If the power of negative thinking is learned behavior, it can be unlearned. We can change. I reject the widely held assumption that "You can't change human nature." In the world of the emotions, nothing is ever all right or all wrong, all good or all bad, all true or all false. We create our own emotional environment, with our families, on the job, and among our friends, by the way we look at things. We can create a negative environment and wallow in it, or we can create a positive environment and succeed in it.

All my professional experience further convinces me that our negative emotions are not even necessarily of our own making. All too often they are planted in our hearts by the force of our culture. They have been imposed on us from the outside. And just as they have been implanted, they can be uprooted. Yet, too often we behave as though we were born with these albatrosses around our necks and can never throw them off. Of course, there are times when we are going to feel bad, depressed, anxious, or angry. These are perfectly human responses to the pain of life—at certain times and over a reasonable period. In the appropriate setting, negative emotions even have their positive value. They are part of our biological survival kit. In moments of peril, fear spurs us to behave in a way that saves our lives. The adrenaline rush of anger gives us added strength to meet emergencies. Even periods of depression, which rarely benefit modern man, allowed our cave ancestors to husband their energies in, say, a time of famine. When bad things happen to us, we are entitled to a decent interval of the appropriate negative emotion. The mother who loses a child, the breadwinner who loses a job, the patient with a terminal diagnosis have all certainly earned their unhappiness. But what we are concerned with here is not the negativity that attaches to a single event and that time will cure. We are concerned with the people who put a bad psychological overlay on top of everything they do—for example, the person who wallows endlessly in guilt. We are concerned with free-floating anger, chronic depression, habitual low self-esteem, attitudes that spill over and contaminate the whole of our lives. We are concerned with the "habit" of feeling bad—the bad habit that can be broken.

The answer is not cockeyed optimism or going around with a mechanical smile pasted on our faces. I have no faith in gimmicky prescriptions for healing the human heart—say, the "power of positive thinking," or Coueism. (Back in the 1920s, Emile Coue, a French psychotherapist, urged his followers to recite, "Day by day, in every way, I am getting better and better." I don't know if they got better and better. But Coue certainly got more and more famous.)

Blind faith is not only unhelpful, it can be fatal. Remember the shocking photographs of those people who died in Guyana a few years ago—some nine hundred of them. They had given their minds and wills to the self-styled Reverend Jim Jones. Jones told them to take a cold drink spiked with cyanide and follow him to nirvana. And they did so.

Mindless optimism also explains the unnecessary suffering that a member of my own family recently went through. I had a friend who was dying of cancer. She learned very close to the end of her life of a method whereby she was supposed to be able to shrink her tumor by "thinking" the right thoughts. My friend had always been an insecure person, and she died believing that she had not tried hard enough in using this "therapy." She thought of herself as a "hopeless failure" at dying, just as she had been at living. I wish that she had thought differently about herself early on, as her negative preoccupation may actually have caused enough stress and emotional disruption to increase her cancer risk.

Just mouthing positivism and repressing negativism is a dangerous form of self-delusion. We all know of people—particularly young people—who have been brainwashed by cults and who go around with a look of rapture on their faces twenty-four hours a day. They have not found happiness. They have achieved mindlessness. They have given up their priceless individuality. They have handed over their minds to some high priest and have docilely joined his flock.

I want the people I work with—my patients and students—to think for themselves. I try to help them to recognize the truth that in the end we are all responsible for ourselves. I want them to understand how deceiving it is to go around brainlessly chanting slogans. I want them to replace the all-American nonsense that says "wishing will make it so" (when the wish is patently absurd) with realistic expectations.

The Bette Midler song *Delta Dawn* is a touching picture of what happens when the mind fixates on a hopeless hope. Delta Dawn—with that flower she's got on—goes down to the railroad station day after day waiting for the man who jilted her years ago. Dawn's is a pathetic and heartbreaking case of the triumph of fantasy over reality.

At the other extreme, I reject the Pessimist's Armor. That is the defense you often hear from people who are trying to protect their emotions by saying: "If I expect the worst, then I won't be disappointed." The Pessimist's Armor is merely another negative habit. And permanent pessimism is as much a lie as mindless optimism. Permanent pessimism breeds a feeling of helplessness in us. It leads us to act on the fallacious assumption that the pessimistic outcome is the only outcome. If we are convinced that everything must turn out badly, we begin to act in a way that fulfills the prophecy.

There is also an element of Magic Thinking in the Pessimist's Armor. There is an unspoken, maybe even an unconscious, belief that "If I imagine the worst, then it won't happen." I will have more to say about Magic Thinking later.

I favor leaning moderately to the optimistic. There is a great line in Marguerite Yourcenar's *Memoirs of Hadrian:* "If I must deceive myself, I should prefer to stay on the side of confidence, for I shall lose no more there and shall suffer less." I'm with Hadrian. We ought to consider all probable outcomes of a particular situation. Some will be happy outcomes, some will be unhappy, and others will reflect every shade of fortune in between. When you have taken into account all likely outcomes:

- You will not go around feeling as helpless as you will if you are convinced that everything must turn out badly.

- You will be better prepared to deal with bad news. You will not be crushed by an unexpected unhappy outcome.

- You will make better decisions because you are using complete information—not just good or bad outcomes— to plan your life.

I urge my patients and students not to think like either Pollyanna or Chicken Little, but to think hopefully yet realistically. Wary optimists, that is what we should be.

"WHY DO I ALWAYS ACCENTUATE THE NEGATIVE?"

Thus far, we have learned that negative emotional habits cripple our lives. They reduce us to less than we can be. We also know that if we have them, we are hardly alone. We are in good company. People who have negative emotional habits number in the millions. We know further that our torments are not exclusively of our own making. We are going around bent under cultural clichés heaped on our collective backs over the centuries.

But we can change. We do not have to live shackled to negative emotions. We can become free human beings exercising our own wills, instead of emotional serfs chained to society's clichés. But before we find out how to break our negative emotional habits, let us find out how we got them in the first place.

LINDA R., a film editor: "I think of the worst thing that can happen. And I feel I'm such an unworthy person that it probably will happen. I deserve it."

MOIRA B., a socialite: "I've got everything and I don't enjoy anything."

LEONARD G., a geologist: "I don't want to be close to anybody. Suppose they die?"

Why do so many of us allow ourselves to become controlled by such a bleak vision of life? Why do we wrap ourselves so tightly in these insecurity blankets? There is no simple answer. Obviously, formative childhood influences and experiences are crucial. What were we taught and how were we treated when we were growing up? What emotional models are we copying? But just as often, our emotional reactions are inexplicable, almost mystical products of the time and tides. One day, we can stand up to anything. The next day, we are knocked over by a feather. On Monday we simply refuse to be available for rejection. On Tuesday, our pores are wide open. And we cannot explain the change. The mountain-and-molehill syndrome comes into play too. If your negative habit is fear of rejection, you may be devastated because you think a friend snubbed you. But if the incident happens on the same day as your husband suffers a heart attack, the perceived snub probably shrinks to insignificance.

MOST LIKELY TO EXCEED

Who are the likeliest candidates to form emotional bad habits? Who is likely to carry a normal emotion to excess? Maybe all of us, at one time or another. But there are certain traits that crop up again and again in people who are prone to develop habitual negative behavior.

THE CENTER OF THE UNIVERSE

One such common characteristic I call the Center of the Universe Syndrome. Those who exhibit this syndrome tend to see whatever happens in terms of themselves alone. They are like the sun at the center of an emotional universe. And everybody else's feelings orbit around theirs.

Here is the Center of the Universe Syndrome at work in its simplest form:

Al calls Jim for a tennis date. Jim sounds remote as he turns Al down. Al jumps to the conclusion that Jim must not like him, or thinks he is not a worthy opponent, or is bored by him. Al has placed himself at the center of the emotional universe. Not only his own, but even Jim's. He has ignored all other plausible explanations for Jim's cool tone: that Jim may have just learned that his company has gone belly-up; that his wife is leaving him; that the "thing" on his arm has been biopsied as malignant.

Al could see Jim's behavior only in terms of himself. He is at the hub of the universe in all his transactions with others. It never occurred to him to ask: "Anything on your mind, Jim? You seem a little down." Instead, Al instantly assumed that Jim thought of him as a lousy athlete or drew some other negative conclusion. Jim, along with everybody else, has to orbit around Al's emotional sun. Like Al, we may become so absorbed with ourselves that there is no energy left to understand others, except through the distorting prism of our self-absorption. We are the Center of the Universe.

THE FLAW DETECTOR

Do you carry around a portable flaw detector? If so, you are a strong candidate for slipping into emotional bad habits. I stumbled onto the idea of the flaw detector through my husband's work. Leon Russianoff is a distinguished classical clarinet teacher. He and his students often go to hear other clarinet virtuosos perform. But they listen differently than we would. They turn on their flaw detectors and seem more intent on spotting what the player is doing wrong than on what he or she is doing right. They are not there simply to enjoy the music. They are listening for the slurred arpeggio, the faulty phrasing, the weak attack.

This may be the way that serious musicians learn from each other. But it is a terrible way for the rest of us to go through life. "Sure, he's loving tonight. But I think I detect the signs already. He'd dump me in a minute." "It sounded like a compliment. But what did she *really* mean?" "What was that look the boss gave me this morning?" "My friend said he liked my novel—what else could he say?" High-risk candidates for negative habits say: "Sure, this apple looks beautiful. It's ruby red and shiny. But just let me look close enough and I'll find the worm hole." Their flaw detectors are always turned on high.

THE TRIBULATIONS OF JOB

We all occasionally feel that the gods have conspired to ruin our day. But some of us convince ourselves that the gods have conspired to ruin our lives. I am reminded of the Biblical Job and his endless tale of woe. And so I call this attitude the Job Complex: "Why does everything always happen to me?" I have one patient who invariably opens our session telling me: "You aren't going to believe what happened now." People who have the Job Complex see themselves as pawns of a malicious fate that is out to do them in. Life is perpetually raining on their parade. They are permanent victims: "Let me put on my victimization glasses so I can see the world through poor little me. Sure enough, here come my victimizers."

What I tell patients who suffer from the Job Complex is to try to get a little sense of proportion into their perception of persecution. None of us is so important that the entire apparatus of the universe was designed to ensure our personal unhappiness. God, the Life Force, whoever or whatever is up there, has to be too busy to spend all the time devising schemes just to thwart you or me. If we are believers, do we think that God, with all the nearly six billion living souls in his charge—not to mention all those presumably in heaven—has singled us out for his unremitting attention? If we are nonbelievers, doesn't it defy our rational minds to imagine that everything and everybody is out to get us? Over time, the hassles, the grief, the hard luck—along with the good luck—are fairly evenly distributed. But many of us do not believe it. We believe instead that we are destiny's stepchildren, as doomed as Job.

THE MATHEMATICS OF GUARANTEED UNHAPPINESS

We are likely candidates for forming emotional bad habits if we practice what I call the Mathematics of Guaranteed Unhappiness. In this math, the bad always outweighs the good. If ten things go right in a day, each of these events is assigned one "plus" point. If one thing goes wrong, it is assigned ten "minus" points. Consequently, most days must end up in the negative column.

TRAPPED IN THE WRONG LANE

We are candidates for habitual negativity if we see our behavior as unchangeable. We are what we are. The world is what it is. It won't change and we can't change. This attitude is like the sinking sensation we get when we take a wrong turn on an expressway. That's it. There is no turning back. We are doomed to the end of time—to be headed in the wrong direction.

ASKING THE UNANSWERABLE

If you find yourself always asking unanswerable questions—the Cosmic Why? and What If?—you are again a likely candidate for negative emotional habits. "Why did this have to happen to me?" "What if twenty years ago I'd married Robert instead of Sam?" "Why was I born?" I continually hear these futile speculations from students and patients. They ram their heads against the stone wall of the unchangeable until their brows are bloodied. Instead of concentrating on what they can alter in their lives in the future, they are fixated on what is past and beyond alteration. They wear themselves down by this pointless and exquisite form of self-torture.

We can all recognize parts of ourselves in the preceding profiles of the candidates for negative habits, probably more than we care to admit. But, if I may paraphrase Lincoln, it's normal to feel bad—and behave badly—some of the time; but when we find ourselves acting negatively all the time, we need help. And my message is that there is help.

Barbara U., a college dropout: "I copied my mother. She was always fretting about something. She was always mad at somebody. I grew up thinking you weren't *supposed* to be happy. We're born in sin, that's what my mother taught me. So just try to lead a good life and maybe you'll get your reward in heaven. You sure aren't going to get it down here. I guess my strongest negative habit is dissatisfaction. I've learned to use it to make my mother feel guilty over me. I use it over other people to get my way too. If something goes wrong with a boyfriend or on a job or anything, I call my mother and manipulate her. I work her around to telling me it's not my fault. It's my usual bad luck. I know that things don't work out for me. Anyway, I've become used to dissatisfaction. If all of a sudden I was satisfied, who would I be?"

There you have the classic negative outlook. "I'm hopeless. Life's hopeless. Nothing is going to change. So what's the use? I may as well wallow in my misery." I'm reminded of the ten-year-old class bully who was sent to my office when I was a school psychologist. I finally asked him if he liked being feared and disliked by the other children. "No," he said (and remember, we are talking about a ten-year-old), "but if I stopped, I would disappoint my public." I often detect that attitude in the Barbaras and other negative-prone personalities I see. They are addicted to their negative self-images. How would their friends recognize them without their albatross, without their insecurity blankets? How would they recognize themselves? The fault becomes the person. And they fear disappointing their public.

SOCIAL SUICIDE

—■—

Untreated negative habits kill a part of us. Sieges of prolonged guilt, depression, obsession, and anxiety can destroy chunks of our lives that can never be recovered. They cause us to commit social suicide. Marie E., a thirty-two-year-old teacher in a private girls' school: "I know I can't come out a winner, so I refuse to compete." Costanza W., a housewife: "When I'm depressed, I'm so focused on myself that I lose the joy of living." Laura P., a library administrator: "Sure I'll be happy. The day I land a man." What all these patients are telling me is that they are consciously throwing away a portion of their lives. Because Marie lacks confidence, because Costanza is sunk in depression, because Laura hasn't got a man, they have put their lives on hold. They are wasting days, months, years that can never be brought back. They are committing social suicide.

THE HEALTH PERIL

The damage that negative emotions do to our spirits is fairly obvious. The habit of depression deprives us of joy. The habit of guilt tortures our consciences. The fear of rejection leads to social suicide. Self-flagellation begets self-loathing. But our physical health also suffers from habitual negative behavior.

Researchers are increasingly finding that how we behave emotionally and how we feel physically are linked. Take stress, which can be the byproduct of losing a job, having a marriage fail, or a fight with a friend. Dr. Redford B. Williams of the Duke University Medical Center says: "What we're finding is that stress has definite biological effects—on hormone production and blood pressure for example. And these effects, in turn, have implications for coronary artery disease ... [also] people seem to come down with colds or suffer flare-ups of arthritis more often when they are under stress." Stress has also been shown to inhibit the body's capacity to manufacture interferon, a natural protein that curbs viral infections. Rejection, anxiety, and anger are all stressful and do indeed appear to inhibit the body's capacity to resist or recover from sickness.

In one study, sixty-nine women who had undergone simple mastectomies were asked how they felt about the seriousness of the disease and about how it would affect their lives. Five years later, these cases were reviewed. Nearly 75 percent of the women who had responded to the initial question with a fighting, positive spirit were still alive. Of those who had accepted their condition with resignation or hopelessness, only 35 percent were still alive five years later.

Another British study found that persons who suffered deep grief at the loss of a spouse experienced a lowered activity of T cells, one of the blood cells that attacks disease. There is a whole new medical specialty emerging that concerns itself with the connection between our feelings and illness. Psychoneuroimmunology is the new science that explores the link between the brain and the nervous system, where our defenses against disease begin.

Clearly, when we let our negative emotions run riot, it is as though we were pumping dangerous substances into our systems. We are poisoning ourselves. We should not let our bad emotional habits go untended, damaging our health along with our happiness. And we do not have to, as we shall learn.

SUMMING UP

Let's sum up what we have found out thus far about our negative emotional habits.

- The emotional bad habit is much like a physical bad habit, an ingrained, reflexive response that we make without even thinking.

- A Gresham's Law is at work here. Bad feelings tend to drive out good feelings.

- Emotional bad habits often occur in clusters. Low self-esteem, self-flagellation, and fear of rejection, for example, form one such common cluster.

- Negative emotions such as grief, sadness, and despair, when they are connected to actual painful episodes, are an inevitable and natural part of life. They have a beginning and an end. But we are concerned here with chronic, free-floating negativity, the kind that colors everything we do and sticks like psychological napalm.

- Cockeyed optimism or mindless pessimism are both wrong attitudes. Hopeful realism is the healthiest posture.

- We are likely candidates for emotional bad habits if we exhibit the Center of the Universe Syndrome; deny that we can ever change; carry around a flaw detector; have the "why me?" Job Complex; continually ask unanswerable questions; or give more weight to our negative than our positive experiences.

- Negative emotional habits, while sabotaging our happiness, are also likely damaging our health.

- Many of our emotional bad habits are foisted on us by our culture.

- We are not stuck forever with our negative emotional habits. Unlike our eye color or height, our behavior can be changed.

Chapter 2

SHEDDING THOSE CULTURAL CLICHÉS

When Estelle P. came to me, she was forty-two, a housewife with three teenage sons and a hard-driving businessman husband. She also had one of those vague umbrella complaints: "I always feel useless and vulnerable." As Estelle talked, I could see why.

Her husband had Estelle's job description all worked out for her. She was first of all his wife, next the mother of his children, and finally, essentially, a baby-sitter for his elderly mother. By the time she finished these roles, there was not much of Estelle left.

Estelle never went out in the evenings because she was expected to "be there" whenever her husband came home. And he kept ragged hours. She had once thought of taking college courses one afternoon a week. But she lost her nerve. She was expected to "be there" when her children came home from school. Her mother-in-law lived around the corner, and Estelle was expected to "be there" to take her to the doctor, shopping, or to church. She was also expected to "be there" to answer the woman's half-a-dozen daily phone calls, mostly a litany of her aches and pains and complaints that nobody paid any attention to her.

Estelle's basic negative emotional habit was guilt. She was obsessed by a vision of what she was supposed to be and racked by guilt whenever she failed that vision.

As I have said, negative emotional reflexes are largely implanted by the culture, and guilt is no exception. Estelle was accepting a batch of cultural clichés of what her life was "supposed" to be. A good wife is her husband's helpmate, his "better half," always at his beck and call. A good mother always places her children's wishes ahead of her own. A good daughter-in-law uncomplainingly puts up with a querulous old woman. As a result of trying to obey all these cultural pressures while denying her own needs, Estelle, not surprisingly, felt useless and vulnerable. Yet, whenever she tried to stray from the cultural beaten path, she was plagued with guilt.

My objective with Estelle was to help her see that she had a right to seek out her own values. Of course, this is more easily said than done. People like Estelle have had their feelings beaten into the ground. The sudden responsibility of having to figure out what they want for themselves can be terrifying. Sometimes I have to perform something similar to cardiac resuscitation on them—in this case emotional resuscitation—to reawaken their deadened feelings. I may begin with lofty and provocative questions just to jolt them—"What would you be willing to give up your life for?" That one makes us concentrate hard on our deepest values. Or I may ask them about the simplest impulses—"What would you really like to be doing this very instant?"

Whichever way I proceed, my objective is to help a person like Estelle understand that she has a right to her own feelings and a right to self-realization. She need not be the slave of the judgments of others, of the crowd, of the culture.

In this country, we refuse to put up with political

tyranny. So why do we tolerate cultural tyranny so slavishly? From childhood on, we are bombarded by *Ought-tos*, *Supposed-tos*, and *Must-nots*. We are told how to think, how to feel, how to behave, even how to look. All too often, we accept these dictates unthinkingly—as Estelle did. We tolerate the theft of our individuality. We don't question whether the culture's clichés fit our lives, what we are and what we want out of life. We put on these *Supposed-tos* and *Ought-tos* and *Must-nots* whether they pinch or sag, as though we could all wear the same size clothes.

THE PRISONER OF SEX

Ruth B. came to my office and said to me: "I called my mother to tell her I'd been named the company treasurer. She says, 'The next time you call, I hope it's to tell me you're getting married.'" I might add that this conversation took place in the 1980s, not the 1950s.

Nowhere is our culture more tyrannical than in the subordinate role it assigns to women. This remains true despite the women's movement (to which I wholeheartedly subscribe). It remains true even after one demeaning sexist barrier after another—professional, educational, and social—has fallen. We still haven't come all that far, baby. Ruth's mother still thinks that "wife" is a better title than "company treasurer." No matter what words they use, the complaint that I am hearing from my women patients, again and again, boils down to this: "Why do I think I'm nothing without a man?" I became so concerned with the prevalence of this feeling in women that I wrote a best-selling book on the subject. The reason why women feel this way is that our culture tells them to.

Joan V., nineteen, a nursing student: "I was brought up

in a small, religious town. You were supposed to be married by the time you were twenty. My parents are starting to get antsy. And I feel the pressure. I haven't landed a guy yet. It doesn't make me feel good about myself. Then I start thinking, Who would want to marry me?"

Chalk up another victim of cultural oppression.

CULTURED UNHAPPINESS

Another negative habit that our culture encourages in women is helplessness. We are actually taught it. My female patients tell me again and again that they feel helpless. How well I know what they are going through. In my day, women were virtually trained to be helpless as a seductive asset. It was another way, supposedly, to snare a man. I might have been able to change a flat on my bike in two minutes. But, according to my mother, I wasn't supposed to let on. Far better to stand there, helplessly seductive, until a mini-white-knight on a Schwinn came along to rescue this damsel in distress.

I am not sure the world has changed all that much since then. Women who manage fifty-million-dollar budgets for Fortune 500 companies still pretend that they can't get a cork out of a wine bottle when men are around. Linda L., a labor lawyer by day: "The only way I can get men to like me is by being a cute little kitten." You see, if you can show men how helpless you are, then they will feel macho. They will see that you need them to protect you. One of them will marry you! That is what the culture teaches women.

Learned helplessness is just another form of social suicide. The woman who practices it is deliberately killing off her capacity to grow. And what happens to the woman who has learned helplessness when she reaches middle age or old age and finds herself widowed, divorced, or separated? The culture taught her to be seductively helpless in order to snag a man. But it did not prepare her to manage her affairs, hold down a job, or function as a whole human being—without a man.

Lest we think that only women are cowed by our culture, let me tell you about two of my male patients, Irwin C., a laboratory technician, and Ed S., a history instructor. Neither of these two men had ever had a mature relationship with a woman.

Irwin assiduously avoided dating because he was short, as he put it to me, "six and seven-eighths inches below the national male average." Women are "supposed" to prefer tall men. So Irwin made up the girls' minds for them. He rejected himself before any girl could reject him. Why? Because, in his eyes, he failed the culture's height test.

Ed, the history instructor, had never dated again after a fiasco in his sophomore year in college. He had fallen in love with a girl who dropped him for a basketball player. One woman preferred a jock to a quiet scholar. So Ed accepted that all women must be the same. In any case, he was not taking any chances on finding out otherwise, after that first painful experience. Both of these men accepted a cultural notion of how they were supposed to see themselves. And in the battle of the sexes, they both saw themselves as losers.

WHAT IS NORMAL?

Patients come to my office and ask: "How am I supposed to feel when my best friend suddenly stops calling me?" "How am I supposed to act when my husband is so cold?" "What should I say when my daughter is so self-ish?" They have a touching faith that there is a "Right Answer," a "Correct Response," an "Ideal Solution." They want to believe that "up there," somewhere, is a big book that will tell us how we should think, feel, and act in any given situation. They are asking, "What does the culture expect of me in this situation? What is approved behavior?"

The last thing I want my patients and students to do is to pursue a chimera labeled "normal." The quest for the right, the accepted, the *normal* response incarcerates us in a prison of clichéd thinking. It strangles our individuality. It makes us one of the herd, driven by the cattle prod of conventionality. One of my patients hooked on guilt told me that all the while she was growing up she was told, "If you don't behave like the rest of us, you're not part of this family." These parents were saying, in effect, "Get in line, kid, follow the leader."

As soon as we think that we have to find the *one* right answer, we have branded all alternatives as wrong. Life is rarely that certain. It is more like roulette than a true-false test.

The beginning of maturity in our lives is the recognition that there is no one magic way, that there are endless ways of dealing with the same set of facts. Maturity means accepting responsibility for ourselves and finding our own solutions. Yes, we say we want personal freedom, but freedom means choices and choices are tough to make. No one can hand us the answers. Look at what happened to people who blindly followed a leader who claimed to have found *The Way*—Hitler in Nazi Germany, for example. We need the courage to think for ourselves and overthrow the tyranny of ideas that don't make sense or do not work for us. Until we can do so, we will go around desperately clutching our insecurity blankets, lugging an albatross around, or feeling depressed, angry, or rejected because the culture told us we should feel that way. We will keep on playing those losing games—and losing.

WHAT WILL PEOPLE THINK?

One of the surest clues that you have become hooked on negative thinking is if you are continually asking yourself, "What will people think?" That phrase is a red warning flag. If you find yourself asking it often, if the opinions of others dictate how you behave, beware. You are on dangerous ground. The phrase is almost always an indicator of faulty thinking. And erroneous thinking lies at the heart of most emotional bad habits.

- Guilt: "What will people think if I leave my child and take a job?"

- Fear of rejection: "What will that gorgeous guy think if I try to start a conversation with him?"

- Low self-esteem: "What will my friends think if I try to get out of their blue-collar world?"

- Self-flagellation: "What will the boss think when he finds out I lost the contract?"

In each case, the red flag is flying. It is warning us that we are thinking incorrectly. It is tipping us off to an emotional bad habit. Rather than asking, "What will people think?" we should be asking, "What do I think? What is right for me? What do I want for myself?"

- "I think I need this vacation with my girlfriends—and away from my husband. It will be a complete change. My mother-in-law won't like it, but God knows I need it."

- "Having dinner alone in this restaurant gives me a chance to think and to study the people around me. And I don't much care what other people think about my being here by myself."

- "Maybe it was nervy of me—the way my friends said—to apply for that job with no experience. But I think I can handle it."

- "So my father's always complaining about my wanting to be a musician. But it's my life, and I'm me, not my father."

The above are all examples of healthy thinking. The green flag is flying, telling us we are on the right road. But if we are constantly frightened over what other people might think, then our lives do not belong to us. They belong to others. So look at these words—"What will people think?"—as a warning. Regard them as one of those signs we sometimes see on the exits from expressways: "Wrong Way—Go Back." We are thinking in the wrong way when we place the opinions of others before our own. Back down and ask yourself instead, "What does my exaggerated concern with the opinions of others tell me about myself? What emotional bad habit does it signal?" And, more important, "How do I change what I think? What do I want out of my life—for me?"

THE DESPERATION TO BELONG

Why do we buy into these false values so often implanted by the clichés of the culture? The answer lies in our desperation to belong, to be among the "in" group. The fear of being left out is one of the most deep-seated that we face. A little girl spills hot chocolate on her new party dress. "Look at the mess you've made," her mother scolds. "If you go around looking like a slob, nobody's going to like you. Boys won't like you. Nobody will want to marry you when you grow up. *And you'll end up all alone.*"

Here we have gone from a splotch of Hershey's on a pinafore to the ultimate disaster—ending up alone. Not being part of the group. The lesson has been implanted in the child early. The worst thing that can happen to any of us is not to belong. And the most foolish thing we can do is to fail to follow the rules that govern acceptance into the club. And so we go through our days blindly obeying the *Supposed-tos, Ought-tos,* and *Must-nots* that we accept as the dues of belonging. Instead of standing firm on our own sense of what is right and wrong, we kneel to the judgment of the herd.

WHERE IS IT WRITTEN?

When I see patients whose negative emotional habits are based on a blind acceptance of cultural dictates, I say to them, "Ask yourself, 'Who said so?' 'Where is it written?' " When Joan V. told me that she felt miserable because her parents expected her to be married by age twenty, I said, "Joan, where is it written? Who said so?" Of all the possibilities open to an attractive, intelligent young woman, where is it written that the only acceptable option is a wedding? Who said so?

To Joan's mother, it is more important that her daughter be married than anything else. But Joan does not have to believe everything her mother believes. And it would certainly be a mistake for her to act on her mother's cliché-ridden beliefs.

If we want to shed our negative emotional addictions we have to break out of the prison of clichéd thought. We have to begin to learn to pivot around a column of confidence in our own judgments. I will have much more to say about this later.

"DESERVE"
IS A DANGEROUS WORD

The culture also lures us into emotional booby traps by baiting us with false expectations. Somewhere out there is the rosy notion that if I follow the rules, if I behave in a certain way, I am *entitled* to certain prizes: "They owe me. I did all the right things. So I deserve the good life [usually seen by my female patients as a superhusband, two adorable kids, and a grassy colonial in Connecticut]." "I've done everything he wants, I deserve better." "I played by the rules, I'm entitled to more out of life." "All I want is what other women have." I run into these expectations all the time. I get the feeling that many of my patients have swallowed a television commercial as their vision of the good life. It is "supposed to" be theirs. They "deserve it."

If I had my way, I would banish the words *deserve, owed,* and *entitled to* from the English language. All they do is set us up for disappointment, resentment, and rejection. Thinking we have something coming, or that we are owed, is a surefire prescription for disappointment. If we don't get what we think we are entitled to, then obviously we were cheated!

Annette R. was not a patient of mine. Actually, I had never met her, though we were neighbors one summer on Long Island. One day Annette stopped my car and said out of the blue: "My psychiatrist told me I need to make a friend. I went to Smith and I know you went to Barnard. I know you're a Ph.D. I think you should be my friend." Not "I'd *like* you to be my friend," but "You *should be* my friend." I don't know what they were teaching in college in her day, but one thing Annette believed was that she "deserved." She deserved friends from what she saw as the "right" background. The culture had implanted her with those expectations.

33

Going through life believing that we are owed, that we deserve or are entitled to, is another negative emotional habit. It sows in us the seeds of bitterness when we do not get what we want. We can hope for some things. But we are on thin ice if we "expect" gratitude, kudos, applause, and love. When we start thinking that we have bought the right to happiness, we have set a trap that we are likely to fall into ourselves.

SUMMING UP

What can we do about these cultural clichés that entrap us?

- We can learn to challenge the *Supposed-tos, Must-nots,* and *Have-tos.* Whenever the culture starts telling us we are *supposed* to feel guilty, or rejected, or helpless, or unappreciated, we should remember to ask ourselves, "Who said so? Where is it written?"

- Whenever we find our behavior overly influenced by "What will people think?" remember, the red warning flag is up.

When we gain the strength and maturity to start thinking for ourselves, we are well on the way to breaking free of habitual negativity. We can throw off our insecurity blankets. We can stop wasting our lives through social suicide. We can replace bad habits of mind with positive beliefs that offer us a chance at happiness.

Chapter 3

CAN YOU CHANGE?

The first step in breaking our negative emotional habits is to learn the difference between "I can't" and "I choose not to." I am still surprised at the number of people who can't tell the difference, people who come to me to prove that they *cannot* change. They come not to be cured but to prove that they are incurable. They are depressed. And they are convinced that they are doomed to depression. They are life's rejects. And they think they deserve to be rejected. They feel helplessness, and they are helpless to change. They seem to be saying defiantly, "That's me. What are you going to do about it?"

Louise D., a thrice-married real estate broker: "I'm a human doormat. Men walk all over me—and walk out. It's always been that way." Kirk T., a high school teacher: "I always assume everybody else is better than me. I can't remember when I thought otherwise." Diane R., a computer programmer: "I'm a fortune-teller. I predict misfortune, and sure enough, it always happens." If these patients can establish that they cannot change, that even after therapy they still could not change, it proves that their negative behavior is not their fault. It is in the genes, a part of their character, their parents' fault, dyed in the wool, their fate. Whatever, there is nothing to be done about it.

I have known people who deliberately behave in a way to match the particular pathological label that they have chosen. They decide that they are rejects, or pessimists, or hysterics and proceed to act out the role. The therapist is expected to put the Good Housekeeping Seal of Approval on their disability. They are now certifiably star-crossed. They cannot change.

When I face this attitude, I tell the patient, "Please rephrase that. Don't say 'I can't change.' Say, 'I do not choose to change.'" I can usually gauge the success that I am going to have by the way people react when I say that. If they are receptive, we will probably do well. If they are resistant, we are in for a more difficult time. I call it the Rigidity Quotient. The less rigid the patient is about his or her capacity to change, the more hope of success. And vice versa.

A TRADE SECRET

I will let you in on a little trade secret. The therapist does not have a black bag of magic tricks. What we have is the capacity to detect erroneous thinking, incorrect perceptions, distorted attitudes, *emotional bad habits*. And, if we are successful in helping you, it is usually because we were able to help you spot that condition in yourself and help you to change yourself. We were able to straighten out your thinking.

People often simply fail to recognize negative behavior in themselves. The negative emotional habit is like a grammatical error that we have been making for years.

But once the mistake has been pointed out to us, we never make it again.

Do you remember the last time you went to an amusement park and saw yourself in a fun-house mirror? The person with a negative habit is behaving rather like someone looking into one of those mirrors. His erroneous thinking reflects a distorted image of himself. And while the healthy personality in the fun house can laugh at that image and walk away from it, the negative personality accepts the distorted image of himself as real. He judges it as an accurate reflection of what he is. And he lives out that image. As therapists, we try to get you to look at yourself in an unflawed mirror, not a trick mirror.

THE WOMAN WHO COULD NOT CHANGE

Millie G. is a good example of the patient who mistook her negative habit for her destiny. Millie had not wanted to come to see me in the first place. She had been dragged to my office by her lover. In Millie's eyes, she was what she was, and that was that. She was a woman who hated her domineering husband but, out of economic insecurity, was afraid to leave him. She had never worked a day in her life and was accustomed to the material comfort that even a bad marriage provided. She viewed herself as a weak, helpless pawn. She had no interests that I could detect. She was driving her boyfriend away by her apathy and pessimism. That was why he brought Millie to see me.

I saw her whole character in her appearance, in the dullness of her eyes, the slackness in her mouth, in the way she slumped in the chair, in her toneless voice. She spent most of the time that first hour glancing at her watch or at the door. Finding the cluster of emotional bad habits in Millie was not difficult: low self-esteem, depression, and, above all, helplessness.

When I did get her to talk, Millie told me: "I don't need this. I hate all this psychology gibberish. And I hate your women's lib too. All that female-accomplishment crapola. It just makes me feel more worthless than I already feel."

I asked her if she wanted anything out of life. Instead, she told me what she expected: "I look down the road and I know what's ahead. Twenty-five, maybe thirty more years of the same." Millie saw herself in the wrong lane of the expressway of life, and there she was doomed to stay. There was no getting off or turning back. It was rough going. Trying to pull something out of this defeated woman made me feel more like a dentist than a psychologist. Finally I asked: "Is there *anything* you like to do?" Her lackluster eyes brightened briefly as she said: "I like to bake."

I asked Millie to tell me about some of the things she baked. She described one of her favorite recipes—as I recall, a German chocolate cake. I then asked her to invent a fantasy centering around her baking. "I don't know," she said. "I'd just like to take all my recipes and do something with them."

We had a number of sessions over the subsequent months. I kept leading the discussion around to her love of baking and what she might do about it. And then, as sometimes happens in my profession, Millie dropped out of sight. At first she canceled appointments. Then I simply heard nothing more from her.

It was about two years later when I heard about the shop in a posh neighborhood on Manhattan's East Side. I stood outside looking at the display in the window for a time. The pastries looked like works of art. The shop was crowded, and when I asked a clerk if I could see Millie, she told me that the boss was busy. I asked her to please tell Millie that Dr. Russianoff had come to see her.

She came bursting through a door, covered with flour, wiping her hands on her apron. She was absolutely radiant. I scarcely recognized her as the drab woman I'd seen in my office. Then she announced to her startled customers: "Hey, everybody, this is my shrink. If it wasn't for her, I wouldn't be here!" In the course of a conversation in her cluttered little office, Millie told me that she had divorced her husband. She did not need him anymore, she said. She was earning more than he did. The boyfriend had drifted off too. She didn't mind. She had all the companionship she wanted. Anyway, her true love was the shop.

Millie had *chosen* to change.

But many people remain convinced that they cannot change. Why? There are several reasons. Their negative behavior is so ingrained that they know no other self. They cannot imagine themselves a different person. They lack the energy to uproot the old, settled, familiar personality that they have become. They fear changing. (Better the devil you are than the one you might be.) But I have found that one of the main reasons why people refuse even to try to change is that they feel overwhelmed. They are so swamped by their problems that they feel incapable of regaining control over their lives. They are twigs swept along by a tidal wave. They are drowning in a sea of negativity. And they feel helpless.

EMPTYING A CAN OF WORMS

Leonard G. is a prime example of a patient paralyzed by what he regarded as an overwhelming situation. Leonard was a thirty-four-year-old out-of-work geologist from the oil business. At first he was unable even to discuss with me the details of his discontent. "My life is just one big can of worms," was the way Leonard put it.

"All right," I agreed, "your life is a can of worms. So let's take the lid off the can, grab just one worm, and slap the lid back on. Quick." I held up an imaginary worm. "Okay," I said, "which one is this?" Leonard thought for a moment. Finally, he said: "I never allow myself to get too close to anyone. They might die."

I asked him what he meant by that. Leonard told me that his father had died when he was an infant. His mother had died when he was seven. He had gone off to live with his grandparents until he was twelve. Then they died within a few months of each other. Thereafter, he had gone to live with a none too receptive married sister and her husband. As a consequence of these shattering early losses, Leonard had tried to shape a life of total self-sufficiency. He had deliberately gone into a lonely profession. He lived alone. His vacations were solitary backpacking trips. He had no close friends and no romantic life at all. The loss of his job, however, had pushed him to the breaking point. The job had been his only lifeline. The loss of it had awakened him to his total disconnection from everything and everyone. And when he lost that last link to life, he finally sought help.

Leonard's insecurity blanket was woven of threads of pessimism, catastrophizing, and alienation. He had virtually worked himself into emotional exile. And so we began with that first worm, his fear of risking intimacy.

Sometimes the beginning of a cure is as simple as introducing people to reality. In Leonard's case, I asked him to talk about people he had known through the years. "Think," I said, "of someone who has done you a nice turn. Think of a pleasant evening. Who did you spend it with? What did you do?" We then brought our talks around to the fact that numerous people who had offered him kindness and friendship had not died, literally or figuratively—they had not *abandoned* him. In reality, he had abandoned them out of his fear of intimacy. And in so doing he had abandoned himself.

When I tell people "The only person who can abandon you is yourself," it usually startles them. It is often their first introduction to a hard but important truth: ultimately, we have to take responsibility for our own lives.

I gave Leonard an assignment, a task in what we call "behavior modification." He was to give a call to the former colleague at work with whom he had felt most comfortable, and he was to invite this man to lunch. He did, and as luck would have it, this fellow had heard of a job lead for a geologist in another oil company. Leonard thus created his own good luck, since he called for an interview and got the job. We had coincidentally dealt with another of the worms in his can (besides his fear of intimacy), Leonard's anxiety at being unemployed. While he was out of work, he had had too much time on his hands, too many hours to wallow in his feelings of alienation. When he went back to work, he again had a focus in his life. And so, by dealing with that first worm, his fear of intimacy, we had pulled two more worms out of the can—his economic insecurity and his obsessive dwelling on himself.

What happened to Leonard often happens with my patients who feel overwhelmed by their difficulties. Once we can get that first worm out of the can, we often discover that it is entangled with others. As we deal with one worm, it pulls the others along with it. The can starts to empty much faster than we expected.

What I am trying to get Leonard to do now is to risk intimacy with someone of the opposite sex. And there is a blue-eyed researcher down the hall at his new job and . . . Well, we will just have to see.

What I had done with Leonard, and what I usually do with overwhelmed patients, is to help them break their generalized discontent into its component parts. I try to help them to get their negative habits sorted out and reduced to manageable size. If we can handle our negative behavior in small pieces, we can begin to eliminate it, piece by piece. Our little victories, no matter how tiny at first, begin to breed a sense of control over our lives. We begin to shake off the paralysis that comes from feeling overwhelmed. We learn that we do not have to change overnight. And we do not have to change everything at once. One worm at a time.

EXCUSES, EXCUSES

I suppose I have heard every excuse in the book as to why people can't change, why they can't do something they should do—including: "My goldfish died."

When we are habitually depressed, feeling helpless or worthless, it is as though a terrible lethargy overtakes us. We wallow in a trough of despair. And it is easier to stay put than to try to pull ourselves out. Excuses provide the rationale for inaction. Excuses are the knife we use to cut the lifelines that people throw us. Excuses are the mask behind which we hide, the crutches on which we lean. We rely on excuses to avoid risk, to explain failure, to resist change, to protect our egos. The excuse is our way of saying: "You see, it's not my fault."

Interestingly, high intelligence is no defense against excuse-making. My brightest patients do not necessarily use their high IQs to understand and solve their emotional bad habits. They are just more inventive at finding excuses to stick to their bad old behavior.

Granted, it is not easy to abandon cozy alibis. When you dread getting out of bed in the morning, you can invent a dozen reasons why you can't make that job interview or start hunting for a new apartment. Inertia keeps you in a trough of apathy. The emotional force of gravity is all on the side of staying there. Overcoming inertia means going directly against what you feel. It means that if you feel rejected, you must get out there and risk rejection again. If you are morbidly shy, you must pretend to be bolder than you are. If you feel helpless, you need to act as though you have some control over your life. All this is hard.

But, if we can clear that first hurdle and rouse ourselves from our lethargy, then we can reverse the emotional gravity. We can make it work for us instead of against us. If we force ourselves, however depressed we feel, to go to a party, we will probably find ourselves at some point engaged in a conversation that distracts us from absorption in our depression. Sociability displaces gloom. The mind cannot contain both attitudes simultaneously. At least not at the same intensity. If we drag ourselves over to the sailing course at the yacht basin, or start studying Italian for a trip next year, or begin painting that awful brown kitchen, then for a few hours at least we will not have time to wallow in our negativity.

Commitment. Involvement. Engagement. These are the best medicines against emotional paralysis. Nature made us to be curious, exploring, creative creatures. The inert state is an unnatural one. Excuses keep us inert. The way to stop making excuses is simply to stop. Set a statute of limitations. Say to yourself: "I wallowed for six months making excuses why I couldn't go back to college. Time's up. Where's that application form?"

The road to hell, we are told, is paved with good intentions—and excuses are the paving stones.

COPPING A PLEA

People also resist change by an attitude that I call Copping A Plea. Copping A Plea is a form of emotional sloth. A little boy I saw when I was a school psychologist offered me an early and amusing example of it. Georgie had been sent to my office because he had a high IQ and low grades. Georgie's explanation was simple and, as far as he was concerned, unchangeable. "Why do you do so poorly in class, Georgie?" "Because I'm lazy. I admit it. I'm just lazy." No excuses. He was what he was. Lazy. He had copped a plea. Georgie was voicing what I also hear from my adult patients, though more subtly: "I am guilt prone." "I am a rejectee." "I am inferior." "I am a pessimist. And I am not responsible for myself. I am what I am." They too have Copped A Plea.

SAYING IS BELIEVING

When we say "I can't do it"—whether it be carry a tune, face a job interview, or initiate a conversation—the words go from our mouths into our ears and then to our brains, where they stick. Saying is believing. "I'm a failure. I'm stupid. I have no talent. And I never will. I can't change." The very sound of our voice confirms the verdict. How much better for our ears to hear, and our brains to register, "Yes, I can change. I can at least do my best to change. I can try."

Emerson tells us, "A man is what he thinks all day long." If we spend our days wallowing in feelings of helplessness, inferiority, or anxiety, then we are helpless, inferior, and anxious. If, on the other hand, we elect to change, we have taken that first indispensable step toward ending these losing games. Maybe a psychotic cannot change, or someone missing a Y chromosome, or a drug burnout. But for the rest of us garden-variety troubled human beings, the door to change is always open. We just have to choose to walk through it.

Spiritual payday in my profession is when a patient or

student calls to tell me, "You changed my life." What they really mean is:

- I helped them to recognize their negative emotional habit.

- I convinced them that the habit could be broken.

- *They* decided they to break the habit.

Regardless of our age, profession, sex, religious preference, or tax bracket, the power to change lies within us.

YOU CAN ONLY
CHANGE YOURSELF

Yes, we can change ourselves; but we cannot necessarily expect to solve our emotional problems by changing someone else. This is a fundamental mistake that I encounter again and again in my patients. "If only my husband were more thoughtful, I wouldn't feel so unhappy." "If my mother would stop picking on me, I wouldn't go around stricken with guilt all the time." "If my boss didn't lose his temper every half hour, I could enjoy my job."

The first time I saw Gertrude L., she still had the bruises on her body from her last beating. She was not the sort of woman you would cast in the role of battered wife. Gertrude was a college graduate who worked for a literary agency. She did, in fact, have the dream house in Connecticut, the husband (a stockbroker), and the two children. However, her husband, Roy, was an alcoholic. And when he got drunk, he beat her.

Gertrude's negative habit was anxiety. But she wanted me to cure her of anxiety by telling her *how to change*

Roy. She clung tenaciously to the marriage the way a drowning person clings to a lifeboat, even one with a hole in it. Her objective was to save her marriage at all costs. She felt that something in her behavior provoked Roy's drinking and violence—and her anxiety. Gertrude had convinced herself that Roy's alcoholism and wife abuse were her fault! A conclusion that Roy encouraged. She felt that if she behaved differently, then Roy would change. And I was supposed to accomplish this for her. In the meantime, the beatings were becoming more severe and she was becoming increasingly anxious. Gertrude was afraid that Roy might kill her in one of his drunken frenzies.

I wanted Gertrude to understand the only real options available to her. She had two choices: she could change the environment that made her unhappy—that is, get out of her marriage with an alcoholic wife-beater; or she could change her attitude toward her fate and learn to accept it (the choice I hoped she would not make). The one thing that she could not change, from everything she told me, was her husband. For years Roy had resisted all her efforts to have him seek help—from their minister or from professional family counselors. When she suggested he try Alcoholics Anonymous, he socked her. Like so many alcoholics, Roy denied his illness. He would not come with her to see me. Overcoming his alcoholism was something that would have to begin in Roy's heart. Gertrude's choices were to live away from it—or to learn to live with it. The only life she could change was her own.

In my experience, there are few recorded cases of someone saying: "You are perfectly right. I know I am ruining your life by my failings. I am dreadful. I am selfish, hypocritical, and deceitful. I am glad you pointed out my faults to me, you see. Because I am going to stop being all those terrible things and become the person you want me to be." If you are lucky, you may persuade the person who is destroying his or her life—and yours in the process—to seek help and to change. But you are not going to finish reading this book and make the other person, the spouse, the parent, the boss, or the lover you always wanted him or her to be. If your negative emotions are caused by someone else's behavior, remember, if they do not choose to change, you really have only the two options that Gertrude faced. You must change *your* environment, or change *your* reaction to the situation. I expect my husband, Leon, to behave leonly. Just as you have to expect that Joan will act joanly. Or that the Prescotts will act prescottly. Of course, they can change. And you can help create an environment that will encourage change in them. But you cannot do it for them. Recognizing that fact frees us to focus on the real challenge: To take control over our own lives.

I like the way my colleague Sonya Friedman explains it. Yes, other people's behavior is beyond our control. But we can change what *we* think, what *we* say, and what *we* do. We control those levers. And that is enough power to start changing our negative responses to life. We can replace guilt-ridden behavior with guilt-free behavior. We can change abject compliance toward others to assertiveness for ourselves. We can go from self-flagellation to self-respect. And we can alter the current of a dozen more of those emotional habits from negative to positive.

We can change.

SUMMING UP

What have we learned in this chapter about change? Let's review.

- The first step in breaking emotional bad habits is to acknowledge the difference between "I can't change" and "I choose not to change."

- Using the technique of Emptying a Can of Worms can help us attack our discontent by dealing with it one problem or symptom at a time.

- Remember that the only person who can abandon you is yourself, that you have to take the responsibility for your own life.

- Instead of "Copping A Plea"—being emotionally slothful and ignoring your own potential for change—try "saying is believing": state a positive behavior change or attitude and focus on it, move toward it in your daily life.

- Recognize that you cannot change others; you can only change yourself.

You've made a beginning.

Chapter 4

■

"AHA! I SEE!": RECOGNIZING YOUR EMOTIONAL BAD HABITS

My husband often says to his clarinet pupils: "Tell me when you're playing wrong." I know what he is getting at. If we can become aware of our negative emotional habits by ourselves—if we know when we are playing wrong—it is far better than having someone else point it out to us. The shock of self-recognition is a powerful teacher. If we can say: "That's it! Now I see what I have been doing," then we are far more motivated to change. When criticism comes *at* us rather than *from* us, our reaction is often either denial or defensiveness. And when we deny or defend our negative habits, we are in effect reinforcing them. We are affirming them through deliberate concealment.

One winter afternoon, I was listening to Alicia L. discuss her negative habit, her feeling of helplessness, when suddenly she stopped short. She looked at me wide-eyed and said: "I see what I'm doing! I'm always showing Fred

49

that I can't get along without him so that he won't dare leave me. I'm suffocating him with my helplessness. And that's what's driving him away." I could not have diagnosed Alicia's behavior more precisely, though I had tried. When I had essentially said the same thing in earlier sessions, I got denial and defensiveness from Alicia. "I don't do that." Or: "Fred always *used to* like to fuss over me!" Suddenly, Alicia recognized when *she* was playing wrong.

THE FLASH OF INSIGHT

All that we as therapists can honestly do is to throw on the lights so that our patients can see for themselves where they are. We can lead them, we hope, to experience the Flash of Insight that Alicia had. We seek to create an environment of self-discovery. Or, to put it another way, we are trying for one magic moment to get people to stand outside their own shells. We want them to be able, if only for an instant, to step outside themselves so that they can indeed say: "Aha! So that's me!"

I remember vividly the most crucial Flash of Insight in my own life. At the time, I was seeking help from a distinguished colleague, Bertrand Frohman. I am utterly sympathetic to the patient who has negative emotional habits, because I have been there. My problem was that by age fourteen, I was six-foot-two and weighed under one hundred pounds. Yet, my dream as a young girl was to be a sex kitten. Instead, I went through high school and college feeling like a freak. By the time I met Bertrand Frohman I was a woman, an adult, and my height was a negative, all-consuming crippling obsession. I equated my essence with my height. All other facets of myself were dwarfed by this part of me.

TURNING OUR
HEADLIGHTS AROUND

One day Frohman said to me: "Every time I ask you something, you manage to turn it around into something wrong with you. Your height. Your personality. Your intelligence. It's as though you're driving along at night and your headlights are supposed to be shining on the highway so you can see where you're going. Instead, you've got them pointing backward so that they are blinding you. You can't see anything but your own failings. You don't see anything else that's going on around you. You don't really see other people. You're so absorbed in what a man might think about your height that you don't give yourself the right to judge *him*. It's highly possible he's not perfect. What is it that you might not like about *him?* Turn those headlights around so that you can see something besides yourself."

Flash of Insight! Suddenly I had this vivid image of myself careening along a highway in a blinding glare of self-absorption. Bertrand Frohman's words were literally a turning point in my life. I turned the lights around and instantly saw with crystal clarity exactly where I was.

I woke up the next morning and said to myself: "All right, I'm not a cuddly little blond and I never will be. So I'm going to start living my life as what I am. I am going to stop rejecting myself." That's what I had been doing. I had been removing myself from the competition before it even started, as a form of pain prevention. I was carrying out social suicide. I had been making up other people's minds about me for them. I was too tall. Therefore, I was undesirable. But now I was going to take a new tack. Yes, I was tall. That was part of me. And not necessarily a bad part. But it certainly was not all of me. I was not my height. I was going to stop beating myself and start enjoying myself.

Here is a milestone of maturity—when we start living our lives according to the realities. Not with what might have been, or what can never be, but with what *is*. I had at last become aware of what I had been doing to myself. That awareness had to precede change. I was tall. That was the unchangeable fact. I therefore decided to start living my life as what I was, instead of cursing my fate for what I was not. Rather late, I was gaining maturity (and better late than never).

My new attitude must have communicated itself. After a lifetime of rejections by men, actual or self-inflicted, I started dating fairly often and also began making a number of just plain friends, who coincidentally happened to be men.

GET IT IN WRITING

The Flash of Insight is awareness in its most dramatic form. Usually we become aware of our negative habits more slowly and less spectacularly. Nevertheless, awareness is the requisite first step on the road to change. A problem recognized is a problem halfway solved. The drug addict's first step toward recovery is that moment when he or she can say: "I am an addict." The alcoholic's road back to sobriety begins with the words *I am an alcoholic*. The emotional addict's first step toward recovery begins when he or she can say: "I am addicted to anxiety—or depression, or helplessness." The first step in shedding an insecurity blanket is to recognize that we are wrapped in it.

I use one fairly down-to-earth technique in helping my patients and students become aware of what is troubling them. I ask them to keep a notebook. This approach is especially helpful in the beginning, when your dissatisfaction may be a formless, unfocused blob. You don't know exactly what is troubling you, but you know you are not happy with yourself. You are suffering from some vague malaise. But you can't quite put your finger on it.

Patients often come to me with such umbrella complaints as: "I don't like who I am." "I'm always bored." "When am I going to be happy?" When I hear these formless complaints, I often recommend that the patient keep a notebook. Keeping a notebook can help pinpoint our feelings. Sir Francis Bacon said it best, long ago: "Writing maketh an exact man." When we start to record our feelings, we force our minds to focus. And from the shapeless mist of our unhappiness, the outlines of our specific problems start to emerge. Just as you tune a radio from the hum and static between stations to a clear signal, you start to tune in on your true self when you start to put your feelings into words.

Start by writing down how it feels when you feel bad. Let's say that as you put words to paper you recognize that what you are trying to express is a sense of helplessness, or anger, or depression. When did you first begin to feel that way? What do you think may have triggered the emotion? With whom and with what times and places do you associate the feeling? Are you possibly modeling your behavior after someone else's? Do you really want to be like that person?

After you have written down as much as you can about the past history of your negative emotions, start recording your present daily encounters with them. Keep track of the *what*, *why*, *when*, *where*, and *who* of the feeling. In time, you will see patterns begin to emerge. Let's say that as often as five times a day, you find yourself recording these kinds of incidents. You forgot to call your mother, and you felt guilty. Someone called to ask you to serve on a school committee. You said, "no." And then as soon as you hung up you felt guilty. You passed along a semi-scurrilous piece of gossip about a friend. And now you are tortured with guilt. Before, you knew only that you felt a kind of uneasiness about yourself. But now the notebook makes your problem unmistakably clear. You do not have to be Sigmund Freud to see the root of your unhappiness. You are guilt prone and guilt ridden.

Or let's say that you don't like who you are. You do not admire that person. But you are not sure why. At the end of a week of entries in your notebook, you begin to realize what it is that you don't like about yourself. The entries may deal with instances where you felt that you were rejected; or they may record the several times that you flagellated yourself to a pulp; or that you worried yourself sick repeatedly about things that never happened. The notebook again helps you to target your particular emotional habit. It tells you that you are habituated to fear of rejection, or low self-esteem, or hystericalizing. You now have something with which you can come to grips. You are no longer grappling with smoke. You have achieved awareness, and awareness is the step that has to precede change.

I have patients who suffer from extreme passivity. They are such compliant personalities and so eager to please everybody that they really don't know what they feel about themselves. They have turned themselves into psychological doormats. I tell them to start keeping a notebook to record their most basic feelings—when they feel hungry, for example. And, when they have that feeling, what do they crave most? What would it feel like to be eating it? This may sound elementary, almost childish; but I am trying to put these passive people in touch with their feelings, at any level—a capacity they have lost because of their excessive passivity.

Once they have been reconnected with their own feelings, on even so basic a level as eating, we move on to a higher level. They can begin to keep track of how they feel about their relationships with a weak-willed husband or a tyrannical boss or a friend who keeps dumping on them. They have begun to feel again. They have reawakened an awareness of self that was suffocating under a blanket of passivity.

REPLAYING THE TAPE

Keeping a notebook will not only help you to diagnose your negative habits, it can serve as a therapeutic tool. Let's consider those instances where you recorded feelings of guilt. Here you can employ a technique that I call Replaying The Tape. Take the instance where you felt guilty because you did not call your mother. You know from long experience that conversations with Mom rarely run under half an hour. And when they do, she feels offended. You had a dental appointment that morning at the time you usually call. And so that day you did not have time. But you did call her that night. Besides, you were not aware, until you began writing down your feelings, that you call your mother most days. By Replaying The Tape—by reviewing the experience with the help of your notes—you are able to put your behavior into perspective rather than mainlining another shot of guilt.

Let's take an entry from the notebook of one of my patients, a woman whom I will call Louise D., whose emotional bad habit was her conviction that she was a social reject. The entry dealt with a friend who had asked to borrow Louise's wok to make Chinese food for a party— and then didn't invite Louise. Louise agreed to lend the wok to her friend in such a way that afterward she felt like a doormat and wanted to kick herself all the way to Chinatown. Louise had said, "Uh, okay. Sure. I guess you can borrow it. What time do you want me to bring the wok over?" All this was said in the tone of an injured mouse. Again, Louise felt that she had been rejected.

I said to Louise: "Imagine that you are replaying the tape of that conversation. How else might you have handled the situation? You might have said, for example, 'Fine. But you'll have to pick the wok up before six. I have plans for tonight.' You would have felt much better about yourself with that response."

Going over the notebook and thinking about alternative responses—Replaying The Tape—won't change the past. But it can cue us to better ways to behave in similar situations in the future. If you don't like what you said, practice saying something that makes you feel better about yourself. If you don't like what you did, think of what else you might have done. Imagine how you will handle a similar occasion the next time.

Or suppose your notebook shows a series of entries describing feelings of depression. Try to recall other periods in your life when you felt depressed. What triggered them? How long did they last? What helped you to pull out before?

NOTEBOOK OF AN AGING COVER GIRL

Dolores R. came to me when she was forty-five. For years Dolores had been a leading model. You probably saw her finely sculpted face, in her palmier days, peering from the covers of the toniest fashion magazines.

Dolores's chronic negative emotion was anxiety. She had difficulty in being more precise with me. Consequently, it was hard for either of us to get a grip on her problem. I persuaded Dolores to start keeping a notebook. When did she feel anxious? Under what conditions? With whom? At any particular time of day more than others? As she came in for her weekly sessions, we went over the notebook. It turned out to be a litany of complaints. She complained about her husband. She complained about her two sons. She complained about her friends. As we discussed the catalog of her discontents, the root of her anxiety began to reveal itself.

Dolores had been a stunning beauty. Her standard modeling fee had been one hundred dollars an hour, and she was one of the first of her profession in that league. She had made her beauty her entire identity. Her face was not her fortune—it was her obsession. A hairline wrinkle in the brow or the tiniest sag of the chin was a natural disaster. And now, at age forty-five, Dolores's glamour was fading, and her sense of herself along with it. She feared that her very essence was abandoning her. Her chronic complaining about everything and everyone was Dolores's way of lashing out at a world that she thought was deserting her. And the people nearest to her were her easiest targets.

What was she now if she was no longer the cover girl? She had no idea. Consequently, she was frightened, unhappy, and in the constant state of anxiety that she had described on her first visit. But, thanks to her notebook entries, we were now finding clues to her problem.

We began focusing on what Dolores had instead of what she was losing. We began thinking about what she could change and what she had to accept. Before her modeling career took off, while she was still in college, Dolores had been a music student and a promising pianist. She had completely lost touch with that part of herself in the competing demands of her career, marriage, and motherhood. During one of her sessions, I asked if she had heard any good concert pianists lately. No, she had not. She did not have time for that sort of thing nowadays, she told me. I gave her an assignment. She was to catch a Claudio Arrau concert that was coming to town. Obviously, I was trying to rekindle her interest in music. And, in time, she indeed started studying the piano again.

The last time I saw Dolores, she was organizing an amateur orchestra in her suburban town. Her crowning achievement was the night when she was the soloist in a performance of Grieg's *Concerto in A Minor.* I was no longer dealing with a self-absorbed and fading beauty, but with a human being who was more than her face. The negative habit, the anxiety that had gripped her for years, began to dissolve. I would like to take credit for her new self. But more credit belongs to Dolores for recognizing the anxiety-ridden woman she had sketched in her notebook—and for determining to change herself.

Sylvia L.'s problem was different from Dolores's. But in both cases I was dealing with unhappy women. And in both cases keeping a notebook proved invaluable. Sylvia told me: "I'm always being upset by something someone says. It'll stick to me like glue all day long. Sometimes for days. I let things fester. I start thinking about it and get angrier and more resentful or more hurt the more I think about it. I'm always nursing a grudge over somebody's words, mulling them over in my mind, even when I'm lying awake at night in bed. The only thing that pushes out one set of words is the next thing somebody else says that upsets me."

In a way, I was surprised to learn of the pain she felt, because Sylvia always presented a cheerful face to the world and had a marvelous sense of humor. However, I did occasionally detect a certain frantic quality in her cheeriness. But even as she told me what was making her miserable, she had a way of saying it that made both of us laugh.

I told Sylvia that I wanted her to buy a notebook and start writing down everything people said that upset her. At the next session, we went over a lengthy list. The very first item Sylvia had recorded was a conversation with her friend Jeanine. Jeanine had said, "Did you ever notice, beautiful women never seem to have a sense of humor?"

"Why did that upset you enough to put it in the notebook?" I asked. "Because," Sylvia said, "everyone knows I *do* have a good sense of humor. And I figured this was Jeanine's way of saying I wasn't good-looking."

She stopped dead in her tracks. And then we both burst out laughing. In that instant, as she heard the words come out of her mouth, Sylvia experienced a marvelous Flash of Insight. The lights had gone on inside her head. And she understood exactly what she had been doing. Again, it was a case of the student telling the music teacher, "Here is where I am playing wrong." She had suddenly recognized in herself the Center of the Universe Syndrome. "I took a perfectly innocent thing a friend said, and managed to turn it into an insult against me."

We continued down the list of upsetting things that people had said to her during the week. In almost every case we found the common thread: Sylvia turning a general comment into a personal criticism, a reflection into a rejection, an insight into an insult. She had written down that she had gone to a movie, a French comedy, with a new date, and afterward he had said, "The Knicks' game was on tonight." Sylvia's instant translation of his comment? "I didn't really want to go to this movie with you. Obviously we don't have anything in common. This relationship is going nowhere in a hurry." We had another good laugh thinking that one through.

In Sylvia's case, as in the other cases, the notebook helped to lead the patient to a state of awareness. What the patient wrote about his or her feelings led us from generalized discontent to specific understanding. With the problem recognized, we were halfway to a solution. Awareness must precede motivation. When we discover what lies at the source of our negative moods, then we can be motivated to change.

AFTER AWARENESS

I did not have to listen very long to Esther E. to detect her negative habit. Esther was the wife of an owner of a chain of drugstores. And her response to a problem was to become hysterical. She and her husband had gone to a dance at their country club. Her husband had danced too often, in Esther's judgment, with another woman. When she and her husband got home, Esther became hysterical. She also described to me an incident when she lost a credit card. Instead of reporting the loss, Esther became hysterical. As a result of her failure to report the loss, whoever took the card charged several high-priced items on it. When she learned of this, Esther became—you guessed it—hysterical.

After recounting a string of these incidents, Esther looked at me sheepishly and said: "I guess I'm an hysteric." It was not exactly a Flash of Insight. But at least a glimmer of recognition. More important, she had recognized it herself. "All right," I said. "You do hystericalize. Now, when do you want to stop being hysterical?"

This head-on approach often produces surprising results. When I ask patients, when do you want to stop feeling worthless, or anxious, or helpless, or angry, or depressed—when do you want to break your negative emotional habit—some will answer, "Yesterday," or, "Right now." But some will just look at me blankly, as though they wonder if I am serious. Do I really expect them to change? Am I really going to try to tear away their insecurity blanket? When I asked Esther: "When do you want to stop hystericalizing?" the problem was out in the open at last. She had to examine her motivation. Was she really prepared to do something about it? Was she truly ready for change? Or did she want to keep on wallowing in hysteria?

Bertrand Frohman, who got me off my tail kick, had a very direct way of dealing with the issue of motivation. Psychiatrists do not ordinarily make house calls. But, as Frohman once explained it to me, a bedridden woman had pleaded with him to come to see her. As soon as he entered her bedroom, she handed him a box of matches. "Open it," she said. He did, and inside he found a dozen or so burnt match sticks. "Every one of those," she announced defiantly, "stands for a therapist who failed me." Frohman took out one of the unused matches. He lit it, blew it out, put it back in the box, and said, "That'll be one hundred dollars." Sometimes we have to be jolted into knowing whether we want to change or keep on clinging to our negativity.

Magda R., a patient of mine, had the opposite attitude of Frohman's match lady. She had total faith in therapy. Magda was married and involved in an affair. Her lover, too, was married. She came to my office because she was haunted by guilt. Guilt had become her emotional obsession. Sex outside of marriage went completely against her upbringing and religious convictions. She came to me under the impression that a therapist would tell her exactly what to do about her situation. Magda behaved as though she could hand me the Gordian knot of her tangled life and say: "Okay, cut through it."

I talked to Magda for some time about her affair, how and why she had gotten into it. I asked her to tell me what she really wanted from it. I listened through a number of gauzy explanations. Then she blurted out something that seemed to shock her more than it did me: "What I really want is for his wife to die!"

At least we now had it out in the open: awareness of what she was really thinking and feeling. "All right," I told Magda. "Obviously, you are not going to kill her. So let's get down to your realistic options. You could divorce your husband. Your lover could divorce his wife. Then you and he could marry and you could live together guilt-free. Is that what you want?" She had no immediate answer.

In subsequent sessions, Magda's attitude toward her husband, her lover, and the affair began to crystallize. We had forced to the surface her first real understanding of her feelings. She came to see that she did not really want a divorce. Her husband was not all that bad. He had actually been quite decent to her. And, in her way, she still loved him. But she felt an irresistible physical attraction to her lover. Her fantasies about the death of her lover's wife were a mental trick to keep her love affair hopeless and romantic. She and her lover were thwarted and star-crossed—because this woman stood in their way. She fantasized about what could not be so that she would never have to face what actually could be: that she and her lover could marry, if both of them were really willing to break up their present marriages.

Magda had achieved awareness on two levels. She finally saw the affair for what it was—a romantic diversion. She was looking for excitement, not a new husband. She also became aware that how she handled her life was up to her. I had helped her to find herself, but she now had to make the hard choices. She recognized her various options: continue the affair and suffer the guilt; reexamine her moral beliefs and thus possibly overcome her guilt; drop the affair if the price of the guilt was too high, but lose the lover—and so on. But, most important, she came to understand that neither I nor any other therapist could hand her a prepackaged solution plucked off the shelf. I could help her to understand where she was. I could throw on the lights, in a sense, to help her find her own way out. But, in the end, she had to choose the way. She had learned that great lesson of maturity: we are all ultimately responsible for ourselves.

As for Esther, with the habit of hysteria, as soon as she told me that she wanted to stop hystericalizing "now," we began to make progress. She had made the crucial breakthrough to awareness and moved on to motivation. We began to devise alternatives to her habitual hysterical responses to problems. We Replayed The Tape. What else might she have said to her husband after the dance, rather than freaking out? How might she have better handled the matter of the lost credit card?

What Esther came to recognize in time was that hysteria was not an inescapable facet of her being. It was not a part of her, like her nose. It was a learned reflex. A bad habit that she had grafted onto herself. It was her acquired reaction to stress. And just as she had acquired it, she could rid herself of it. Just as she had formed the habit, she could break it.

She called me recently. "I feel so much more self-respect now," she said. "After my tantrums, I could always see the disgust in my husband's face. He never said anything. But I could see it, and I knew I was driving him away from me. Now, I stop when something upsets me. I make myself a cup of coffee. I sit down and I start thinking. What should I do? What makes sense? And I feel . . . I don't know . . . so much more adult about myself." I felt pretty good, too, after Esther's call. I had helped her to see her situation for herself. And I had helped her to accept that breaking her negative emotional habit was ultimately up to her. In short, I had helped her to help herself. And that is not a bad definition of what my profession is all about.

SUMMING UP

———■———

What Dolores, Esther, and Magda had all achieved was awareness. You can achieve awareness on your own by asking yourself these questions:

1. What part of my life is it that I am unhappy with? What part of my character or my behavior displeases me?

2. Am I expecting someone else to solve the problem for me? Or am I prepared to accept responsibility for myself and for changing myself?

3. What can I do to change? What am I doing now that I should stop? What am I not doing that I should start doing?

When you have answered these questions you have arrived at the required state of self-knowledge. You may well have experienced your own Flash of Insight. You are ready to break down the problem into bite-size pieces that you can handle. Awareness will lead to motivation. You are now getting ready to send your negative emotional habits packing.

Chapter 5

THE ONLY PERSON WHO CAN REJECT YOU—IS YOU

Hell hath no fury like a woman scorned, the poet tells us. Men do not enjoy being dumped either. Few experiences are more painful to us than being rejected. Nothing can erode our sense of self-worth faster. Being unwanted, being shut out, being spurned hurts deeply.

Of all the emotional bad habits I deal with in my practice, the rejectee syndrome is possibly the most common. I am constantly dealing with patients cut by the two-edged sword of rejection. They either think that they are worthless goods—turned down, turned away, stamped DISAPPROVED—or they become so fearful of rejection that they will do anything to avoid a rejection-loaded situation. They are not going to give anybody a chance to reject them. And so they hide from life. They commit social suicide. Fear of rejection is one of the losingest of losing games. As painful as rejection is, I am convinced that much of the pain is self-inflicted. Richard P., a civil servant: "I don't go for job interviews. You can't be turned down for something you didn't apply for." Nancy M., a social worker: "When I see that bored look in a guy's eyes, I know that the ax is about to fall, and I get out of the way quick."

The roots of the rejection-prone personality usually go deep. Listen to this confession of Lyle R., an actor who took my course on negative emotional habits:

"I was abandoned at the age of four. That set the tone for the rest of my life. When I was still young, I understood that I was alone in this world and that there was no one else I could count on. I trained myself to be abnormally self-reliant, I guess. I grew up in a kind of isolation, like one of those 'bubble kids.' I have great difficulty asking anybody for anything. I am independent to a fault. I always seem to be saying, 'I don't need anyone.' Then afterward, I feel so alone.

"I naturally expect others to fail me, to let me down. And they usually do. My father deserted me. One wife and two live-in girlfriends left me. Friends disappoint me. I can smell rejection coming a mile away. So I either do something to trigger it from them, to get it over with. Or I get myself out while the getting is good.

"The theater is a world of constant rejection. Acceptance is the exception. Rejection is the norm. Yet, I still don't handle the rejection well. I've had my successes, but the continual rejection beats me down. I also wanted to write for the theater. But I've given that up. I can't work up the motivation anymore. Why write plays that won't be read and won't be produced?

"I try to think about how I should cope with rejection in my personal life and in my work. I am slowly coming around to accept that I can't hack it alone. I need other people. I need friends. I need professional interaction. Let's face it, I need love. But the old habits die hard. And more often than not, I still find myself withdrawing instead of plunging in."

Lyle's story reveals the classic outlines of the rejectee personality.

- Rigidity: "I expect others to let me down or leave me."

- Hopelessness: "Why write plays that no one is ever going to see?"

- Avoidance: "I trigger rejection or leave people before they can leave me."

But at least Lyle is on the right track. He is arriving at awareness. He knows where he is at this stage in his life. And he knows what he has to do. He has to connect to other people, even if it means risking rejection. And I am now working with him, helping him to do so. But many of my patients and students have accepted what they see as society's verdict. They are rejects, wallflowers at the ball of life. Even worse, they have done society's dirty work: they have unilaterally declared themselves rejectable.

Beverly M. is a prime example. Beverly is no raving beauty. But she is certainly attractive enough. She works as an office manager in a modeling agency. Listen to Beverly (and I'm sure you will hear her negative habit coming through loud and clear):

"There's a photographer at the agency who's been asking me out. I figure he must be getting turned down by the models. Otherwise, why is he bothering with me with all those gorgeous creatures around? Can't you just see it? I go out to lunch with the guy and afterward he's taking pictures of one of those long-stemmed lovelies at the agency. And he's going to keep his mind on me? So I keep turning him down."

You heard the same thing that I heard. Beverly has her flaw detector turned up on high. She'll find that worm hole in the apple. Beverly was not rejected. She rejected herself. After working with countless people who are hooked on rejection, I am convinced that only we can reject ourselves.

Take a situation that looks on the surface like a clear-cut, open-and-shut case of rejection. Mary Ann McC., shy and rejection-wary, slips uncertainly into a cocktail party. Much to her astonishment and delight, a handsome, well-dressed man immediately comes up to her and initiates a conversation. They find that they both saw the same Meryl Streep movie recently. And they both love her. They never miss any of her movies. They both have the same favorite pop group and have all their tapes. They both coincidentally spent vacations in Ireland last summer and can't wait to get back. Mary Ann was starting to experience "that certain feeling" when the guy excused himself to get a drink.

He never came back. The next thing Mary Ann knew, he was talking animatedly with a blond stunner in a black dress with a plunging neckline. Soon afterward, those two were headed out the door.

Mary Ann told herself that she was a fool to get her hopes up. Of course, it had to end that way. She was a born rejectee. She never should have put herself in the position where someone could reject her again. She vowed that this was the last party she was ever going to.

A clear-cut case of rejection, right? But was it? Of course, Mary Ann read it that way because the insecurity blanket she lugged around was the certainty that she was a rejectee. All that this incident did was to confirm what she already knew. The experience also confirmed her tendency to pull back into her shell—to commit social suicide.

THE THREE WINDOWS
OF PERCEPTION

Looking at this situation as a problem in handling perceived rejection, we can see that Mary Ann made two mistakes.

1. She rejected herself.

2. She decided not to risk rejection in the future.

Let's reconsider how she behaved. The rejection-prone personality tends to see him- or herself in the worst possible light and at the center of a negative universe. Remember the Al and Jim conversation over the tennis game? Jim said no, he could not play, and Al immediately assumed that *he* had been rejected. This is precisely what Mary Ann did: she looked at the situation and put herself down as a loser.

Actually there are *always* at least three ways to look at any given set of facts. I call them The Three Windows of Perception. Each window reveals a different view of an identical situation. When the handsome man left the party with another woman, Mary Ann looked at the encounter through a stained glass window darkened by her habitual fear of rejection. She simply saw herself dropped in favor of someone more desirable.

But let's look at the same scene through another window. This one is made of plain, untinted glass. It reveals only the outward facts of a situation. Through this plain glass window, we see a man and a woman talking. We see the man leave her and then talk to another woman. We see the man and the second woman leave the party. No interpretation. No conclusion. Just the facts. But there is a third window. And this is the one that Mary Ann, locked into her habitual negativity, never looks through. It also happens to be the most complete reflection of any event. For this window is multifaceted and reveals all possible explanations of what happened. In the case of Mary Ann's perceived rejection, Window Three may reveal that:

- The man had come to the party specifically to meet the woman he left with. She may have been his fiancée, his lover, or his wife, for all Mary Ann knew. She simply did not have the facts.

- Or, the man was an extrovert, an office politician. He always makes it a point to meet and charm everybody he can at any social gathering.

- Or, the man was genuinely attracted to Mary Ann and was making a mental note to look her up at some future point.

- Or, it is also possible that he *did* find Mary Ann less desirable than the woman he left with. She may, in fact, have been rejected for someone else.

The point, however, is that there were three ways to look at Mary Ann's encounter—Three Windows of Perception—but Mary Ann immediately seized on only one: the one that put her in the worst possible light, and the one that confirmed her self-image as a loser.

I often employ the Three Window technique in dealing with patients and students who feel habitually rejected. What I am training them to do is to recognize the alternative perceptions of any encounter with another person:

- Window One: The cold facts of what happened

- Window Two: Your perception of what happened

- Window Three: All possible explanations of what might have happened

The healthy personality, the person who will not allow him- or herself to be rejected, has learned to look through Window Three in encounters with other people. But the Mary Anns will usually say: "Sure, I can look through Window Three and see all those possible reasons why I got dumped. But I know the *real* reason. It's me!" To which I say: "Show me the proof. Prove to me that all those other explanations are false." When we feel rejected, we have to put that question to ourselves: "Where is the proof? Why isn't a less damaging explanation just as possible?"

When you feel that you are being rejected by somebody else, it is really you who are rejecting yourself. You are colluding with the other person in assuming the role of rejectee. I cannot stress this point strongly enough. The only person who can reject you—is you.

RISKING REJECTION

Back to Mary Ann's encounter. The second mistake she made was to decide to avoid risking rejection in the future. As Richard Silvestri, a colleague in my field, has written: "If you aren't rejecting and being rejected, then you just aren't living." The point is not to *avoid* rejection, but to learn how to *risk* rejection in ways that are not destructive to your self-esteem, and to cope.

I have another patient who told me that she would not do any socializing "until the energy level is right." This young woman had, in effect, put her life in cold storage. She was not going to start living until she reached this mysterious "energy level." Which is another way of saying that she was committing social suicide. Her excuse for not engaging life reminded me of an old Arab saying:

"Appetite comes with eating." And, I would add, life comes with living.

The key in learning to handle rejection is to recognize this fact: you have *the right* to reject—and so does the other person. It is important that you can go into any situation involving potential rejection with that understanding clearly in mind. You are not going to like everybody. Everybody is not going to like you. You do not have to accept everybody. Everybody does not have to accept you.

When a social encounter has an unsatisfactory outcome, don't reach automatically for your insecurity blanket. Don't assume that you were rejected again because you are too fat, too thin, too short, too tall, too shy, or too aggressive. You have to rid yourself of the feeling that you are somehow on the slave-trader's block and that someone has pinched your biceps and checked your teeth and found *you* wanting. Learn to function in the marketplace of friendship, of work and love, instead of running away. You are not always going to win. But when you have learned to hear the word *no* without wilting, you are on your way to breaking the rejectee habit.

Once you see the social encounter in these terms—that either person has a right to reject—you then take the pressure off your ego. And once your ego has been trained to handle rejection, you will stay in the game instead of crawling into your shell every time an encounter does not turn out well.

Take another situation I spoke of earlier. This one not only looked like a prima facie case of rejection, but it seemed that the rejectee had had her face rubbed in it. That was Louise D., whose friend wanted to borrow her wok for a party but did not invite Louise. It was entirely possible that her friend was having a party only for fellow workers from her office. It could have been a birthday party for her father and only the family was invited. It could be that her friend was having other friends over whom she knew that Louise disliked. The explanation did not have to be the one that Louise immediately seized upon—that her friend deserved the Sheer Gall Award of the Year for inviting her wok to the party, but not Louise.

Mary Ann, Lyle, Louise, any of us who habitually fear rejection, have to learn to hear *no* without falling apart. We have to grant others—a friend, the boss, the director, the stranger at a party—their right to reject, while we reserve our own right to reject. And we must learn to risk rejection. Every time we take a social risk, we win with ourselves. Every time we avoid such a risk, we lose with ourselves.

BEHAVIOR MODIFICATION: LEARNING TO RISK REJECTION

Behavior modification is one of the most successful tools for helping people who are hung up on rejection. It is an approach that you can employ yourself. Let me use the case of Denise C., a college student, as an illustration.

Denise was sent to me by her mother after she went into a tailspin because a boyfriend had left her. She had become so despondent that she had flunked out of college. She had become socially inert. Denise virtually had *rejectee* branded on her forehead.

Even before the failed romance, Denise's idea of behavior at a party was to stand there and hope someone else would make the first move. On the rare occasions that she did initiate a conversation, she made sure it was with the mousiest-looking person in the room. She was always trying to put herself into a low-risk or no-risk situation.

I told Denise that she was not to turn down any party invitations. Instead, she was to cultivate them. Then I gave her a behavior modification assignment. The next time she found herself in a social situation, she was to initiate five conversations. Furthermore, she was to start with the person who looked most interesting to her and work her way down.

At our next session, Denise told me that she had indeed been invited to a cocktail party. I asked her if she had carried out her assignment. She waffled for a moment and then said: "I went in the front door. I looked at this room full of people and I marched straight out the back door."

I told Denise that her assignment still stood.

A few weeks later she told me about the next party she had gone to. She had walked up to the best-looking man in the room and introduced herself. "And he looked right through me," she said. "I wanted to drop through a crack in the parquet floor." But by then I think she was more afraid of failing me than facing rejection, because she kept on introducing herself to people. She struck up a conversation with a young woman, and it turned out that they had friends in common. They had a long, pleasant chat. Denise went on to her next quarry, and the next. She now seemed to the other guests like someone involved and worth knowing. And, much to her astonishment, two people came up and introduced themselves to her.

Thus it went in her subsequent social encounters—some successes, some failures. Acceptance and rejection, the normal round of life. The important thing is what was happening inside Denise's head. She was learning, not how to avoid being rejected—but how to risk rejection. Which is another way of saying she was learning how to engage life. She was seeing each encounter not as a do-or-die, will-I-be-accepted or will-I-be-rejected final exam, but for what it was: people chatting at a party. Her fate and her self-image did not hang on every single encounter.

PRACTICE, PRACTICE, PRACTICE

Denise was also learning a social skill. She was practicing and getting better all the time. I cannot over-emphasize the importance of practice in replacing negative emotional habits with positive behavior. We take it for granted that we have to train our bodies through constant effort to master a physical skill. No one would expect to read a book about tennis and then step on the court with a smashing overhead and a deadly backhand. You expect to practice, practice, practice. You are not going to read this or anyone else's book and learn how to overcome the rejectee syndrome—or any other negative habit. Again, you need to recognize the importance of practice. You can make your own behavior modification assignments—direct yourself to initiate conversations, interview for jobs, audition for parts, whatever—and keep at it until it all comes naturally. Just as we need practice to achieve proficiency on a golf course or a dance floor, we become adept through constant repetition of social skills, too.

THE ROOTS OF REJECTION

Overcoming rejection is obviously not simply a matter of behavior at cocktail parties. My most serious patients have devoted their lives to feeling rejectable and the acid of rejection has eaten deeply into their self-images.

Take Betty M. I call her The Pleaser. Betty had a long history of rejection by men. After she related to me a series of these disasters, I detected a pattern. In the most recent case, Betty had gone to live with Hal. She was determined to *please* him. She studied his likes and dislikes as though she were preparing for a college final. She learned Hal's favorite recipes from his mother. She was by nature an early riser, but she stayed in bed late, because Hal liked to sleep in. She did not like to stay up late, but she did so because Hal and his friends did. In fact, she dropped her friends, because Hal did not like them. Instead, she tried to make his friends her friends, though they were not her type.

Yet, the more she tried to please Hal, the more he found fault with her. And the more he found fault, the more she tried to change, to anticipate his every whim and wish, to twist herself into a pretzel of compliance. And, in the end, Hal left her.

Betty lost Hal precisely because she spent all her time trying to be The Pleaser. In her desperation to please, she had lost sight of who she was. Consequently, she had drained herself of any selfhood as she tried to cram one persona after another into her skin in a frantic effort to be what Hal wanted. She had become a lump of protoplasm that he could shape at will. And still he never seemed satisfied with the shape he molded Betty into. She thus lost respect for herself and Hal's respect too. And again, she was rejected.

When I saw Betty, she was disconsolate. "Why me again?" she kept asking. Especially when she always tried so hard *to please;* when she did all the right things. Why did men leave her? Why was she always rejected? Was she ever going to be happy?

Betty was carrying a fake ID. Or, worse, it was as if she carried no ID at all. Trying to be what we are not is hard work. It is like lugging a hundred-pound sack of confused identity on our backs. The moral of this story is that you may as well be yourself. At least you will be rejected on your own merits. The authentic self must be the ever-present self. If that means rejection from one source, then move on to another where you are valued for who you really are.

Nancy T. was so rejection-battered that she practiced what I call Preemptive Rejection. She would reject a partner before that person could reject her. The pattern had been set early. As Nancy explained: "I had been going out with this beautiful guy in high school. There was no doubt in my mind that he was going to take me to the prom. Then one day he told me that his mother said he had to take the daughter of a family friend instead. He couldn't ask me. I remember going to my mother, absolutely devastated. And I'll never forget what she said: 'You must have done something to turn him off.' And I guessed I must have. The whole experience was so awful that I tended to avoid men after that. I certainly made no effort to meet them. If I did go out with someone, I backed out at the first sign of trouble.

"Then I met Frank. It was wonderful. We really cared for each other. I know I loved him. Then, about six months ago, we went on a bike ride. I was in a bad mood. I don't even remember why. I guess Frank assumed my bad mood meant I was turning away from him. He shoved off. I haven't seen him since. And I was afraid to call him. I didn't want to go through rejection again. I don't even know why it hurts so much. If I'm not hardened to rejection by now, I never will be."

We went through Nancy's life like a couple of archaeologists in order to excavate the pattern in her behavior with men. The pattern we found was composed of wary, superficial commitment at first, followed by minor misunderstandings that triggered her decision to flee from the relationship. But when we got to Frank, we saw that he had, in effect, turned the tables on her. Her flaw detector was ever at the ready. Nancy suddenly experienced a priceless Flash of Insight. She recognized her own past behavior in Frank's behavior. He had had a few unhappy relationships of his own, Nancy knew. Now, he had forfeited her love out of his own pathological fear of rejection. At the first sign of trouble, Frank had bugged out. Nancy understood. She had done the same thing a half-dozen times in her own life.

I persuaded Nancy to call Frank. She did, and they resumed their relationship. They have now been married for three years and have two children. I also find it encouraging that Nancy has come to understand her mother's role in making her feel like a rejectee in her youth. And she is determined not to hand down that particular insecurity blanket to her own children.

THE EMOTIONAL REHEARSAL

Here is a therapeutic tool that I find works rather well in combatting rejection, the Emotional Rehearsal. We touched on it briefly in chapter 1 when I expressed my preference for moderate optimism and my rejection of permanent pessimism.

When you face a situation that involves the *potential* for rejection, think it through in advance. What are all the possibilities? Let us take a simple example first. You are going to apply for a job. The possibilities here are fairly clear cut. You will get the job or you won't. Or let us say that you are working up your courage to submit your first novel to a publisher. Here there are more possible outcomes: the novel may be rejected; the novel may be accepted; the novel may be acceptable with changes; the publisher says, "Not this time, but let us see what you write in the future"; or maybe the publisher never responds at all. Let us look at an even more complex set of possibilities. You are strongly attracted to a woman whom you know only slightly. You think about calling and asking her out. Here the possible responses are: she says "yes," she will see you; she turns you down because she says she is busy that week; she sounds as though she is giving you a polite brushoff; she informs you that she is going with another man; she turns you down cold.

In all these cases, just thinking through the range of possibilities helps you better to face any one of them. By having thought about what *can* happen, you are better prepared to handle what *does* happen, particularly if the result is negative. You have gone through an Emotional Rehearsal. By putting yourself through the Emotional Rehearsal, your ego is not going to be walloped by the one outcome that you would not let yourself think about. Your response will be more considered and mature.

REJECTION AND CULTURAL CLICHÉS

Look at the role that the culture plays in stirring up our feelings of rejection. Cultural clichés tell us when we are supposed to feel hurt, ought to feel rejected, and must feel left out. The society virtually orders us to set up rejection traps for ourselves by setting up culturally dictated expectations.

Adele is one of my older patients, a widow in her late fifties. She is addicted to the notion that she is going through life unappreciated. Her children don't appreciate her. Her grandchildren don't appreciate her. Her nephews and nieces don't appreciate her. Adele came out of the hospital recently after minor surgery. She told me that she felt ignored and unappreciated all the time she was there. It seemed that she and some of the other patients gathered in the sun room every day and kept an unspoken score of who got the most cards and flowers. Adele was hurt when she thought of some of the people who sent her neither.

Adele is also of the school of etiquette in which people start waiting for the thank-you note almost as soon as they mail the gift. One of her nieces never thanked her for a graduation present. Adele was not only hurt by the niece, she could barely speak to her sister, the girl's mother. Adele felt hurt and rejected. Patients frequently tell me that they perform acts of kindness, generosity, and unselfishness and never receive the appropriate pat on the back. I hear wives who tell me that they go to enormous lengths to please their husbands and never get any credit, never get thanked, never receive a grateful hug. The script goes something like this: "Every morning I get up at an ungodly hour to prepare a nice breakfast for my husband. He never expresses the slightest appreciation. He is supposed to thank me. He did not. So I am supposed to feel hurt."

There we go again, paying the price of cultural clichés. People are *supposed to* send you flowers and cards when you are in the hospital. When we do good deeds, somebody *ought to* place the laurel on our brow. And if they don't, we are *expected to* feel bad, neglected, rejected. Where is it written? Where is it written, except in etiquette books, that someone must send flowers or candy or thank-you notes or give you compliments and accolades? Adele's niece may have exhibited bad manners by not thanking her aunt for a gift. But Adele set herself up for disappointment by her expectation, her feeling that she *deserved* gratitude.

As for husbands, they don't know the half of what wives do for the family. The husband doesn't know that the wife waited three days for the plumber. Men don't stay home from work for those things. Men have been conditioned—by women—to believe that these chores get done magically while they are away. I tell women who feel underappreciated: "Don't expect any great satisfaction, except the inner glow of a task well done."

My feeling about our getting strokes is simply this: Don't do something for the applause. Do it because it gives you satisfaction, or pleasure, or pride. If you get the bouquets and the accolades, the thank-yous and the get-well cards, enjoy them. If you don't, be philosophic about it. Virtue is still its own best reward. Do not allow yourself to be crushed, to feel rejected because someone else did not obey the cultural clichés. Don't set rejection traps for yourself and then tumble into them.

HIDDEN CONTRACTS

A family conversation:

FATHER: Mary, I want you to help me put my papers together for that tax audit I've got with the IRS on Monday.

DAUGHTER: Dad! It's Saturday afternoon, I'm going to the beach with the gang. I'll help you later.

FATHER: Later! Can't you hear? I've got to go to the IRS Monday. After the hundreds of times I've taken you to the beach, you can't even give your father one lousy afternoon?

DAUGHTER: I'm sorry, Dad. I didn't realize when you took me to the beach as a kid that I was making a deal to help you with your income tax today.

What we have here is a Hidden Contract. The Hidden Contract is an assumed agreement with another person. The father, in this case, raises an obligation that his daughter knew nothing about. Because he gave her time when she was young, she is to give him time now that she is grown up.

Let's take some other examples:

- I'm an old-fashioned girl. I gave myself to you because I was sure you were going to marry me.

- I invite you to my parties, therefore I expect you to invite me to yours.

- I hired you when you had absolutely no experience. Now that you are useful, you have an obligation to stay with the company.

- Dad and I bought this house with the flat because we figured when you got married, you'd live with us. You and Sarah can't go and live by yourselves now.

The conditions of the Hidden Contract are unstated and unilateral. One person sees the contract as binding. The other is not even aware it exists. The Hidden Contract is an open invitation to disappointment, resentment, anger, and rejection.

We have no right to expect others to honor a Hidden Contract. And we are not bound by a contract that exists only in someone else's head. By attempting to hold someone to a Hidden Contract, we are like the person waiting for praise, gratitude, or accolades. We "deserve" to have you keep your end of the bargain. You owe it to us—even if you never knew the contract existed.

If someone—a spouse, a friend, a relative—enters knowingly and willingly into the contract, fine. Then they do have an obligation to us. But we are riding for a fall if we suddenly whip out the Hidden Contract and demand compliance. We have merely found another way to reinforce a negative emotional habit, particularly rejection, as in the following examples:

- I was a fool, an idiot to give myself to that guy. He never intended to marry me.

- We've had them over three times, but they never had us over even once.

- I hired that ingrate when he didn't know his assets from his debits. Now he's starting a company to compete with us!

I tell my patients that a Hidden Contract isn't worth the paper it isn't written on. Do what you do because you feel it is the right thing to do—or the thing that you really want to do. And don't hang around afterward waving the imaginary Hidden Contract, waiting for your reward—or for disappointment.

PERFECTION PARALYSIS: ANOTHER FORM OF SELF-REJECTION

Winston Churchill said it best: "The quest for perfection is spelt paralysis." A wise man indeed. Take the case of Claude W. Like a number of my patients, Claude is in the theater and has real talent. But, when he came to see me, Claude had not been to an audition for months. His career was stalemated. Claude suffers from the ailment that Churchill was talking about: "If I can't do it perfectly, I'm not going to do it at all." I call it Perfection Paralysis. Claude is not alone in his attitude. Many of my patients have put their lives on "hold" until they achieve some unattainable state of perfection. They are socially—and in Claude's case professionally—paralyzed. They are, in effect, rejecting themselves.

What produces Perfection Paralysis? What makes people think they have to be perfect? Again, we do not have to look much farther than our ever-present villain, the cultural cliché. Do these words have a familiar ring? "Don't raise your hand unless you know the answer." "Whatever you do, don't make a fool of yourself." "Here, let Mommy do it. You're doing it all wrong." "If it's worth doing at all, it's worth doing well." (Translation: "well" equals "perfect.")

We are raised on cockeyed notions of perfection. There is supposedly a right way to look, to do, to be. And if we can't achieve that perfect state, what's the use of trying? We are just wasting our own and other people's time.

Perfection Paralysis is almost always implanted early. The child is reared in an atmosphere where great emphasis is placed on orderliness, on achievement, on modeling oneself on the mother, the father, the brother, or the sister who always does things "right."

The parent who gives us Perfection Paralysis is the parent who can spot a stain on a skirt at one hundred paces, who instantly spots the C in an otherwise straight-A report card, who corrects the way a six-year-old thanks Grandma for a birthday gift. The child raised in this perfection-drenched environment grows up—all too often— thinking, *The only way they will love me is if I never make a mistake.* And the best way to avoid doing something wrong is not to do it at all. There we have the perfect preconditions for Perfection Paralysis.

What happens to little Peter Perfect and Prudence Perfect when they grow up? Often, they wind up needing help from people like me. They fall victim to these common consequences of perfectionism:

- Since they suffer an exaggerated fear of failure, they will not attempt many things that they would like to do. Hence, they are often frustrated, bored, and dissatisfied.

- They are indecisive. They become bogged down in a swamp of conflicting choices and can't make up their minds as to which is the one "right" answer.

- They are often depressed. They feel overwhelmed by the perceived necessity to handle a task perfectly. So they remain inert. They don't do anything, and this depresses them. (Interestingly, one possible explanation of stuttering is that the stutterer fears not saying "exactly the right thing." And so his mind is rapidly selecting and rejecting as he gropes for just the right words. Consequently, he stutters.)

- Guilt often accompanies Perfection Paralysis. The guilt accumulates as the person tries to do something and the result is less than perfect. He or she tries again, falls short of perfection, and the guilt increases.

- Social suicide is another frequent outcome of the perfection syndrome. "I'm not going to the beach unless I lose twenty pounds." So she doesn't go to the beach and instead works off her loneliness and boredom by overeating, gains more weight, and hates herself more, on and on ad infinitum.

- Perfection-prone people are often motivated by false objectives. They want to be perfect to impress, or to feel important, or for other specious reasons. They are exhibiting "motivation pollution." Their reasons for wanting to appear perfect are polluted. They recognize this fact about themselves and so choose instead to do nothing.

- Peter Perfect and Prudence Perfect often turn out to be secretive or they lie. They are saying, in effect, "I don't want to be this imperfect me. I can't stand this flawed me. So I won't tell anybody about me. Or I'll tell them things that make me somebody else."

All of which brings us back to my patient, the actor, Claude W. He was raised by a widowed mother who, on the whole, was an admirable woman. She was determined that Claude and his older sister were not going to fall behind at anything just because they did not have a father. She thus set terribly high standards of academic performance, personal neatness, and good manners. Claude told me that the words still ringing in his ears when he thinks of his mother are, "Come now, Claude, you know you can do better than that." Consequently, Claude grew up seeing himself always coming up short. He was perpetually one step behind perfection and constantly struggling to get there.

In time, Claude developed his own imperfect solution to perfectionism. Whenever anything difficult or unpleasant loomed in his life, he would just back away from it. "If I can't do it perfectly, what's the use? I'm just wasting time."

When Claude came to me, as I said, he had not auditioned for a part for months. I asked him why. He told me: "A director asked me to try out for the lead in an off-Broadway show. I'd been recommended by an actress who liked my work. I felt pretty good. Nervous but reasonably confident. So I read. And afterward all the director said was, 'Thank you very much.' I was in a state of shock. I called the actress who'd gone to bat for me. She told me not to take it personally. The director said I'd done fine. But he was under the impression I was taller. And the part called for a tall leading man. In my heart I knew she was just trying to protect my feelings. I didn't get the part because I wasn't up to it. I wasn't ready yet. I just wasn't good enough. So now I'm working harder. When I know I'm perfect, then I'll audition again. And not till then."

What I told Claude, and what I tell my other patients suffering from Perfection Paralysis, is to ask themselves a few basic questions. First of all, who told you that you had to be perfect? (In Claude's case, it was essentially his mother.) Why did that person lead you to believe that you had to be perfect? (In Claude's mother's case, it was to fulfill *her* emotional need to spur her fatherless children to success.) And finally, is it reasonable to expect anybody, including yourself, to be perfect? (For Claude, this unrealistic standard was causing him to commit professional suicide by, in effect, rejecting himself before any director could reject him.) Consequently, he was stalled in his career. What's more, he was fooling himself. The perfection he sought was an excuse for avoiding rejection.

What can you do about Perfection Paralysis? In other words, how do you learn to be satisfied with an imperfect you? First of all, question all those *Ought-tos, Shoulds,* and *Have-tos* that tell you that you have to be perfect. Ask: "Where is it written?" And I can tell you now that it isn't written anywhere.

Think of the things that you want to achieve (for Claude, getting good parts in the theater) and then tell yourself: "I'm going to try to do it. I'm not going to do it perfectly. But I'm going to do it as well as I can." And, as you are telling yourself this, remember, the process of working toward your goal is in many ways more important than the goal itself.

Banish from your vocabulary the expression "a waste of time." It is only another excuse for dodging what you should be doing. Instead, put forth your best effort, and when it is done, Talk Tenderly To Yourself. Be supportive. Say to yourself: "That was a good try. Now we're getting there. I may not be perfect, but I made a good effort." Once you learn to discard perfection as your standard, you will realistically appreciate what you do achieve.

And level with your true friends, the ones with whom you can let your hair down. Tell them that you know you are afflicted with Perfection Paralysis and ask them to tell you to *Stop it!* when they see you slip into that emotional bad habit.

Also, try some imagery. Imagine yourself wrapped in a cloak that has stamped all over it I HAVE TO BE PERFECT. Then imagine yourself undoing the cloak and letting it slip to the floor. Tell yourself that you don't need it anymore. After all, it's not part of your skin. It is not part of you. It is a habit. You got into the habit, and, like the cloak, you can cast it off.

Above all, get over the notion that you are supposed to be some sort of genetic marvel, the perfect human being. I have never met one. And neither have you. Nor are we going to meet one.

I urged all of these approaches on Claude. I also advised him to put the Three Windows of Perception to good use. If he looked through Window One—just the facts—he would have seen an actor auditioning for a part and not getting it. Instead, Claude looked only through Window Two, the one colored by his terror of rejection. What he saw through this window was an actor auditioning for a part, *not doing perfectly,* and consequently being rejected.

Had Claude looked through Window Three (the all-explanations view) he would have seen these possible interpretations:

- Maybe he reminded the director of another actor, whom the director disliked intensely.

- Maybe he was indeed too short for the part.

- And it could actually be that he was not good enough.

The point is that Claude looked only through Window Two, and went into career hibernation. He committed professional suicide.

After one of our later sessions, I said: "By the way, Claude, why don't you find out how tall the leading lady is in that show you auditioned for? I'm just curious." The next time he came to me, he said: "She's five-foot-nine." And Claude is not exactly Boston Celtics stature. We can argue that the director had a clichéd belief that the leading man has to be taller than the leading lady. And Claude could not expect to change the director. He could, however, change his own perception of what had happened. The given reason was likely the real reason why he did not get the part, and not the one that had sent him running away until he was "perfect."

Claude still suffers from Perfection Paralysis, but little by little we are getting him out of that emotional wheelchair.

SUMMING UP

Let's pull together what we have learned thus far about rejection:

- Above all, accept the right to reject, for yourself and others. They have a right to reject you. You have a right to reject them.

- Employ the Three Windows of Perception. Before you conclude that you were rejected, make sure you look through Window Three, at all possible explanations for what really happened.

- Learn how to *handle* rejection, not to avoid it.

- Don't commit social or professional suicide in order to avoid the pain of rejection.

- Don't set rejection traps for yourself by expecting gratitude and accolades.

- Don't be bound—and don't try to bind others—to Hidden Contracts.

- Thinking that you have to be perfect leads to Perfection Paralysis. Tackle the thing you want to do—recognizing that you will not be—cannot be—perfect at it. Leave perfection to the saints. Instead, Talk Tenderly To Yourself: "I made a perfectly good try. I'm getting there."

We ought to look at situations that have a risk of rejection as the lottery of life. Sometimes we are going to win. Sometimes we are going to lose. The only guaranteed losing game is to stay out of the game.

Chapter 6

———————————————•———————————————

TALK TENDERLY
TO YOURSELF

Talk Tenderly To Yourself.
Simple as it sounds, it is one of the most effective techniques you can use for breaking negative habits.

"I HATE ME"

————————•————————

Chief among those emotional habits that you can break
by Talking Tenderly To Yourself is self-flagellation. Let me
cite a memorable case in my experience. One of my most
fascinating patients was an author whom I will call Edward Z. Ed had every reason to feel good about himself.
His books had been critically acclaimed and were com-
mercially successful. He had a lovely wife and two accomplished daughters. Yet, he suffered from habitual
self-flagellation. And, like most self-flagellators, he was
also an expert at the Mathematics of Guaranteed Unhappiness. In Ed's view, two wrongs did not make a right.
One wrong outweighed a dozen rights. If in one day he

sold a paperback edition of his latest book and signed a contract for a new book, but his agent informed him that Hollywood had not optioned a third book of his, all of Ed's emotions fixed instantly on the negative news. He would immediately start flagellating himself. He was a "lousy writer." Whatever made him think he could write in the first place? The movie people sure had his number. On and on, he would continue to whip himself.

Ed told me that he had once worked for three years on a biography of a famous figure. He then turned in the manuscript to his editor—and waited. He waited for a week, and when he heard nothing, he started getting uneasy. When two weeks went by, he fell apart. The manuscript was obviously "terrible." It was evidently so bad that his editor could not even bring himself to comment on it. Whatever made Ed think he was a writer? A *writer*? He was a failure!

After three weeks, when he could not stand the suspense any longer, he called the editor. He learned from a secretary that his editor had been out of the country for a month on business; he was not even aware that Ed had turned in the manuscript. In the end, the book was successfully published. But Ed Z. had wasted three weeks flogging himself, all for nothing.

Do you often curse yourself for being "stupid" or "a fool"? Do you work yourself into a rage because you left your glasses at home, missed a bus, broke a dish, muffed a tennis shot? If you turn everyday setbacks into proof that you are worthless, if you can find no forgiveness in yourself for yourself, then you, like Ed Z., are addicted to the negative emotion of self-flagellation.

Remember "Saying is Believing" back in chapter 3? That is what happens when you berate yourself. The words go from your mouth into your ears and lodge in your brain. You *hear* the verdict—"I am incompetent"—and in time you come to believe it.

Why do we treat ourselves with less understanding and

forgiveness than we would grant even to a perfect stranger? Listen to Ed Z.'s explanation: "When I was growing up, I knew kids who flunked a course 'because the teacher didn't like me.' Or they got fired from jobs because 'the boss was an SOB.' They didn't get into certain colleges 'because I didn't have pull.' They always had excuses for their failures. Listening to those crybabies, I made up my mind that I was not going to be that way. I was not going to be an Alibi Ike, always finding excuses. I was always going to do my best. If I failed, it was going to be my fault, not somebody else's. I was going to be my own toughest critic, kick my own butt, and keep myself moving."

Ed's emotional bad habit, self-flagellation, is particularly common among strivers and conscientious, self-reliant personalities. I told Ed that taking responsibility for himself was admirable—up to a point. I vigorously believe in self-reliance. We *should* set our own goals and then work hard to realize them. But it is possible to follow a good rule right out the window—which is what Ed did. He could not control every element of his life. Sometimes things went wrong that were beyond his control. Yet, Ed behaved as though everything that went wrong was because he had not thought hard enough, worked hard enough, or been smart enough. If his car did not start, he would berate himself mercilessly: "Why didn't I take the damn thing to the garage the first time I heard that *ping*? Why am I so lazy? Now look at the spot I've put myself in."

Ed had gotten it into his head that negative motivation works. But he had succeeded in spite of, not because of, his self-flagellation. He had made it on ability and hard work, not masochism. Negative motivation—telling ourselves how bad we are so that we will start to be good—rarely works. When we flagellate ourselves, all we do is give ourselves a sock in the self-esteem. Let's say you interview for a job but don't get it. You then start whipping yourself: "Why did I turn in such a lousy resumé?

Why did I give such dumb answers to the interviewer? Why did I wear the wrong outfit? No wonder I didn't get the job. I didn't deserve it. I really am a jerk!" There. You proved it again. But negativism is not going to motivate you to do better at the next interview. A self-despising, self-proclaimed failure is, if anything, likely to do worse.

Instead of flagellating yourself, *Talk Tenderly To Yourself.* The Hebrew scholar Hillel said: "If you are not for yourself, who will be?" Wise words. You have a perfect right not to be perfect. Don't say: "I failed," thus rendering yourself a failure. Say, instead: "I made a mistake." Making mistakes is very human—and correctable. A friend fouls up and you will dismiss it with, "Relax. To err is human." You will tell a mere acquaintance, "Forgiveness is divine." Show yourself just as much consideration. Remember, as Hillel reminds us, in the end, the one person you have to live with—and count on—is you. So don't make an enemy of yourself.

If you can forgive yourself for handling a situation poorly, it does not necessarily mean that you are copping out. It does not mean that you are alibiing your way out of responsibility. It means that you recognize that you are as fallible as the next person. In this frame of mind, you can make up your mind to do better next time. You will face the next task with self-esteem and confidence instead of self-loathing and pessimism. You are not ignoring your faults. Rather, you are showing a proper respect for your abilities. You are seeing your failings and virtues in sensible proportion.

When you find yourself beating up on yourself—"You jackass! You dope! You wimp!"—just say: "Stop it! Cut it out! That's my best friend you're talking about!" Talk Tenderly To Yourself. If you feel you must let off steam, do it with a laugh and a smile. Kid yourself gently: "You silly thing. Don't do that again." Just feel the difference inside you when you say something understanding, compared to something demeaning. When you are forgiving and understanding toward yourself, you can virtually feel the soothing balm. But when you are harsh and condemning toward yourself, you can feel the acid eating into your insides. If you make a mistake and curse yourself out, it is like throwing gasoline on a fire. Instead, as the old song says, "Try a Little Tenderness." Use a little of that soothing foam to put out the fire.

There is an expression I use on myself when I have fouled up, and I urge it on my patients and students: "You're okay, sweetheart." When you do something wrong or foolish, instead of finding yourself the most contemptible person in the Western world, just say, "You're okay, sweetheart. Maybe not perfect. But okay." Then you can go on to the next challenge without your self-esteem being battered to a pulp. When we want to Talk Tenderly To Ourselves, finding the right words is crucial. First, carefully think through exactly what happened. If you blew up and told off the boss, instead of flagellating yourself afterward—"You moron! How could you be such a fool!"—think about the facts of the situation. What drove you to behave like that? "He's been riding me for weeks. His criticism is unfair. I just couldn't take it anymore. I lost my temper and I blew up. I see now that this was not the smart way to handle the problem. Okay. I made a mistake. I'm not perfect. I'm like everybody else. Now let's see what I can do about it. Let's think about how I might handle this situation better in the future."

Lois P., a housewife patient of mine, was also addicted to self-flagellation. "Why do you do it?" I asked Lois. "Are you possibly modeling yourself on someone?" She thought about it and—Flash of Insight—said: "Why yes, my mother!" All the while Lois was growing up, she had watched her mother heap abuse on herself for the pettiest mistakes—burning a pie, for example, or getting to a phone too late to answer it. The one episode that stuck in Lois's memory was the time when her mother lost a purse with over a hundred dollars in it. As Lois recalled the incident: "My mother was in bed for two weeks with a sick headache. She never stopped moaning, 'I don't deserve to live. I don't deserve to live.' "

Lois had copied her mother's reaction to mistakes—blame yourself, whip yourself, but never forgive yourself. I told Lois that this was a good time to Replay The Tape. I told her to imagine that she was young again, and that her mother was in bed, devastated by the loss of the purse. Knowing what she knows now, what might little Lois have said to her mother? I gave her a cue as to what I thought would have been helpful: "Mom, I don't think you're doing a good job of raising your little girl to face adversity. I need someone as a model who feels that she can make a mistake without punishing herself for two weeks. I wish you would teach me a better way of coping with life."

Lois's mother had taught her, instead, to pump herself full of "psychological pus." When I used that phrase with Lois, it sounded so ugly that I immediately regretted saying it. But Lois called me the next day and said: "You know, I kept thinking about what you said about the pus. That image was right on target. That's exactly what I was doing. And I'm going to start getting rid of the ugly stuff." I asked: "When are you going to start getting rid of it?" Lois's reply: "Today."

As I try to lead Lois and others like her away from self-flagellation, I say to them: "Learn to accept yourself 'as is.' " Substitute self-understanding for self-loathing. You tolerate imperfections in others. Show just as much compassion to yourself. You say your Aunt Arlene never stops talking. She wears you out. But you forgive her, because she is kind to you and has other wonderful qualities. Your '69 Karman Ghia is ready for the boneyard. But you tolerate all its faults—and repair bills—because that car is special to you. Show yourself as much tolerance. Treat yourself as thoughtfully and forgivingly as you would another person or a piece of machinery. Accept yourself *as is*, warts and all.

I like the image of the mother giving a baby a bath. She holds the child's head gently but firmly as she splashes water over its head and coos to it. Don't be afraid to give yourself a little of that treatment. Be a good mother to yourself. Talk tenderly and lovingly to yourself. It will have the same effect on you as it does the baby—it will build a sense of security, warmth, and confidence.

Remember Edward Z., the writer and world-class self-flagellator? Let me tell you what Ed told me at one of our last sessions. He had gone to Chicago to conduct interviews for his next book. A friend there had loaned Ed his vacant apartment. Ed got up the next morning and energetically began putting together his Do List of all the things he expected to accomplish in Chicago. Almost everything he wanted to do first involved a phone call.

He picked up the phone—and it did not work. Ed began to fume and rage. "Here I go again. If I touch something, it breaks. [Center of the Universe Syndrome.] Now I've managed to break Bob's phone. [Guilt.] If I don't reach those people on this trip, I'll probably never get to see them. And I won't get the book done on time. [Catastrophizing.] What the hell did I do to that telephone? How could I be so clumsy? [Self-flagellation.]"

He let himself go on like that for five minutes. And then, suddenly, he caught himself: "Hey, this is where I'm supposed to Talk Tenderly To Myself." He sat down and started to think the situation over: "Ed, you've had a setback. Now what do we do about it?"

He thought and then began to act. As he later described that day: "First, I checked all the phone connections and extensions to make sure they were plugged in. They were. Then I went to a pay phone and called the phone company's service department. They told me that service had been knocked out throughout Bob's building. Hooray! It wasn't *my* fault! They then told me they'd have a service man over sometime that day. But I'd have to be there to let him in.

"I stayed at the pay phone and made most of my other calls. I managed to schedule my interviews rather easily over the next few days. I *would* finish the project on schedule. I went back to the apartment and said to myself, 'You've probably got several quiet hours ahead. Even the telephone can't interrupt you. What a rare treat. What would you like to do?' First, I put some jazz tapes on Bob's stereo. Then I rummaged through his library and came across *Anna Karenina*. I'd been meaning to read it ever since my college days. I settled in, listened to the music, and read the book. Five hours later, the repairman came and put the phone in order. I'd enjoyed one of my most peaceful days in recent memory. What struck me most was this: that day was going to pass, whether I spent it ranting and raving and flagellating myself, or whether I spent it as I did, constructively and pleasurably. I Talked Tenderly To Myself for a change. And it made all the difference."

Let's go back to some of my earlier observations about Ed. First of all, we are talking about a man fifty-two years old, of rather fixed habits. Yet, he managed to change. That fact itself should inspire the rest of us. Second, Ed told me that he had built up to this breakthrough by practicing. He had been deliberately trying not to flagellate himself for months. He had been saying to himself: "Now stop it. Cut it out." He had worked at Talking Tenderly To Himself until it started to feel natural and comfortable. After all, here was a man who had spent decades acting just the opposite way, habitually finding fault with himself. Now, in a strange apartment in a distant city, he discovered that he could alter the habits of a lifetime. Remember the example from chapter 4, the woman with the guilt complex who felt bad because she was too rushed to call her mother one morning? Instead of abusing herself for being selfish, she could have Talked Tenderly To Herself. She might have said: "Yes, I did not call Mom this morning. I was really jammed for time. But

I do call her every other morning. And I am going to call her tonight. You're okay, sweetheart. You're not such a bad daughter after all."

And remember Denise C., who went into an emotional nosedive and flunked out of college because a boyfriend threw her over? She responded well to behavior modification, including my assignment that she introduce herself to people at parties. But Denise could have spared herself much grief in the first place if she had handled the breakup differently. Instead of Talking Tenderly To Herself, Denise had talked hatefully to herself. She was "undesirable," "ugly," "useless"—because a guy had left her. If, after a decent interval of permissible heartbreak, she had said to herself: "You're okay, sweetheart. Scott may not have appreciated you. That's his privilege. But somebody else will," she could have softened the blow, saved her ego, and hastened her recovery.

We do not motivate ourselves by proving how stupid or unworthy we are. We motivate ourselves by telling ourselves that we are decent human beings, occasionally prone to weakness and vulnerable to error, yes. But capable of change for the better. You might think, for example, that a compulsive eater would be motivated to lose weight by flagellating the fat self. Not so. He or she is more likely to be motivated by liking the thin self buried inside the fat self and wanting to let that desirable self out.

When Henry Ford II fired Lee Iacocca as the head of the Ford Motor Company, Iacocca did not flagellate himself. He did not say, "What's wrong with me? I've got no business in the car business." In effect, Lee Iacocca Talked Tenderly To Himself. He held on to his self-respect and self-confidence, recognized that if he occasionally made mistakes, he made a lot more wise decisions. He simply plugged ahead, undaunted by the Ford firing, and went on to save the Chrysler Corporation.

THE "ME GENERATION" HAD A POINT

When I tell my patients and students to Talk Tenderly To Themselves, they often say that it sounds so self-indulgent, so "Me Generation." To which I answer: "The Me Generation had a point." I find it positive and healthy to ask ourselves: "What do I want out of life?" I find that those who are most vocal about criticizing the Me Generation are usually people who like to control others. They do it by arousing our guilt or crying "Selfish!" or otherwise trying to make us feel unworthy about seeking personal happiness and individual fulfillment. But it is perfectly reasonable to try to please ourselves, as long as we do not step on other people in the process.

Of course, the purely narcissistic personality has never been popular. He or she is seen as self-centered to the point of evil. But all too often people are accused of being selfish and narcissistic when their only crime is that they are working toward bettering themselves. Introspective people are also sometimes seen as self-absorbed. They are not spilling their guts, baring and sharing every emotion with the rest of the world. Their reticence is interpreted as aloofness, when actually they may be quietly studying themselves with the goal of improving.

You have a perfect right to become your own man or woman. In fact, if you don't try to understand yourself and don't aim to fulfill your potential, you will not be of much interest or value to others. So give the side of yourself that is trying to develop itself a chance. Don't be pressured by accusations that you are too self-contained, too thoughtless, too narcissistic, or too Me Generation. Don't be stampeded by clichéd ideas of false humility into being less than you want to be.

SUMMING UP

Let's sum up this business of Talking Tenderly To Yourself with a small variation on the Golden Rule:

- "Do unto yourself as you would have others do unto you."

- Stop beating up on yourself. Stop scolding, criticizing, and putting yourself down. Stop flagellating yourself.

- Instead, start Talking Tenderly To Yourself.

Chapter 7

TO YOU-NESS TO ME-NESS: MAKING YOUR FEELINGS KNOWN

Remember the fable of the blind men describing an elephant by touching it? One man felt the trunk, another the tail, another a tusk, another a hoof. And another stroked the beast's belly. Little wonder that each man described an entirely different animal. The modern equivalent involves five bystanders describing the same traffic accident. What we end up with are five honestly intended but often very different versions.

We all perceive the world differently. Your perception is not mine. Mine is not yours. That should be obvious. It is not. All of us suffer to a degree from nasal-impeded vision. We cannot see beyond the ends of our noses. Which brings us to another priceless tool for seeing our lives more clearly and for breaking our negative emotional habits. It is called To You-ness To Me-ness.

The concept was originated by Wendell Johnson, a

major figure in the field of General Semantics. What Johnson recognized is that the pronoun *you* plus a negative adjective—"you are selfish"—is a potent and often dangerous emotional weapon. I call it the Accusatory You—"You are thoughtless!" "You are stupid." Direct and uncushioned, these words hit us like a punch in the stomach.

Take this situation:

BEN: You are so damned selfish.

HELEN: Why am I selfish?

BEN: Because you expect me to go to that boring office party of yours with all those people you know I don't like.

From this rough start, the conversation usually goes downhill.

HELEN: I'm selfish? How about the time I went to that ridiculous high school reunion of yours. I didn't know a soul there. And I didn't want to.

BEN: Yeah. So you went around with a long face all night. Big favor.

What Helen is getting from Ben, Johnson tells us, is a difference of opinion about her. In such situations, instead of trading insults and escalating the conflict, Johnson advises us to apply To You-ness To Me-ness.

HELEN: Ben *to you*, I'm selfish because I want you to go to my office party. But *to me*, I want you to go because I'm proud of you and want my boss to meet you. We simply have a difference of opinion about me."

The above language is softening and conciliatory. To You-ness To Me-ness allows you to explain how the situation looks from your standpoint; and it gives the other person his or her own face-saving exit. The technique provides for an understanding you—"I appreciate how you feel. I feel different and I would like you to know why." The Accusatory You, on the other hand—"You are stubborn" —only gets people's backs up. And will probably provoke a counterblast. The Accusatory You amounts to throwing rocks at each other; To You-ness To Me-ness is more like waving an olive branch.

THE RIGHT NOTE

Your melody pattern is important in To You-ness To Me-ness. Be sincere—and sound it. The temptation to slip into sarcasm is fatal: "To you, I'm a snob because I don't like rock concerts. To me, I just have different musical taste than you"—said with a smugness that you could cut with a knife—translates as follows: "To me you are an arrested adolescent and a musical Neanderthal, while I am a cultured sophisticate." The other person gets the message. Your melody pattern gives you away. The reconciling, harmonizing value of To You-ness To Me-ness has been lost. You have just engaged in a more subtle form of the Accusatory You.

Edward Albee's play *Who's Afraid of Virginia Woolf?* is a night-long exercise in people's refusal to practice To You-ness To Me-ness. Instead, George and Martha spend the evening verbally punching each other silly with the Accusatory You.

I had a patient, a secretary, Inez G., who was a hard-core anxiety case. Inez was not so much wrapped in her insecurity blanket as sewn into it. One of her many sources of anxiety was her job. She woke up every morning and started worrying about what was going to happen when she got to the office. During her commute, she would start getting nervous just thinking about her boss. Inez described him to me as "the kind of guy who is always creating false pressure. 'Drop everything. Get on this right away.' Then two minutes later, he's back. 'Drop that. I want this done now.' Then two minutes later, he's back complaining that you didn't finish the first job. I get so upset that it's a wonder I get anything done. I start getting defensive and nasty. Then he says I've got a lousy disposition. It's a shame because otherwise I could like this job. Only, I can't take much more of him."

I saw this as a perfect opportunity for Inez to apply To You-ness To Me-ness. The next time it happens, I told her, try something like this on the boss: "To you, Mr. Rossi, it seems that if you bug me, you'll get more work out of me. But to me it has the opposite effect. I react to constant pressure by getting nervous, and it affects my work. So let me give you some reliable predictions about myself. If you will just leave me alone, I'll get the work done. If I'm constantly badgered, I won't. The next time you feel like telling me to hurry up, please try to remember this. Find somebody else to bawl out, because you're not getting your money's worth out of me this way." (The latter is a particularly persuasive argument with bosses.)

After a few weeks, Inez did work up the courage to use a variation on the above dialogue with her boss. And it did work. She told me: "Now he leaves me alone, but he deals out a double dose of his pestering to one of the other girls!" Inez was able to change herself and thus *her* relationship with the boss. But, as we have discussed before, she could not change him.

You can also use To You-ness To Me-ness by yourself. Begin by taking two chairs. The chairs can actually be placed side by side or exist only in your imagination. Now let's recall the case of Ruth B., who told her mother that she had been named company treasurer. Her mother told Ruth that she would rather hear that Ruth was getting married. Her mother's reaction, Ruth said, "took all the joy out of my promotion." Ruth had allowed her mother to make her feel that she had failed at what really counted, which was to land a man. Once again, a cultural cliché was torpedoing someone's happiness.

I suggested to Ruth that she imagine herself in one chair and her mother in another and that she use To You-ness To Me-ness. She tells her mother about her promotion. Then she shifts chairs and assumes the role of her mother.

MOTHER: The next time you call, I hope it's to tell me you're getting married.

RUTH (Back in her own chair): Yes, Mom, I know that to *you* it's more important for me to get married than to have a career. But *to me*, my career is very important at this stage of my life. My promotion was a great source of pride and satisfaction. I worked hard for it. I hoped you might share my joy.

MOTHER: Your sister was married and had two children by your age.

RUTH: To you, Mom, it's wonderful that Beth got married and had kids. And to you it's a shame I haven't done the same thing. But, to me, it would be a mistake to try to live my sister's life, because I'm not Beth. To me, marriage and children may come in time. I hope they do. But to me, it would also be wonderful if you took pleasure and pride in my kind of achievement, too.

This two-chair technique helped Ruth put her situation into perspective. Instead of merely accepting her mother's judgment—that she had the wrong priorities—she was able to understand what was really going on. Her mother and she have a *difference of opinion* about Ruth. And Ruth is a better expert on what she wants out of her life than her mother is. Instead of accepting her mother's idea that a woman is nothing without a man, Ruth has the right to declare her wholeness as a single woman.

The fact that the conversation was imaginary and Ruth's mother did not actually hear the words is not important. The important thing is that Ruth heard the words. She did not blindly accept her mother's verdict about herself. Through To You-ness To Me-ness, she was able to give voice to her own values. She found the right words—words that revealed her mother's insensitivity and her own true feelings about her life and career. Finding the right words is, again, terribly important. The next time she has a real encounter with her mother on this subject, Ruth can draw on these words. To You-ness To Me-ness offers her an opportunity to explore a difference of opinion in words that are reasonable and not hostile. Used properly, they can have a soothing, defusing effect.

THE GREAT AMERICAN ZAPPER

I once had a patient who raised an interesting point about To You-ness To Me-ness: "Suppose the other person is right? Maybe I *am* selfish!" Let's look at a case in point. Betty F., age forty-five, is obsessed with guilt feelings about her father. She was particularly put on the defensive when her father said—with predictable frequency—"You're a selfish daughter." Betty feared that her father was right, that she was a bad child, because, underneath, she did not really like him. Nevertheless, she tried to please him and tried to put on the best possible "good daughter" face. Still her father called her selfish and thoughtless. Worst of all, Betty usually was left in the dark as to what her offense was.

"He always gets me with that," Betty told me, "because I go crazy trying to figure out my crime."

I counseled Betty not to accept her father's blanket accusations at face value. I also warned her not to get defensive or argumentative with her father, either. It would do no good to recite all the wonderful things that she did for him. I know of few cases where people react to that approach by saying: "Why, you're quite right. I hadn't thought of all you do for me. Forgive me. I retract the charge."

Instead, I suggested to Betty that she use To You-ness To Me-ness to find out why her father was dissatisfied with her: "I know, Dad, that *to you* I am a selfish daughter. But *to me* it's not clear exactly why. It would be very helpful to me if you would tell me how I am selfish toward you."

Will Betty necessarily get a satisfactory answer? Maybe not. But at least she will elevate the issue from a George-and-Martha exchange of verbal brickbats to a more civil plane.

It is also quite possible that her father will answer Betty with: "Well, if you don't know, then there's no point in telling you." That line is one of the great zappers in the English language because it is virtually unanswerable. It cuts real communication dead. It reminds me of those Communist purge trials in the Soviet Union in the 1930s where people had to guess why they were being shot. Don't let people force you into this box. When you hear the Great Zapper—"Well, if you don't know what you did, there's no use telling you"—I suggest this response: "I'm sorry you feel that way, because I really would like to know. I understand that *to you*, I should already know and you don't want to bother to explain. But *to me*, it's unfortunate that you feel that way because it gives me no opportunity to understand and solve the problem."

SUMMING UP

—•—

- To You-ness To Me-ness is enormously valuable in dealing with a number of negative habits—guilt, anger, unhealthy love relationships, and others.

- Primarily, the technique helps make clear that your perception is not necessarily my perception. Nobody has a monopoly on the truth.

- The very language of this technique has a shock-absorbing effect. "I know that to you it seems . . . but to me . . ." These phrases have a way of softening our exchanges with others. It is a far cry from the acrimonious and futile "You're a no-good bitch—yeah, well you're a selfish bastard" type of dialogue.

- To You-ness To Me-ness not only helps clarify differences of opinion, it allows us to do so in a civilized way.

Chapter 8

GUILT: BANISHING THE GRAY GHOST

Guilt is the gray ghost of the emotions. It pursues and haunts us, casting a pall over our lives. A few years ago I played a psychologist in Paul Mazursky's movie *An Unmarried Woman*, starring Jill Clayburgh. In it, a young wife is divorced, becomes emotionally shattered, and, among other things, seeks therapy by coming to see me. We get into the issue of guilt, and I tell her something that I believe (in real life as well as on the screen): *Guilt is a man-made emotion*. We manufacture it and then inject the poison into our systems.

Chronic guilt feelings are a common and crippling emotional habit. I have patients who come to me bowed under gunnysacks of guilt. I ask them: "What good did guilt ever do you? So, let's see how we can get rid of it."

I recently had an experience with guilt's deadly, clinging quality. I was on a vacation at a Mexican resort. One evening I was dozing peacefully in my hotel room when I heard a commotion in the hallway. I came out of the room and saw a young girl in a negligee running toward me, pursued by three hotel employees. She was screaming: "Get me out of here! Get me out of this place!"

The girl virtually fell into my arms. As soon as I could get her calmed down, I explained that I might be able to help her. I brought her into my room and her story came tumbling out. The young woman had called the desk and shouted hysterically to the clerk that her husband was trying to kill her. The three employees then raced to her room. She burst out of it and went running down the hall—with them in pursuit. That was when I happened on the scene.

I eventually persuaded her to go back with me to her room, where I met her husband, the meekest, most frightened little man imaginable.

It turned out that the couple were on their honeymoon. She was the only child of blind parents. She had spent most of her life looking after them. She was, in effect, her parents' eyes. And now, having gone off and gotten married, she was stricken with guilt that she had abandoned Mom and Dad.

I talked to her for a long time, and tenderly, I might add. When she was reasonably relaxed, I suggested that she and her husband get into bed and just hold each other. Not talk. Not try to have sex, unless they felt like it. Just cuddle. What I wanted her to realize through this low-key intimacy was that the gray ghost pursuing her was useless guilt, and not this mild-mannered man she had married.

The next day I saw them frolicking in the pool; I hope that it meant they had found a way for her to begin overcoming her guilt. It is an insidious and destructive force, this man-made emotion. Still, the gray ghost of guilt is a hard one to escape, as this bride's torment all too vividly demonstrated.

I am deliberately discussing guilt right after To You-ness To Me-ness because that technique can be especially effective in breaking the guilt habit. Sometimes we create guilt ourselves. Sometimes others try to foist guilt on us. Thus, it becomes important to ask ourselves in guilt situations: "What's going on here?" And To You-Ness To Me-ness helps us to sort out the truth.

Remember Estelle? She was married to the hard-charging businessman who assigned her the roles of wife, mother, and baby-sitter for his mother. Period. That was the be-all and end-all of Estelle. She had once thought of taking college courses one afternoon a week, but she gave up the idea because it made her feel guilty. She was supposed to be at home every day when her boys came home from school. Her husband made that clear. Estelle might have said to Herb, her husband, "I know that *to you* I seem selfish if one day a week I want to take some courses. But *to me*, I am devoting my entire life to you, the kids, and your mother. Most of the time, I don't mind. But to me, it seems I also owe something to myself."

When we look at a guilt situation in these terms, it helps answer the question: "What's going on here?" What's going on in Estelle's case is that her husband is having it all his way. He is manipulating Estelle—through guilt—to make sure that she lives entirely by his rules.

Leah T. finds herself in only a slightly different situation. Leah's negative emotional cluster combines pessimism, catastrophizing, and gobs of guilt. Leah's mother runs a fashion boutique and Leah sometimes helps her out. Leah made clear to her mother that on the fifteenth of the month she was going on a vacation with her husband. "But I'm having a sale on the eighteenth," her mother protested, "and I was counting on you to help me." Although Leah had been telling her mother for months about the impending vacation, her mother just kept on saying: "But I want to have my sale that week."

Leah stuck by her guns—to a point. She went on the vacation. But when she got back, her mother refused to see her. "I can't forgive what you did to me," her mother said. Leah's resolve to stick up for her rights collapsed into an orgy of guilt. She told me that she was now phoning her mother three or four times a day—and constantly being rebuffed.

I said to Leah: "Let's figure out what's going on here. Let's set up two chairs. You play yourself and I'll play your mother". We then proceeded as follows.

LEAH: To you, Mom, I'm a selfish daughter, because I was not there to help you during the sale. To me, I gave you all the warning in the world that I would not be available if you insisted on that date. But you went ahead anyway.

MOTHER: What a selfish daughter. Leaving an old lady to do all that work all alone.

We went on in that vein, until it became clear that Leah did not so much deserve to feel guilty, but rather that her mother had manufactured Leah's guilt by manipulative behavior. As I say, guilt is a man-made emotion.

I told Leah to stop buying her mother's accusations. And I advised her to stop bombarding her mother with contrite phone calls. After all, she had not done anything wrong. Instead, I urged Leah to make just one more call. Then, I helped her to find the right words for it. If her mother still said that she did not want to see her, Leah was to respond: "I'm sorry you don't want to see me, Mother. There is so much I want to talk to you about. And I want to want to help you when you need me. So, when you're ready, call me." Not "if you're ready," but "when you're ready." That one word makes all the difference in the world. When tends to get guilt out of the picture. The obligation is now on her mother. If leaves the power in her mother's hands, and leaves Leah dangling by her guilt. I wanted Leah to have the words that would give her comfort. I wanted her to get off the bad words—"I'm a bad daughter"—and onto good words that would leave the door open for a mutually healthy reconciliation with her mother.

113

LOVE AND UNDERSTANDING

Leah's guilt grew out of the fact that she was a compassionate woman. Her mother was getting on. Her mother ran the shop and lived alone. Her mother counted on Leah. Leah loved and cared about her mother.

Yes, we want to be sympathetic human beings. We all want to be thought of as loving and caring. We want to give and receive love. But it is equally important to be understanding. Understanding is a rich emotion that has more applications than love does across the spectrum of human relationships—with family, spouses, friends, co-workers, and neighbors. Love is how we *feel.* Understanding is a much better guide to what we can *do.* When we are understanding, it means that we are receiving another person's message clearly and ungarbled. With love alone, we are hearing the message through the sometimes distorting filter of intense emotion.

Just as understanding is a better guide to our actions than love alone, so is empathy a better guide than sympathy. Sympathy, as I am using the word, involves close personal identification with the other person's predicament. Let's say you visit a friend who has just lost a husband. You tell her that you can imagine how she must feel. Alone after all those years with Ken. Their beautiful vacations together, over now. Where will she live? How will she get along financially? You are sympathizing 100 percent. You are attempting to experience the same emotions as the widow is going through. But you are not doing her much good. This kind of sympathy is like jumping into the ocean to share the plight of a drowning woman. You are now experiencing exactly what she feels. But if you do that, you can't help her. You can only go under with her.

Empathy, as I am using it, means caring, but maintaining enough distance—remember, you are not the other person—so that you can help and not simply commiserate. You can throw the person a life preserver. Yes, you want to be compassionate toward your bereaved widow friend, and you offer to help however you can in this difficult period of adjustment. But you remain strong and independent, so that she will have someone to lean on instead of someone to drown with her in her grief.

I was much impressed recently by an article I read about what to do when someone in your family has Alzheimer's disease. The article urged, "Try to find a little time for yourself." I would amend that to: "Find *a lot* of time for yourself." When you are considerate of yourself, you will have more to give to others who need you. You will empathize and help them, rather than sympathize and sink with them.

Guilt, love, and sympathy are all closely intertwined. Loretta V. and her father provide a case in point. Loretta came to me in a state of deep depression. It was not difficult to get to the root of her despair. Loretta's father was a widower who had been crippled by an accident the year before. He was now confined to a wheelchair and Loretta looked after him. Loretta had worn herself to a frazzle as her father became more and more demanding.

I convinced Loretta that she needed more time for herself—for her father's benefit as well as her own. She was exhausting herself. She needed a vacation. Loretta thereafter related to me the dialogue that occurred after she brought up the subject of a vacation with her father.

FATHER: I'm your father. After all I've done for you. Now you want to run away from me. Leave me with strangers.

LORETTA: Dad, I'm talking about a vacation, not running away from you. I'm arranging professional nursing care all the while I'm gone. If I go on like this, twenty-four hours a day, I'm going to burn myself out. And then I won't be any good for you or me.

FATHER: Your mother always said you were selfish. Now I see she was right.

After hearing of this dialogue, I explained to Loretta the mental state of a dependent person like her father. The dependent person is in an insecure position. Such people often become adept at manipulating the behavior of those around them to compensate for their helplessness. They are frequently testing the limits, finding out how far they can control the behavior of their caretakers. They are trying to locate the boundaries of permissible behavior. When they finally locate these boundaries, they actually feel more secure. They at least know how far they can go.

Loretta's father had been psychologically devastated by his helplessness. Now, almost unconsciously, he was testing the limits of his control over his daughter. Guilt was his most effective weapon.

Loretta wanted to do right by her father. But she also had to make him see that she was not available for his manipulation. I told her that it was fine, even necessary, for her to empathize with her father's condition. But she was not him. Total identification with and absorption in his life would not do him or her any good. There would be nothing emotionally or physically left of her to give him. She had to get the guilt off of her back. For starters, she had to see the issue of her vacation in To You-ness To Me-ness terms.

FATHER: You're a selfish daughter. Your mother always said it.

LORETTA: *To you,* Dad, I'm a selfish daughter. But to me, going on a vacation will recharge my batteries. I'm going to come back refreshed, with more energy. And then I'm going to have more of myself to give to you and I'll be able to take better care of you.

When Loretta is able to make clear her feelings, her father will feel more secure. He will know the boundaries of his relationship with his daughter. And, he'll stop testing the frontiers of his confinement. He will know where they are.

QUESTIONS WITHOUT ANSWERS

Another exquisite form of guilt is the Unanswerable Question. Indeed, as I said earlier, the constant asking of unanswerable questions is a fairly sure sign that we are addicted to guilt.

Marjorie W. offers a case in point. Marjorie set out to be a model mother to her daughters, Gail and Sally. No excuses for Marjorie. No one was going to find Marjorie's children insecure because they had not had enough love. No one was going to find her children badly educated because they had not gone to the right schools. No one was going to find her children uncouth because they had never had cultural opportunities. No one was going to find her children impolite because they had not been taught good manners. Marjorie was determined to do *everything* right.

But nature played a trick on her. Sally, her younger daughter, was beautiful, glowed with personality, loved school, earned top grades, and made friends easily. But Gail, two years older, was an ordinary-looking, painfully shy, withdrawn, lonely girl and a poor student.

No excuses for Marjorie. Gail's problems were obviously Mom's fault. And so Marjorie spent years torturing herself with Unanswerable Questions. Starting with Gail's birth. Why hadn't she gone to a better obstetrician? The delivery had been difficult. Maybe the child had been brain damaged? Why had she let the teacher put Gail in that "special" class in grade school? It was clearly for slower students. Wasn't it obvious that Marjorie must have favored Sally? Otherwise, wouldn't Gail have turned out just as well?

Marjorie came to me crushed by guilt. What she wanted was for me to provide answers to those unanswerable questions—on her terms. She expected me to tell her how she had failed as a mother. "It *is* my fault, isn't it?" That was what she wanted to hear. Then she could go home with her guilt confirmed by a board certified therapist.

Of course, that is not what I intended for this troubled woman. Instead, I had Marjorie go into some detail about her relationships with her daughters. I came away with a fairly clear picture of a mother doing the right thing for both girls equally—although she refused to give herself any credit for it. And I learned some troubling things about her behavior toward her more accomplished daughter. For example, Marjorie had conditioned Sally to low-key her accomplishments—such as always making the honor roll or getting the lead in the school play—for fear that Sally's triumphs would depress Gail.

I tried to make Marjorie understand that asking questions that could not be answered was about as useful as picking scabs. She was not making anything better, but worse. I asked her: "Do you want to stop feeling guilty? Or do you want to stay mired in it?" Her answer was not surprising for a conscience-stricken mother: "I want Gail to be happier. I want her to do well in school. I want her to have more friends, like Sally."

"Then," I said, "maybe we ought to have Gail in here to see what we can do to help her. But the one thing that is *not* helping you or her is your obsessive guilt. For people who are unaware, guilt is like a contagious disease. You keep reinforcing your own guilt by torturing yourself with the unanswerable Why? Sally feels guilty too. Instead of taking pleasure in her achievements, she is being made to feel that somehow they are a slap at her sister. And while Gail may not be as quick as Sally, she is no fool. She is doubtless feeling guilty herself, because you and Sally feel bad about her. You are generating a cycle of guilt. And it does not have to be."

In Marjorie's case, The Three Windows of Perception proved very helpful. Window One merely revealed two sisters of unequal accomplishment. But Marjorie's nose was firmly pressed against Window Two, where all she saw were two sisters of unequal accomplishment—*because Mother had failed one of them.* I eventually managed to move her to Window Three.

In time, Marjorie came to recognize that not only were we dealing with three members of the same family, we were dealing with three distinct individuals. We did not have three peas in a pod, but three separate pods. Marjorie had been a good mother to both daughters. But Sally and Gail were not hothouse plants who would grow up the same because presumably they were identical seeds raised under identical atmospheric conditions. Through Window Three, Marjorie saw two girls of unequal accomplishment—which could have several possible explanations: they were very different people; Sally may well have been smarter than Gail; or Gail might bloom later than Sally and in other areas—after all, she was only fifteen. The one thing that Marjorie needed to understand was that she did not "own" these two girls, even if she was their mother. She could hope to shape the clay. But she was dealing with two different varieties of clay and could not expect to mold both identically. She was not going to change any of these conditions or rewrite history by torturing herself with unanswerable questions about the past.

What Marjorie had to learn is that there are questions

for which there are no answers. Recognizing that fact is a sign of maturity. Learning to live with it is the mark of wisdom.

IT HAS TO BE SOMEBODY'S FAULT

How deeply the culture infects us with guilt. Religion can be one of the great guilt-makers when it is based on a wrathful God rather than a loving, understanding, and forgiving God. I remember what one patient told me of his early religious training. The clergyman had been talking about sinners going to hell. And then he told his young charges how long they would suffer in hell, if they sinned. My patient still remembered the man's words vividly thirty years later: "Imagine the earth as a steel ball. And imagine that once every million years, a dove's wing grazes that steel ball. When the dove has worn the ball down to nothing, that is when you will be released from hell!" How is that for the ultimate guilt trip? Little wonder that children raised on such horrific nonsense grow up guilt-prone.

A painful story of culturally inspired guilt is told in the movie *Ordinary People*. Young Conrad is consumed with guilt over his brother's death in a boating accident. His mother's coldly contained behavior and her obvious preference for her dead son have not helped Conrad deal with his overwhelming sense of responsibility for the tragedy. He tries unsuccessfully to commit suicide by slashing his wrists.

Conrad later sees a sympathetic psychiatrist who tries to make him understand the accident more clearly. "What have you done wrong?" the psychiatrist in effect asks. And Conrad blurts out: "It has to be *somebody's* fault."

That is what society has drilled into the boy's head. It has to be *somebody's* fault. Someone has to shoulder the guilt. Thus, a cultural conspiracy has driven a youth, at the very threshold of life, to attempt to kill himself. And what his therapist is trying to make Conrad see is that he need not be the slave of society's clichés. Somebody is *not* always guilty.

DO APOLOGIES HELP?

When someone tries to lay blame on us and tries to make us feel guilty, the hope is that we will say: "Now I see the light. I see what a bad person I've been. I hope you can forgive me for the terrible things I've done." I have serious doubts as to whether apologies serve any useful purpose in most situations. When someone makes us feel guilty and that we "owe" them an apology, they are usually seeking a form of control over us. Apologies only have meaning when we ourselves recognize that we have genuinely wronged someone and want them to know that we are aware of it and that we sincerely regret our actions. Otherwise, a pressured apology is just a manipulative device to add groveling to our guilt. I do not find apologies of that kind healthy or helpful.

GUILT-GIVING IS A BAD HABIT TOO

Let me repeat, perhaps ad nauseam, that guilt is a man-made emotion. Thus far, we have dealt with the emotional bad habit of people who feel chronic guilt. But hanging guilt on others is an insidious habit too. Guilt-giving is a symptom of other negative emotional problems. My patient, Alicia, was hooked on helplessness. She is the one who played the helpless female to arouse guilt in her husband so that he would never dare abandon her. But, when I made that diagnosis, you may recall, Alicia reacted by denying it and becoming defensive. And then she experienced that first Flash of Insight in my office. ("I see what I'm doing. I'm always showing Fred that I can't get along without him, so that he won't leave me.") After that, she became more and more aware when she was being manipulative. And the more aware she became, the less she did it.

I knew that Alicia had broken the cycle of acting helpless and inflicting guilt on her husband after the incident of the burglary. She and Fred had returned to their apartment the day before he was supposed to go to California to visit his children by a previous marriage. Let Alicia tell you what happened next:

"I saw this as another situation to make Fred feel guilty. Leave me alone in an apartment that crooks had just broken into? At the same time, I knew that this behavior of mine was driving him away from me. I knew how badly he wanted to see his kids. I thought of how you had made me aware of what I had been doing. I just made up my mind to turn over a new leaf. I told Fred to get packed. I would call the security company to come and change the locks on our doors. I got so involved in all this stuff over the next few days, with the burglar alarm people, the locksmith, and so on, that I barely noticed Fred was gone. And when he came back, he'd had such a wonderful time with his son and daughter. He was so happy. And I showed him the new security system I'd had installed. He didn't feel guilty about leaving me, because I didn't load any guilt on him. Instead, he felt proud of me. And I felt like a useful adult instead of a whining, helpless forty-three-year-old child."

SUMMING UP

Recapping what we have learned about guilt:

- When someone or something makes us feel guilty, ask: "What's going on here?" We may find that we are being manipulated into unnecessary guilt to serve somebody else's emotional needs.

- We need not feel guilty over others' misfortunes and unhappiness—unless we indeed caused them. Our empathy and understanding will help people much more.

- Don't rile up your guilt by continually asking yourself unanswerable questions.

- Everything that goes wrong does not have to be *somebody*'s fault.

- Don't be pressured into making unwarranted apologies. The apology may just be a device for someone to add groveling to your guilt.

- Above all, remember that guilt is a man-made emotion. We can stop manufacturing it and stop injecting ourselves with it.

Chapter 9

ASSERTIVENESS: THE EMOTIONAL GOOD HABIT

Carole L., a government employee: "I was on a plane and this rich-looking woman asked me if I'd mind moving over one seat so she and her friend could sit together. So I wound up sitting on the aisle, which I hate. Afterward, I found myself crying. Why do I let people walk all over me? Why don't I stand up for myself? I hate myself for that."

Jerry M., a systems analyst: "I make tennis dates with this friend. I have to get up an hour early to do it. And we only have the court for an hour. He's always late. I just boil inside. But when he shows up, I don't say a word. I just kind of give him a sickly smile."

Elaine S., an occupational therapist: "My in-laws are always disrupting our plans and announcing that they are coming to stay with us for a week or so. And I never know how to say no."

Carole, Jerry, and Elaine are patients and students of mine. And they are hanging onto addictions labeled Low Self-Esteem, Shyness, and Passivity. They demean themselves by letting other people manipulate them. They take no pleasure in their compliance. Instead, they feel "used," like "doormats" or "damn fools." They do not respect themselves because they make themselves unworthy of the respect of others. They are, in a word, nonassertive.

Fortunately, there has emerged in the past few years aid for the unassertive. The concept of assertiveness training has gained widespread acceptance, and it works in breaking emotional bad habits.

First, let's look at four basic personality types in terms of assertiveness:

1. *The Compliant Personality*. Remember Betty M., The Pleaser? She worked so hard to be and do everything that her lover wanted that she lost all sight of who she was or what she wanted for herself. Betty was the ultimate compliant personality. You could almost see the footprints on her back.

2. *The Aggressive Personality*. The direct opposite of The Pleaser. He is racing up in the fast lane and you'd better get out of the way. He knows what he wants and he is not particularly concerned about how he gets it. The end justifies any means. The aggressive personality's battle cry is: "Hooray for me, and to hell with you!"

3. *The Passive-Aggressive Personality*. The passive-aggressive is docile on the surface and cunning underneath. A passive-aggressive is the secretary who hates filing and makes sure that she does it so badly that somebody else ends up doing it for her. On a more insidious level, remember the classic movie *Gaslight*, in which the "loving husband" makes his wife believe that she is losing her mind? Passive-aggressives are expert "gaslighters."

4. *The Assertive Personality*. Assertive personalities try to win what they honestly believe they are

entitled to—but not at the expense of others. They speak up for themselves—and for others. They do so with the moral force of right on their side. And they do so fairly but firmly. Assertive personalities are what I am trying to make of Elaine, Jerry, Carole, and all my patients and students who are carrying around a doormat for an insecurity blanket.

I often wish that there were a better word than *assertiveness* to describe the state we are after. *Self-assured* might be better, or *self-confident.* Too many people still confuse assertive with bullying behavior. The major difference is that the aggressive personality acts in his or her own selfish interest. The assertive personality acts forcefully, but fairly. The aggressive personality may be feared, while the assertive personality is respected. The aggressive personality uses humor as a weapon to cut, to hurt, to demean. The assertive personality uses humor to create a bond with others or to defuse tense situations. But even if the two words—*aggressive* and *assertive*—sound too close for comfort, *assertiveness training* has entered the language. The concept is invaluable, and so we will use it.

SWITCHED-ON AGGRESSIVENESS

Before we get into the value of assertiveness training in breaking emotional bad habits, let's consider this question: Is *aggressiveness* always a bad word? Is there no place for aggression in our repertory of acceptable behavior? Yes, there is—when we control it, when we use it consciously and selectively, and, most important, when we know how to turn the aggression on and off.

I once took my daughter to the airport. She was to fly

on a student discount fare. As she got up to the counter, the clerk demanded some form of ID, which Sylvia did not have. He tried to shunt her aside. Time was running out and I knew that if something was not done soon, she would miss her flight. I quite deliberately flipped on my "pushy mother" switch, and I bellowed: "Whaddaya mean she needs an ID? Where did the ad say she had to show an ID at the airport?" I saw poor Sylvia cringe with embarrassment. But the clerk's expression said: *Let me get rid of this kook before she does something crazy.* He grudgingly issued Sylvia her ticket. Then I snapped off the aggressive switch, thanked the man, and left. But, ninety-nine times out of a hundred, I counsel assertiveness, not aggressiveness.

HANDLING A
PASSIVE-AGGRESSIVE

I had a patient who was being driven crazy in her own home by a passive-aggressive. Her name was Tina and his was Art. Art was a tenant in an apartment in the house that Tina owned. In the beginning they had been not only good neighbors but friends. They would walk their dogs together, kid around, and tease each other mercilessly.

Then, for no reason that Tina could figure out, Art suddenly became unfriendly. He barely spoke to Tina. When she asked: "Is there anything wrong? Have I done anything to offend you?" Art would just turn away and grumble: "Nope. I'm fine," and disappear back into his shell.

Art's behavior was making Tina an emotional prisoner in her own home. She was uncomfortable whenever Art was around. Tina is a sensitive woman with traces of the guilt-prone and rejectee personality, which had brought her to me in the first place. Art was preying on both habits, her guilt and her fear of rejection. But Tina did not want to throw him out, because she dreaded the confrontation. Also, until his mood change, Art had been a model tenant. And so she went on trying to mollify him and getting the cold shoulder for her trouble.

I told Tina that she was being manipulated by a passive-aggressive. He was controlling her mood and her environment and apparently enjoying the power. In her concern to know what *she* had done wrong, this man was, in effect, "gaslighting" her.

I suggested that the next time Tina saw Art, she could say this—and this only—to him: "I don't know what the problem is. But when you are ready to talk about it, let me know. I'll be here." (Notice, I recommended, "when" not "if," thus leaving the psychological leverage in Tina's hands.) Then I advised her to resume her normal behavior around the house as much as she could. "Don't let his behavior control your behavior," were my parting words as Tina left my office.

The next time she came to see me, Tina told me about her last encounter with Art: "I came through the yard, walking my dog. I saw Art and gave him a big smile. I said: 'Hi' and stopped only long enough to give him the little speech about discussing the problem *when* he was ready. Then I just kept right on going. I was walking 'assertively,' you might say. The next morning, I almost fell over. Art said: "Hi, Tina. How ya doin'?" And then he offered to drive me to the garage where my car was being fixed!"

What Tina had done was to send Art a loud, clear message. She was not available for his rejection. By her assertive self-assurance, she made clear that she was going about her life, regardless of his behavior toward her. When Art realized that fact, he knew that he no longer exercised control over her. And he gave up the game.

Art provides a relatively mild case of passive-aggressiveness. The ultimate passive-aggressive personality appears in the musical *I'm Getting My Act Together and Taking It on the Road*. The husband is manipulated by his wife's suicide threats. In effect, she says: "Leave me and I'll kill myself." When the husband meets an intelligent and assertive woman, he is unable to free himself from his psychological bondage to his wife. The wife controls him through the ultimate passive-aggressive weapon. If he abandons her, he will be responsible for her death.

SOFT ASSERTIVENESS

A husband and wife have a fight over a dinner invitation. Ben, the husband, is annoyed because Lucille, his wife, has agreed that they will go to dinner at the home of people whom Ben can't stand. Ben becomes abusive. He calls Lucille "an invitation junkie." She couldn't turn down the village idiot, he bellows. "It's a good thing you're on the pill," Ben says, "because you don't know how to say 'No' to anybody."

Later, they go to bed, and Ben is in the mood for sex. Lucille now faces a problem. She feels angry over his earlier abuse of her. And her angry self wants to reject him. However, her loving self wants him. The two selves are in conflict. Earlier, she had been a receptacle for his ridicule. Now he wants to make her a receptacle for his desire. If she gives in, she will feel as though she has betrayed her justifiably angry self. It is also a sticky situation because her husband has now escalated the earlier scrap over the invitation to the more sensitive issue of sexual rejection.

Here is another opportunity to apply assertiveness training techniques. And let me stress that assertiveness need not be a grim, relentless pursuit of our "rights." We can also use softening behavior and humor to achieve assertive ends. In this case, Lucille says to Ben: "Yes, I want the cuddling, the warmth, the intimacy. But you made me mad tonight. You were impatient and abusive toward me. My anger is justified. And I won't feel good giving in to sexy old you without a fight. So why don't you let me push you away. A symbolic push. And then you come on to me. Tell me all those sweet nothings. Woo me! Seduce me!"

Our injured party has used humor assertively. She has also taken another assertive tack that I much approve of. Again, it is a matter of finding the right words. She has cued the other person to the healing phrases that she needs to hear. She has given her husband predictability about herself. She has behaved shrewdly, amusingly, yet assertively. And this is far better than she and Ben turning their backs on each other, which is all too often how such domestic wars are waged.

As you can see, handling situations where assertiveness is called for can include some complex behavior, moves and countermoves, ploys and counterploys. Elements of playacting may be involved. But then, much of life is role playing. The important question is whether our acting is for positive or negative ends.

Let's look at another example of the assertive use of words. This one also involves modern mores and sex. I increasingly hear from my single female students and patients that they hate carrying condoms. But with the fear of AIDS and herpes, they feel that they ought to protect themselves. One of my patients, Isabelle S., a young teacher, told me: "It's agony for me to carry those things. No matter how pretty they make the packages, men are still offended. It goes against their romantic ideals. And mine too, I guess."

We talked about assertive language, words that would make her intentions perfectly clear without giving offense. What Isabelle and I worked out—and what she is now saying to men—is this: "What I'm about to say is not a reflection on you. But, I made a contract with myself. As long as these health threats exist, I'm not going to have sex with anyone who does not wear a condom. Period."

We had discussed in advance all the negative reactions that she would probably encounter. But Isabelle is sticking to her words. She is convinced that her attitude is intelligent and defensible. It is also assertive. In a firm but reasonable way, she is making absolutely clear where she stands.

THE ASSERTIVE VOICE

Assertiveness is a state of mind. It is a posture, a certain quality in the voice itself. When we speak clearly and with certainty, people will tend to take us at our word. We project authority, an air that we know what we are talking about. The melody pattern of our voice signals our firmness and confidence, or our fears and insecurity. There is a great authority vacuum out there. And people who at least sound as though they know whereof they speak are the ones who usually fill that vacuum.

I still recall with horror the time a friend visited me with her four-year-old. Little Mark took a fancy to a Steuben crystal bird on my coffee table and started playing with it. His mother said: "Mark, Mark darling, please. Please put Penny's bird down, honey. Please, Mark." Those were the words. But the melody pattern said: *I know you never listen to tiresome old Mommy, Mark, you adorable little devil. I don't expect you to listen now. But I do have to say something for Penny's sake.* So Mark indeed ignored her and went on fidgeting with my high-priced bird.

But, after the bird survived the first drop to the floor, I could not take it anymore. "Mark," I said, "put the bird down." I did not raise my voice. But my melody pattern was coolly unmistakable in intent. I meant, *put the bird down.* His mother did not. My tone had been assertive, his mother's compliant. And the child heard the difference. When I spoke, Mark put the bird down.

BROKEN RECORD

One of the most effective techniques yet devised for becoming an assertive person is "Broken Record." Broken Record is essentially another way of finding the right words. The technique helps us to form the true message we want to transmit. It keeps us from being distracted from our goal. It makes clear to the other person that we know what we want and that we are not about to be sidetracked.

Remember Leonard G., the out-of-work geologist, and how we emptied his can of worms? Another of Leonard's emotional bad habits was his passivity. It came out when he told me about a camera that he had bought from one of those perpetually "going out of business" stores. When he got home, Leonard realized that the camera was defective. Not only that, but the camera had been misrepresented; it was a cheap knock-off of the brand he thought he had bought. He told me that he had taken the camera back, but the clerk had told him: "Sorry. All sales are final."

"Do you still have the camera and the sales slip?" I asked. Leonard said yes, he did. "Okay, Leonard. Then I am going to tell you about Broken Record." We began by deciding exactly how he wanted this matter of the camera resolved. Leonard said: "Well, I want my money back."

"Fine. Then that's your message. You want your money back. Keep repeating it to yourself aloud again and again until your ears plant the thought firmly in your brain. Then, go back to that store and tell them, 'I want my money back.' Say it courteously, *but firmly*. And *do not alter the message*. Do not be diverted. Do not be distracted. You are going to be like a broken record. You want your money back."

At our next session, Leonard reported his encounter at the camera shop. He had said to the clerk: "I bought this camera here. It's defective. It's not the model I was told it was. I want my money back."

"All sales final," the clerk said and started to move away.

"I want my money back," Leonard said calmly but more firmly. The clerk shrugged and told Leonard he would have to see the manager. The manager came over, looked at the camera, saw the defect, and said: "No problem. I'll get you another one."

"I want my money back," Leonard said.

Now the manager was getting red-faced. "Look, pal, you don't like this model. For another fiver, I can give you a top-of-the-line fast-speed . . ."

"I want my money back."

The manager now tried a waxy smile. "Okay, I'll tell you what. You want your money back, I'll make an exception in your case. I'll give you a credit slip for the amount of the camera."

"I want my money back," said Leonard.

And, in the end, Leonard got his money back.

Leonard had behaved like a fisherman who will not let the fish off the hook—no matter how desperately it wiggles. The fish hook was his constantly repeated refrain: "I want my money back." Leonard had asserted himself. And he had won. Broken Record had given him a singleness of purpose that communicated itself to others. Not only did the technique have the desired effect on the store manager, but the sound of Leonard's voice, firm and unwavering, gave Leonard confidence too.

I also taught Broken Record to Marge A., who had an assertiveness problem at home. Marge felt that she was the designated doormat in her marriage with Stan. Which was what brought her to me. Marge's emotional bad habit was low self-esteem, which Stan's behavior reinforced. The way Marge put it: "I always have the feeling that what I want doesn't count—even I don't count."

Stan was not a bad man. He was just thoughtless. One of Marge's pet peeves was that Stan rarely bothered to tell her where he was going to be or what time he was coming home. He then became defensive if Marge questioned him. Marge was defensive too. And her complaints about his insensitive behavior usually ended up in shouting matches, with Stan, in the end, managing to completely bamboozle Marge. By the time the shouting stopped, her original complaint had somehow gotten lost in the verbal wreckage. Stan always managed to leave Marge crying and convinced that the spat had been her fault.

Marge's situation is not at all unusual. She shares it with millions of other women. I wanted her to crawl out of the common female trap in which women go into a situation with a perfectly legitimate gripe and come out feeling like the culprit instead of the victim.

I believed that Broken Record could help Marge stay on target. It could keep her vision clear even when Stan started throwing verbal sand in her eyes. And so we worked on Broken Record responses for her most common run-ins with Stan.

One night a few weeks later, Marge had dinner in the oven, ready to serve at eight. By nine, Stan had still not arrived. She called his office and got no answer. She was angry. By ten o'clock, she was scared. He had been taking a new drug for his angina and Marge wondered whether he had had a heart attack. Was Stan in a hospital? Was he lying dead in the street? She found herself glued to the window, staring out, hour after hour. But, one corner of her mind was also rehearsing a Broken Record response that she and I had discussed. Finally, at midnight, Stan came rolling in. He had obviously been drinking. Marge suppressed her twin urges—to embrace him because he was all right, and to strangle him for what he had put her through. Instead, she swallowed hard and, as calmly as she could, said: "Stanley, dinner has been ready since eight o'clock and now it's too late to eat it. There are any number of things I would have liked to do tonight rather than wait for you. *In the future, I would appreciate it, when you are going to be late, if you would call and let me know ahead of time.*"

STAN: What's the big deal? Save the dinner for tomorrow night!

MARGE: Stanley, *in the future, I would appreciate it, when you are going to be late, if you would call and let me know ahead of time.*

STAN: I don't get you. My boss invites me out for drinks. Then he asks me to have dinner with him. What am I supposed to do? Spit in his eye?

MARGE: *In the future, I would appreciate it, when you are going to be* . . .

STAN (now thrown off balance and angry): You're so selfish! You give me a pain you know where. Christ, I'm going to bed, and to hell with you and your dinner. You spoiled the whole evening!

MARGE: *In the future* . . .

Did Marge's Broken Record work? Will Stan change? Will he call her the next time he is going to be late? Will he be more thoughtful in the future? Maybe yes; maybe no. But, whether he does or not, the Broken Record has

helped Marge to win with herself. She was able to crystallize her feelings in a phrase. She did not allow herself
to be distracted. She did not allow herself to be drawn
into a shouting match with her husband. With calmness
and dignity, she pivoted around her newfound column of
confidence and stood up for her rights. She never lost her
temper. Never raised her voice. And she went to bed
without crying and without the usual feeling that she had
been in the wrong. In fact, she went to bed feeling good
about herself. And it is even possible that Stan got the
message.

SUMMING UP

What have we learned about assertiveness? We know the
following:

- Compliant, aggressive, and passive-aggressive behaviors are essentially unhealthy and we need to develop
an assertive approach to life.

- Aggressive behavior is recommended only in rare situations and only when we have our hand firmly on the
on-off switch.

- We can deal with aggressive and passive-aggressive
people by making clear that we are not available for
their manipulations.

- Assertiveness need not be strident. It can be expressed
through humor and subtlety.

- Broken Record is a highly effective technique for achiev-
ing assertiveness and for making unmistakably clear
what we want and where we stand.

Chapter 10

"SORRY, I'M NOT AVAILABLE"

Rejectees give off signals that say: "I am rejectable." People who feel inferior say and do things that set their inferiority feelings in italics. Pessimists invite disappointment. I'm reminded of a mean little trick they used to play in my girls' school. Somebody would sneakily Scotch tape to some kid's back a sign saying: KICK ME. And the poor kid would go around all day wondering why everyone was laughing and giggling at her. That is how many of us are going through life. Perhaps unknown to ourselves, but obvious to everyone else, we are carrying signs that say: REJECT ME, or ANGER ME, or DISAPPOINT ME.

Some of the people I see in class or in my office remind me of vending machines. They seem to have buttons on them. By their behavior, they seem to be saying: "You want some guilt out of me? Okay, push the top button. You want self-loathing? Try the middle one. You want to see some anger? Hit the bottom button. I'll always come through."

Others invite unhappiness by a more complicated route. We have all met the guy at the party who instantly impresses everybody by his brilliance and wit. But, as the night wears on and he never shuts up, his style begins to wear thin. We start to OD on his compulsive need to be the center of attention. Here is a person saying, in a roundabout way: "Dislike me." And we do.

I have occasionally used in this book the phrase, "Don't make yourself available." Many of the techniques we have considered so far are really ways to give people predictability about ourselves, to transmit the message: "I am not available for rejection . . . or guilt . . . or hysteria . . . or whatever it is you are trying to dump on me."

Broken Record, for example, is designed to make it unmistakably clear that you are not about to be bullied into retreat or detoured down an emotional side street. You know what message you want to deliver, even if you have to repeat it a dozen times. The whole point of assertiveness training is to communicate to others: "I am not available for your dumping." The objective of To You-ness To Me-ness is to demonstrate that you are not about to become the prisoner of somebody else's opinion of you. You are not going to be maneuvered into feelings of selfishness or anger or low self-esteem. Instead, you are announcing: "You and I have a difference of opinion about me. To you, I'm selfish. To me, I'm self-concerned. To you, I'm too tall. To me, you judge people by superficial standards. To you, I'm incompetent. To me, I'm a good worker who gets rattled by your constant criticism." The reason why it is important to recognize cultural clichés is so that we will not be taken in by them. Instead, we can stand on our own two feet and say: "I'm not buying that. It doesn't fit me. Because I'm a woman, don't expect me to behave helplessly. Don't expect me to hide my talent under a bushel." "Where is it written?" and "Who said so?" are also ways of declaring our emotional independence and giving predictability about ourselves. We are not going to follow the herd blindly down Negative Alley. Replaying The Tape helps us to recognize past situations where we may have failed to give predictability about ourselves. As we recall our past actions, we may see where we virtually invited second-class treatment. We were going around with that KICK ME sign on our backs. But now we are tearing it off.

DON'T TAKE THE BAIT

Doris G. is an expert at giving people predictability about herself. Doris is not a patient of mine. She is a friend who long ago shed her insecurity blankets, if she ever had any. Doris's husband, Russell, however, is a deeply neurotic man. And the way she handles his bids for sympathy are models of how not to make yourself available for someone else's neuroses.

Russell suffers from a Sears catalog of ailments, real and imaginary. Recently, he underwent treatment for serious high blood pressure. Soon afterward, Russell told Doris: "I can't take it anymore, I'm going to kill myself." Then he looked at Doris expectantly.

The following dialogue ensued:

DORIS: Russell, I wish you didn't feel that way. But if you feel that unhappy . . .

RUSSELL: Don't you care? I'm your husband. I tell you I'm going to kill myself, and you act as though I'm talking about the weather.

DORIS: I wouldn't want you to live a life of misery.

RUSSELL: I'd be leaving you and the kids in the lurch, wouldn't I?

DORIS: Yes, and we would miss you terribly. But if you are so dissatisfied with your life . . .

RUSSELL: I would think it would drive you crazy just to hear me talk about it.

DORIS: I'm sorry, my love. I just don't feel suicidal myself. I love life. I wish you did, too.

RUSSELL: You know, I just remembered. The doctor told me those pills might have a depressing effect on me. Maybe he can switch me to a different prescription.

Doris knew enough not to make herself a receptacle for her husband's neuroses. She simply was not available for Russell's emotional manipulation. She gave him plenty of predictability about herself. Doris is also a good example of providing empathy instead of sympathy. Instead of jumping into the river with Russell, she gave him enough rope to pull himself out.

GIVING THE RIGHT SIGNAL

If someone hands us something, say a book, our reflex is to take it. If someone hands us a load of guff, our impulse may be to take it, too. But why should we? And if we don't accept it, then whoever is dishing it out is stuck with it. That is what predictability and availability are all about. You have a perfect right not to be lured into somebody else's emotional game-playing. You have the right to say "no."

If a husband wants an "open marriage" and the wife would feel vulnerable in that situation, she has a perfect right to protect her own interests. She has the right to say "no."

You have a perfect right not to be emotionally whipsawed by others. You can learn to cue people, with the right words, as to what you will and will not tolerate.

Let's take the case of Miriam P., an executive secretary who has been going out with a man for the past six months. Miriam is strongly attracted to him, but he is forever disappointing her. He tells Miriam that he will call tomorrow, or Friday, or Saturday, and then he doesn't call. His thoughtlessness is painful to her—and disruptive of her plans. My advice to Miriam is to give him predictability about herself. Tell him something along these lines: "Don't say you'll call me tomorrow if you don't intend to. Say you'll call me when you can. It's unfair to expect me to wait for a call that may or may not come. I don't like it." These words protect her dignity. They also put her in a position of shared control in the relationship.

All too often we give the worst possible predictability about ourselves. We make ourselves available for shabby treatment. Take the starry-eyed woman who endows a man with the combined qualities of Clark Gable and Saint Francis. She "invents" him as her ideal. Then she starts to berate him for not being what she invented. The fellow says: "Hey, what's going on here? This is a case of mistaken identity. You're hanging the wrong guy. I'm getting out of here." She has made herself available for abandonment and has virtually conspired to make sure it happens. Or take Adele, smarting because her niece did not send her a thank-you note. Adele is poised, ready, and available for rejection, sitting there like a duck in a shooting gallery, just waiting to be hurt.

You cannot reject somebody who is not available for rejection. You cannot put down somebody who is not available to be put down. You cannot castrate a man who is not available for castration. You can reduce your vulnerability by letting those around you know how you are going to react, by giving them predictability about yourself and by making clear what you will or won't put up with from them.

YOUR SPINAL COLUMN
OF CONFIDENCE

———————————————— ■ ————————————————

If we did not have a spinal column, our bodies would collapse like punctured balloons. It is much the same with our emotional posture. The chronically depressed person, the helpless female, the rejectee, the catastrophizer all have about them an almost visible emotional sag. They lack a spinal column of confidence. They give off the message that they are available for emotional exploitation. On the other hand, we all know people who give off the opposite signals. They revolve around a spinal column of confidence. They give clear signals about what they will or will not tolerate. Their column of confidence holds them upright. We can almost see it, like a second backbone providing psychological assurance. And we respect the message these people give off: "Treat me with respect."

We can nurture such a column of confidence in ourselves. We can learn to achieve a posture of self-assurance. We begin by assuming a certain physical stance. We say to ourselves:

- I am holding my shoulders square, not slumped.

- The seat of my pants is planted firmly in the chair—not three inches above it.

- I am leaving space between my arms and body and under my chin.

- My feet are planted firmly on the floor.

- There! Now I feel comfortable and composed. I can start to feel that column of confidence running up and down my spine.

- I am also giving myself plenty of time to think. I am not about to be stampeded into saying or doing something before I am ready, before I have thought it through. I am not available for manipulation. I am not going to allow anyone to use me as the trash bin for their anger, their neuroses, or their emotional blackmail. There is a strong, stable "thereness" about me, a certain authoritative weight. My thoughts, words, and deeds are all emanating from a column of confidence.

I had a patient, Vicki P., a student in whom I wanted to implant a column of confidence. Let me tell you how we proceeded. Vicki's negative habit was a rock-bottom opinion of herself—subzero self-esteem. Vicki is the one I quoted in chapter 1: "I never seem to say the right thing. I never do the right thing." During our sessions, she was constantly shredding tissues.

Vicki had been raised in the shadow of an older sister. Her sister had habitually put Vicki down: "She made me feel that whatever I said or did was stupid." Vicki had accepted her sister's judgment of her and carried it into adulthood. She had a marvelous capacity for turning almost anything that happened to her into proof of her inferiority.

I had her carry out behavior modification to overcome her feeling that nobody would want her friendship. I assigned her to make lunch dates and to join a hiking club. I taught her to Talk Tenderly To Herself whenever she thought she had done something stupid. But mostly, I helped Vicki build her spinal column of confidence by Replaying The Tape. We went over some of the most scarring childhood conversations with her sister that she could remember.

As the weeks passed and we employed the above techniques, Vicki turned out to be an apt pupil. I was working with first-class ore. Underneath her insecurity blanket of inferiority feelings, Vicki was a highly intelligent person of strong character—if only I could get through that blanket of suffocating low self-esteem.

Until now, nobody had ever told her that she could look at her life differently. Nobody had shown her that her feelings of inferiority were disposable and not permanent. I was telling her things that were virtually revelations. I was demonstrating to her that her problem was one of perception—how she saw herself, or, more accurately, how she let others dictate her opinion of herself. And above all I was demonstrating to her that this perception could be changed for the better. After several weeks, I asked Vicki to describe how she felt about her early relations with her sister in light of her newfound knowledge. Here is what she said:

"If I had been old enough to understand these things, I would have asked myself, 'What's going on here?' I'd Replay The Tapes of some of those conversations where she made me feel like an idiot. And I'd start to ask myself, 'Why is she always doing this? Is she an authority on my intelligence?' The truth is she was eight years older than I. She'd been the center of my parents' attention for years before I came along. And she was not happy that I came and broke up her monopoly. So, she did quite a number on my self-esteem when we were kids at home. But she sure was no authority on my intelligence. She was not a fair judge of anything about me. Now I've arrived at a point where I'll be the judge of my ability. Not her."

In time, I could virtually see Vicki's column of confidence grow, lifting her up taller and straighter. I could see the chin held level and the shoulders squared. The hands folded in her lap. The calm look in her eye. The tissues unshredded. Vicki was beginning to revolve around her column of confidence.

Let's take an identical set of facts and see how a person like Vicki, with a column of confidence, reacts to that situation, compared to someone with a psychological spine made of Styrofoam. The boss is coming to the office over the weekend and tells his assistant to leave a cer-

144

tain important file on his desk. On the way in on Monday, the assistant remembers, to his horror, that he forgot to leave the file out for the boss.

The tower of Styrofoam presents the worst elements of contrition and defensiveness: "Oh, my God, Mr. Rossi, what a stupid thing! I'm so sorry. I probably ruined the weekend for you. I made you come in for *nothing*. I feel like the biggest jerk in the company. I was sure my secretary would take care of the file. I was sure I told her, I guess. But of course it's really my fault, isn't it. Of course it's my fault, my fault, my fault. . . ."

The confident personality pivots around his or her column of confidence and shows empathy toward the boss, but does not grovel. "That was careless of me, Mr. Rossi. I'm sorry. It must have been annoying to come all the way in and not find the file. I hope you had something else lined up to do and that I didn't cause you too much inconvenience. I don't think it will happen again."

A column of confidence communicates itself to other people. We are all attracted to assured behavior. We all respect calm speech, carefully reasoned thinking, and cool judgment. Our overeagerness and sweaty palms make other people uncomfortable—and suspicious. And that goes for our dealings with bosses, teachers, bank loan managers, and prospective lovers, for that matter.

The confident personality has the self-control to walk into good situations—and walk away from bad ones. The person revolving around a spinal column of confidence does not slink or flee from a rebuff, but walks away with dignity and pride intact. The confident personality does not have to protect the ego with icy disdain. He or she deals with an unsuccessful social encounter with this attitude: "*To you*, this relationship is not worth pursuing. *To me*, that is unfortunate. We might have given something to each other."

People who pivot around a column of confidence are in sync—internally in dealing with themselves and externally in dealing with other people. We can build that core within ourselves. We can condition ourselves to stand up straight emotionally. And from that stand-up posture, we can slip our emotional bad habits off our backs.

SUMMING UP

Let's summarize what we have learned about giving people predictable signals about ourselves, how to tip them off as to what we are—or are not—available for.

- Learn the techniques of assertiveness training.

- Use Broken Record to make our intentions unmistakable.

- Practice To You-ness To Me-ness to clarify differences of opinion about us, differences that may encourage people to think they can dump on us.

- Replay The Tape to spot past unassertive behavior and to devise more assertive future responses.

- Reject culturally imposed roles that do not fit us.

- Give people the words that crystallize our meaning and that help to cue their behavior toward us.

- Develop a column of confidence, including a physical posture that signals to people that we are firmly rooted and not available for their manipulations.

Chapter 11

———————————•———————————

INFERIORITY: CHASING
THE NOBODY BLUES

People tend to take us at our word. If we think we are inferior, they will be inclined to accept our judgment and treat us accordingly.

- Roberta W., a school administrator: "I suffer from psychological leprosy." Not surprisingly, people do tend to treat Roberta as though she has a communicable disease.

- Charlotte M., a student: "My mother was always telling me, 'You should hang your head in shame.' " And Charlotte does have a hangdog look about her.

One of the most touching cases of low self-esteem I ever encountered was Skip, a boy I counseled when I was a school psychologist. I was administering a test to him and asked him to define an apple. Skip said: "It's a red thing. It's round and you can eat it." He immediately followed up that perfectly good answer with: "Wrong, right?" He was so habituated to feeling inferior that the only "right" condition for Skip was to be "wrong." At a tragically early age, this boy saw himself stuck in the wrong lane for life.

Virtually all of us have an Achilles' heel, a weak spot on our psyche. I once talked to a world-renowned female physician. I asked her if she considered herself a success. There was a pained silence. And then she said: "No. I'm fat." Here was one of the most valuable human beings I know. And she could be brought low by one word—*fat.*

Most of us are plagued from time to time by such feelings. Others of us are dogged continually by them, hooked on the habit of feeling worthless. Of all the negative emotional habits I treat, low self-esteem is one of the most common and one of the most easily triggered.

I had a patient, a housewife, Lorraine T., who wanted to be a writer. She wrote furtively, in between household chores and raising her children. She never said a word about the writing. Then one night after the children had gone to bed, Lorraine nervously handed her husband a typed draft—her first short story.

"What happened?" I asked eagerly. "He sneered," she said. "He flipped through a couple of pages, looked up, and laughed at me. I tore the story up and threw it in the garbage can. And I cried my heart out that night. I haven't touched the typewriter since." Lorraine's reaction is all too common for a person whose insecurity blanket is low self-esteem. She had a Humpty Dumpty ego. One tap and she fell to pieces. You will also notice that she looked only through Window Two, knew nothing about To You-ness To Me-ness, and ended up committing partial suicide by not writing any more.

I am now working with Lorraine to master those techniques. And I have persuaded her to sit down again at her typewriter. One of her assignments was to bring me her latest short story. I read it. And I would say that as a literary critic, her husband is a flop. She obviously can write. I have also persuaded Lorraine to enroll in a short-story course where her talent will get the nurturing it deserves.

But her initial behavior—letting her husband's scorn crush her—is the classic reaction of people whose negative habit is poor self-esteem. They go around waiting to have that judgment confirmed. They do not question the qualifications of the judge. They already believe themselves inferior or untalented; the fact that someone else says so merely confirms how right the other person is. I am helping Lorraine say to herself—and to her husband—"What's going on here? Who is he to dismiss my writing talent?"

MUTUAL ENTRAPMENT: MARRIAGES MADE IN HELL

Frequently, people with low self-esteem have a way of finding each other. It would not be surprising if Lorraine's husband, for example, has his own share of inferiority feelings. Such couples often find a perverse security in each other. They are not threatened by a spouse or lover who has the self-assurance to walk out on them. They are rolled up in the same insecurity blanket, mutually entrapped.

Ellen and Bill are the most profound case of Mutual Entrapment in my clinical experience. Both were intelligent, yet plagued by feelings of inferiority. They both held nondemanding civil service jobs. And their marriage resembled two parasites feeding off of each other's neuroses.

Bill, a weak man at work, was a terror at home. His dinner-table conversation was an endless recital of Ellen's failings. His power trip was to pull himself up by pulling her down. "Can't you even get dinner on the table at a decent hour?" "Can't you drive the stupid car, stupid?" "If I hadn't married you, nobody else would have looked at you twice." "I don't want sex with you, because you just haven't got it."

Ellen took his chronic criticisms to heart. She was constantly asking herself: "Now what did I do wrong?" She honestly believed: "I do everything badly." "I'm a lousy wife." "I'm a poor excuse for a mother." "I should never have been born." She was forever telling Bill "I'm sorry" for this or that alleged failure on her part. Her life was one long apology for her existence.

Ellen was also a battered wife. And she was convinced that her behavior provoked Bill to beat her. In other words, it was her fault.

What small victories Ellen did achieve she dismissed as meaningless. (With Bill agreeing, of course.) He had taught her well the Mathematics of Guaranteed Unhappiness. Her defeats always far outweighed her victories. She was elected president of her garden club, worked hard, and did a good job. She ended her term, however, convinced that she had been a failure. (Bill agreed.) For along with her other negative habits, Ellen suffered from the Impostor Syndrome. If only the members knew how unqualified she was, they would never have elected her president. They just had never caught on.

As I listened to this woman, I knew exactly what she had done. Ellen had entered into a contract. Ellen was saying, in effect, with Bill's concurrence: "You keep telling me I'm worthless. And I'll keep on believing it. Then you'll feel more important than I. And because I can do this for your ego, you won't leave me. And that's what I need." Mutual Entrapment.

Yet, some secret part of Ellen was desperately trying to crawl out of this hell. On the side, she was stashing away money. When she had saved enough, she finally worked up the courage to leave Bill and went to stay temporarily with an aunt out of town. The next day, Bill killed himself.

Bill had lost the one source of validation in his life—

his control over Ellen. And, with his death, this tortured man added the final charge to his indictment of her. Not only was she a stupid, sexless wife and poor mother, she had driven him to suicide. Ellen came to me a few years later, still a shattered woman, her low opinion of herself confirmed by this tragedy.

What I worked on first with Ellen was awareness. I wanted to move her to a point where she could say: "Aha. So that's me. That's the role I played for Bill." We replayed The Tapes of her confrontations with him over the years. We examined the steady torrent of insults and abuse that he had heaped on her. Was it justified by the evidence? Was she a terrible wife, a bad mother, a poor driver, a failure as president of the garden club? What she eventually came to understand was how she had colluded with Bill to confirm his overriding need: to prove that he was better than somebody. Ellen provided the somebody.

Once she was able to understand the manipulative nature of Bill's behavior, she was freed of her belief that she was always wrong. Her only reason for accepting his judgments was her own sense of inferiority and her morbid need to hold on to him. This self-defeating attitude is not at all uncommon. I have numerous patients who cling desperately to unhealthy, destructive relationships. They feel that they must belong, even to a domineering parent, even to a disastrous marriage. Being left alone is the ultimate terror.

I also had Ellen carry out imaginary conversations with Bill—a retroactive form of To You-ness To Me-ness—using her new self-awareness: "*To you,* I was lucky you married me. Otherwise, no one else would have. *To me,* based on the men I have attracted since you've been gone, it seems you were wrong. To you, I was a lousy driver. To me, I was a nervous wreck because of your backseat driving."

I persuaded Ellen to Talk Tenderly To Herself, also retroactively. Bill's suicide had been a devastating blow to her. He had managed to harm Ellen right up to his dying breath. He had left her a crushing load of guilt as her inheritance. Ellen had to see that she was not really the cause of Bill's suicide. She was not obliged to lead a miserable existence with him so that he could sustain the illusion of his superiority over her. I told Ellen that she was to Talk Tenderly To Herself, to forgive herself, and not to let the gray ghost of guilt consume her.

Then we moved from the past to the future. Here our objective was to build a column of confidence around which Ellen could revolve. Without Bill to knock down whatever confidence she built up, she began to blossom. Ellen was not an unattractive woman. And she indeed started to go out with other men. In her long bondage to Bill, she had forgotten that all male-female relationships do not have to be sadistic and destructive. Bill represented one sick man, not all men. Her successful relations with other men friends, women friends, and colleagues began to reverse years of inferiority feelings. I could almost see that column of confidence straightening Ellen's spine.

It was a long, slow process. The gains took place over the course of years, not overnight. But Ellen did eventually shed her negative emotional habit. She stopped feeling and behaving as though she were worthless. She gave her victories the weight they deserved. She abandoned the Mathematics of Guaranteed Unhappiness. Ten years after the destruction of her first marriage, she was working, still in the civil service, but now at a high-level job as public relations director of her agency. And she was married to a loving and supportive man.

TRYING TOO HARD

In the above case, Ellen's long addiction to feelings of inferiority had been deliberately fostered by her husband— with malice aforethought. But an inferiority complex can also be caused by the best intentions gone awry. Kenny was a case of mine who illustrated a worthy goal pursued in the worst way.

He was ten years old, and he had been sent to me, as school psychologist, because his teachers wanted to know why he never paid attention in class and always appeared to be "out of it." Kenny was a wan-looking little boy. The first thing I observed was that he never smiled. It was also difficult for him to open up. But finally one afternoon after several dead-end questions, I managed to get a response. Kenny had had a particularly bad report card the week before. I asked him what had happened when he brought the report card home. "She lay down on the bed and cried," he said. Any other reactions? I wanted to know. "When he came home, he said he was going to send me to a farm where I'll have to work all the time."

"He" and "she." He never referred to his parents any other way. These impersonal pronouns were my first clue to what might be troubling this boy. I made an appointment to visit his parents at home.

Two things struck me immediately when I arrived—the obvious poverty of the family and their intense pride. The house was tiny, barely more than a cabin on an unpaved road outside of town. Besides Kenny, there were three younger sisters crowded into it. But everything was neat as a pin, the rooms, the furniture, and the children.

The father was a taciturn, stern-faced man who obviously ruled this roost. Kenny's mother looked frightened and kept glancing out of the corner of her eye at her husband, as though she feared displeasing him.

I learned that day that both the mother and father had been reared on farms doing back-breaking chores. Kenny was their first born—and a son. *His life was to be different.* He was to *make* something of himself. And the father's approach was to keep the boy under constant pressure. Kenny's home life amounted to an endless recital of his failings. His father was constantly warning him to do better, and punishing him with a strap when he did poorly. The mother, out of fear of her husband, went along. Thus, when Kenny's father was not leaning on the boy, his mother was crying over his inability to live out the family dream.

Out of the best of intentions, these parents were virtually addicting this boy to guilt and low self-esteem. Kenny's impersonal "he" and "she" when he talked about his parents was his way of insulating himself from them. The words *Mom* and *Dad*, which should have connoted warmth, security, and understanding, were absent in his home life. And so Kenny numbed himself with the neutral pronouns.

I now understood why he was such an unhappy child; why he was so clearly "out of it." Kenny's feelings ran something like this: "I'm disappointing 'them.' I'm worthless. I'm nobody. I'm hopeless. So they don't love me. What's the use of trying. I wish I'd never been born. I wish I could just disappear." Few sights are more heartbreaking to see than a child of ten who has already given up on life. That was Kenny, when I first worked with him.

I saw his parents again, and I tried to make them understand that we inspire children to do well, we do not terrify them into it. We need to provide a secure home harbor from which the child sails into the world feeling loved and secure, if he is to do well. I made some headway. But the father was a tough nut to crack. I concentrated my efforts on Kenny. But it is difficult to reach a child of that age with abstract psychological insights. Kenny needed to be shown, not told.

154

I learned from his teacher that the class was soon going to begin a project called "My Home Town" to show the children how a community works. "Is there anything that Kenny does well?" I asked the teacher. She laughed and said: "Window gazing. Maybe we could make him be a window shopper on Main Street." Then she added more seriously: "Actually, he draws fairly well." The next time Kenny came to my office, I gave him a pencil and a sheet of paper and asked him to sketch me. The result was not a bad likeness. I went back and talked with the teacher, and I suggested my idea to her. Thus, when the parents came to the school auditorium and walked down Main Street of "My Home Town," one shop was "Kenny's Art Studio," with his sketches of his classmates tacked to the wall. Kenny was a hit. And I suppose payday for me was to see that little boy smiling. His parents were smiling, too.

I am not naïve enough to believe that this single experience marked the end of Kenny's ingrained habit of low self-esteem. But I hoped it might be the beginning of the end. The lesson this child provides for adults hooked on the habit of feeling inferior is to look for the root. Were these feelings possibly imposed on us by others intentionally—as in the case of Vicki with her jealous older sister? Or were they unintentionally saddled onto us by well-meaning but poorly guided parents, such as Kenny's? Whichever the explanation, here is a place to ask: "What was going on there? What made me feel that way? *Who made me feel that way*—and why?" If we can get at the root cause, we may begin to realize that "inferior" is not what we are; it is what we have been made to feel. And, with the arrival of awareness, we can begin to apply the appropriate therapies—and end this losing game.

THE HELPLESSNESS HABIT

Helplessness and a sense of inferiority are closely bound together. The psychologist M. E. P. Seligman has done invaluable work on the personality that becomes hooked on helplessness with a subsequent loss of self-esteem. Seligman's useful idea for overcoming helplessness is that the way we look at what happens to us may be as important as what actually happens to us. If we can change the way we regard a situation, we can change the way it affects us. People who feel helpless tend to look at situations, Seligman says, as Stable, Global, and Internal. Let us say you lose a friend through something you said or did. If your reaction is: "I always screw up my friendships," that reaction is Stable—that is the way it is and that is the way it always will be. So you behave in future relationships as though breakups are the inevitable outcome of your friendships.

The lost friendship also confirms that "I can't do anything right." That reaction is Global. Everything you do always turns out the same way—badly.

Next, as you explain the breakup: "It was all my fault." That behavior is Internal. You always look inside yourself to find the culprit. Everything is always your fault.

The person who looks at the events of his or her life as Stable, Global, and Internal will almost inevitably feel helpless. For if all things are indeed ordained to turn out badly because of the kind of people we are, then our situation truly is hopeless. We exercise no free will. We are pawns in a losing game in which the rules never change. We are displaying those unmistakable symptoms of the negative-prone personality. We see ourselves at the Center of the Universe, flaw detector turned up high, suffering the tribulations of Job—"Woe is me, condemned to foul up to the end of time."

We need to learn instead to see things not as Stable, Global, and Internal, but as variable, depending on the time, the place, and the people involved. What happens to us is not always the same, not a confirmation of what always was and always will be. It is one page in the book of our lives. And the future pages still remain to be written. Our behavior is not locked into our genes, encoded into our chromosomes, a fixed part of our character. We have merely responded so consistently and predictably that our behavior has hardened into a habit that *seems* like part of our genetic makeup.

We can break the habit of seeing our helpless behavior as "Global"—"I always do everything wrong"—by remembering that there are several potential outcomes of a particular situation. The dice can come up in innumerable combinations. Nor do we have to accept that things are Stable, that they will always turn out the same for us. Virtually the only way we can ensure that things will always turn out wrong is by behaving as though they must turn out wrong, by habitually taking the pessimistic course. "I won't call my friend back, because she won't want to patch up the friendship after the way I screwed it up." Finally, we can get off the kick that "It's always my fault" by using The Three Windows of Perception. Your friend was cool to you during your last conversation and hasn't called back since. You assume that you haven't heard from her because of something you did. Maybe she had to leave town suddenly because of a death in the family. Or perhaps she has slipped into her own state of acute depression. Or maybe she is upset because you didn't want to join her tennis foursome. You don't really know.

You might call her and bring the conversation around to the foursome. You might say something like: "*To you*, sports are important. *To me* they are not really my thing. But I recognize that we don't have to have identical interests to be friends. And I want you to know that I value the interests we do share."

And if you did indeed lose a friend, do not say to yourself: "There, you miserable reject. You did it again." Say to yourself instead: "That was too bad. I wish I hadn't acted in a way that spoiled the friendship. Maybe I'm not perfect. But I am capable of changing. And I'll try not to repeat the same mistakes next time. You're still okay, sweetheart. You're not so bad."

In time, your emotional habits will not be seen as Stable, Global, and Internal. And they will not lock you into a state of helplessness. You will start to see that other doors are open to you.

THE IMPOSTOR SYNDROME

Have you ever dreamed that you were walking around in public, naked? It is a fairly common dream. And it rarely has anything to do with sex. Rather, the nude dream reveals our fear of having our disguises stripped away. The nude dream is a symptom of the Impostor Syndrome, another negative emotional habit I treat.

It is surprising to find out how many superior people suffer from the Impostor Syndrome. In fact, the genuine second-rater is often insensitive to his or her second-ratedness and, consequently, does not feel inferior. But many intelligent, able, hardworking people are habitually frightened that they are not intelligent, able, or hardworking enough.

Research psychologists have found that as many as four out of every ten successful people are hooked on the Impostor Syndrome. They believe their success is all a hoax perpetrated on an unsuspecting world, and they fear that they are going to be "found out." One major novelist of my acquaintance and one of my husband's most brilliant musician colleagues both suffer from the

Impostor Syndrome. One of the finest actors who ever walked across a stage or stepped before a camera often said that in his heart he was always a poor boy from a Welsh mining town and did not deserve his success. The actor was the late Richard Burton. I could name several other celebrities who still fear being unmasked as frauds.

The Impostor Syndrome is more common early in people's careers. It is particularly prevalent among people who have pulled themselves up by their own bootstraps—people like Richard Burton—who rose from humble beginnings. Self-made successes and people who are the first in their family to go to college also commonly experience the Impostor Syndrome. It is also found frequently among women who succeed in nontraditional professions—high finance, upper-level management, and engineering, for example. The Impostor Syndrome may be secretly tormenting the seemingly cocky hot-shot in your office.

The Impostor Syndrome is something that a healthy personality outgrows. Most people come in time to recognize that their success is entirely deserved. But for others, the inner suspicion that they are frauds is a chronic and crippling habit.

Abe T., a management consultant, was brought to me by his wife, Marsha, because their marriage was falling apart. Marsha's complaint was that she might as well be a widow. Abe was married to his job. Twelve-hour days and seven-day weeks were the norm. And when he did come home, he was too tired or preoccupied to have any time for Marsha or the children. The couple had been on one disastrous vacation in the previous eight years. Abe had brought his work along and had cut short the vacation by a week.

Abe defended his workaholism by saying: "I'm doing all this, breaking my back for you and the kids. Do you think it's for me? Who needs it?"

Abe needed it. Underneath his excuse that he was out there breadwinning for his family was a less attractive explanation for his fanatic devotion to his job. Abe was consumed with fear that he was not good enough. In his secret self, he believed that the only way he had succeeded in the company was by outworking everybody else. And the only way that he could hold on to his place was by continuing to do so. In his heart, Abe felt like a fake. He could never compete with his colleagues by working normal hours. They were obviously smarter than he was. He would just outsweat them. He was convinced that he was an impostor, substituting drudgery for talent, hours for ability.

Most people, after enough victories, finally have the security to recognize that they are not wearing a mask. Most people become in their own eyes the accomplished person whom the world sees. But, for the Abes of this world, the Impostor Syndrome is a form of inferiority feeling that can haunt them throughout life. Here he was, a successful man in his forties, and still unable to enjoy the fruits of his labor, still running scared and wrecking his marriage in the process. All because he could not shake off the Impostor Syndrome.

What I attempted to show Abe first was that he was not alone. I helped him to understand that at some point probably everyone he worked with had felt like a fraud about to be exposed. He was hardly unique, particularly in his competitive world of strivers and overachievers. The difference was that the others came in time to see their success as merited, while Abe still saw his success as a fluke. I told him, without using names, of famous patients I had helped who suffered from the same emotional bad habit. I wanted him to recognize that he was in good company. We were working toward awareness.

Next, I had Abe tell me about his work in detail. I asked him to describe to me various projects of his that had succeeded. I wanted to know what his superiors had said about these achievements. What emerged was that the praises and the raises had always related to the brilliance of Abe's ideas, not to the number of hours that he put in. Inspiration, not just perspiration, had led to his success. In fact, on numerous occasions his bosses had urged Abe to take more time off. They recognized that they had a valuable property. And they were not eager to see Abe burn himself out. Abe never entirely believed them. He assumed that the talk about time off and vacations was just their way of recognizing that he was a hard worker. Abe's reaction on hearing this was to beam with pride, and to show them that he could put in even longer hours.

It took months to bring Abe to a state of awareness. We finally got him to distinguish between the quantity of his work and the quality of it. Through our extensive Replaying The Tapes of his conversations with his bosses, it finally became clear what they were praising him for: it was not for being a workhorse, but for being a gifted innovator. And in time he came to see what he was doing to his wife and children. He had taken the marriage for granted. It was the firm foundation—always there for him to come back to, no matter how many hours he spent on the job, no matter how many business trips he made. But now that foundation was crumbling, and the threatened loss scared him.

Abe has changed. His wife had wondered if he ever could. He himself had never believed that he could. But he did. Now, instead of swamping a project in sheer hours, he puts in all the time necessary—and no more. At long last he has learned to delegate authority to able subordinates and not try to screw in every last bolt himself. As a result, another facet of Abe's capacities has emerged. He has come to be seen not simply as a talented, insecure drudge but as a leader and manager. And I learned that some months ago he was named a partner in the firm.

The Impostor Syndrome is not a common form of low self-esteem. But it can be a crippler. It robs people of the pleasure of their successes. It leads them to suffer unnecessary anxiety and puts a strain on their families. It is another emotional bad habit, and it can be broken.

MAGIC THINKING

———■———

There is another force that grips some victims of the Impostor Syndrome. They are carrying out a form of Magic Thinking. In the beginning of their careers they worried that they were unqualified—yet they succeeded. Therefore, they come to believe that the way for them to continue to succeed is to keep worrying that they will fail. They stand logic on its head. If they convince themselves that they are frauds, they will not be unmasked as frauds. This is an insidious form of superstition. My goal is to help these people see that what is succeeding for them is not mental mumbo-jumbo, not Magic Thinking, but their own talent.

This is a good time to look a little deeper into this phenomenon of Magic Thinking. I have a patient who is a catastrophizer. When she hears a fire engine, she always imagines that her house must be burning. So far, it hasn't happened. So she keeps imagining it is her house—to make sure it is not. Magic Thinking.

Another patient tells me: "I just read a book that says, 'Wishing will make it so.' " I answer: "I don't believe it."

Patient: "You gotta believe. Otherwise, it doesn't work."

Again, Magic Thinking. And again, I don't buy it. Believing in Magic Thinking is selling your intelligence for a mess of voodoo. It is, in the end, escapism from reality. If we deal in Magic Thinking, we lose effective control over our lives. We cannot shape our own destinies because we are depending on some form of hocus-pocus to do the job for us. Magic Thinking diverts us from taking the practical steps necessary to cope with life and substitutes superstition for intelligent action. The magic I recommend is to make Magic Thinking vanish.

THE IDENTIFIED PATIENT

———•———

Remember Vicky P. from chapter 9, the young woman whose older sister always made her feel stupid? As Vicki put it: "I was supposed to be the dumb one in a bright family." Other preassigned family roles that I run into among my patients are The Selfish Daughter, The Problem Child, The Hypochondriac.

These Identified Patients, not surprisingly, often wind up in therapy. I try to help them to understand "what's going on here." In their particular family, the father may be The Breadwinner; the mother may be The Queen Bee; the older brother may be The Model Son. In Vicki's case, she was The Dumb One in a Smart Family and expected to fail as part of her role. By portraying the Identified Patient, she helped the others hold on to their own roles— Smart Sister, Long-Suffering Parents, Big Brother.

I vividly remember a family who came to me; I'll call them the Greens. The son was a pupil in the school where I was the staff psychologist. Peter Green, age fourteen, was rowdy and incorrigible. He skipped school. He stole some of his mother's jewelry to buy pot. He picked fights with bigger boys and, consequently, was always being beaten up, as though he was looking for punishment. Virtually every teacher and student had a low opinion of him. But no one had a lower opinion of Peter Green than Peter himself.

After I had talked with him a few times, I decided to call a family conference. It was not long before I understood the psychodynamics of the Green family. It became clear that the father and mother did not get along. But, rather than face the failure of their marriage, they denied it. In their eyes, they would get along fine if it were not for their wacky kid. Peter was not simply addicted to negative behavior; his parents were practically ladling out the negative narcotic for him. He was the alibi for their marital failure.

When I saw the three of them together, Peter gave an Academy Award performance as The Bad Seed. He sulked. He squirmed. He made smart-aleck asides under his breath. When I asked him questions, he answered with a grunt. He behaved far worse than he did when I saw him alone. Peter had colluded with his parents to be the Identified Patient in the family. And the collusion was taking place before my very eyes. His delinquency conveniently explained the strife between the mother and father. There was nothing wrong with their marriage except for this delinquent that they had spawned. Subtract Peter and his mischief and they would have had to face the hard truth: The marriage was a shambles. He helped blind them to that fact. Consequently, they made no real attempt to save this troubled boy from himself. All they did was roll their eyes in long-suffering exasperation over his behavior. And Peter went on playing his part, The Identified Patient.

It is painful for a fourteen-year-old boy to have to accept that his parents do not get along. And it is more painful still to recognize that they are, however unintentionally or unconsciously, using him as the scapegoat. Identified Patients face difficult choices. They can either believe that they are indeed The Bad Seed, The Klutz, or whatever role they play, or they have to recognize that their families are using them, however unwittingly, to serve their own emotional needs. And this latter choice can be more painful than continuing the Identified Patient role.

With young patients like Peter, I try to build their self-esteem, but without disparaging their families' behavior. In trying to help older Identified Patients, I have proceeded along these lines. First, I try to make them become aware of the position in which the family has placed them. I help them to ask: "What's going on here?" I want them to realize that they have been maneuvered into a role. I want them to see that this manipulation works only if they allow themselves to become part of the collusion. I want them to understand that they do not have to stay shackled to the part of Problem Daughter, Black Sheep, Family Doormat, or Dumb One in the Bright Family.

Virtually our whole bag of therapies can be useful in helping the Identified Patient: Talk Tenderly To Yourself ("Okay, sweetheart, they're trying to make you feel helpless again. But you proved today, on the job, that you can be pretty resourceful."); Three Windows of Perception ("Window Three tells me that one reason my sister may always put me down is because she is envious."); Replay The Tape ("Mom, it would have helped me if you had not given me money when you learned I was spending it on dope. I wish you had tried to get me professional help."); To You-ness To Me-ness ("To you, I'm The Junkie, The Bad Boy, The Troublemaker. But to me, I'm a confused kid trying to grow up in a world where it seems that everyone does drugs.").

Being the Identified Patient is a particularly insidious condition because the family, the very people who should be pulling us out of our insecurity blanket are, perhaps unconsciously, trapping us in it. But once we understand our entrapment, we can begin to free ourselves. The cure eventually helps the family too, because then all its members will more likely face up to their problems rather than hide behind and blame the Identified Patient.

TREATING MARILYN MONROE

I said earlier that low self-esteem and the Impostor Syndrome are no respecters of fame or fortune. The case of Marilyn Monroe is tragically apt, a woman who clearly had both of these negative emotional habits. Recently, a magazine made me a tantalizing offer. I was asked to write an article telling how, as a therapist, I would have treated Marilyn Monroe.

To me, as well as to two generations of Americans, Marilyn Monroe has always been a compelling enigma—the sex goddess, the woman who appeared to have it all, yet who took her life at the age of thirty-six. We still wonder what made Marilyn tick—and fall apart. Was she an idol, a victim, a pathetic creature who needed mothering, a sex object with threatening sexual power, or a human sacrifice on the altar of phony values?

I eagerly took up the magazine's offer. I started out by admitting that I had never met Marilyn Monroe. All that I knew about her was gleaned from her movies and from newspapers, magazine articles, and books. I began by recalling some of the things I had learned about Marilyn: for example, that she showered several times a day, changed her clothes frequently, and was compulsive about every detail of her appearance—yet she always felt that she was flawed. What comes through here is a woman who—unsure of her inner resources—felt that she had to make it almost wholly by externals, by her face and body. What also comes through—not surprisingly—is a woman obsessed with warding off age and trying not to grow up. She is hanging on to childlike habits of helplessness and needs a man to take care of her. She is saying: "Make me happy." "Make decisions for me." "Show me your love night and day." "Love me no matter what, and like me too." "Be my father. Be my mother." It would have taken a saint of a man to live day in and day out with so emotionally demanding a person.

I further expect that Marilyn Monroe would have interpreted any lack of attention as a sign of waning interest in her and a signal to move on to the next man. Many women brought up in our culture can identify or at least sympathize with much of her behavior. And that is one reason why the fascination with Marilyn Monroe's life endures, not only among men because of her "sexiness" but among women who see in her a fellow victim of sexual stereotyping.

As Marilyn's therapist, how would I try to help her? I would first try to move her away from the negative messages that obsessed her. "How much longer can I hold on to men—and my public? My breasts are beginning to sag. My complexion is going. Then, what am I?" I would encourage her to Talk Tenderly To Herself and to think about and applaud her smallest successes as a human being, and not just the glittery successes of a star made of celluloid.

Marilyn lived in an environment where she felt the need for constant reassurance. She felt that her worth was measured in her ability to arouse in others a desire to take care of her. I would head her in the opposite direction. I would try to show her that we can create our own emotional environments. We do not have to inhabit an environment that others create for us—in her case, the artificial world that the studio moguls and their publicists dreamed up for her. I would help her to stand on her own two feet and to overcome the need to have others think for her and take care of her.

I suspect that the reason why Marilyn Monroe never achieved sustained intimate relationships was that she was scared that if she bared her inner self to others, they might find her empty. She likely suffered from the Impostor Syndrome: "Let me flee before they find me out." I suspect that Marilyn did see herself as an impostor—

poor little Norma Jean Baker, born into nothing, coming out of nowhere, and now the object of global adulation. That was a heavy burden to carry, particularly for a young woman who was not sure what she really was when the cameras stopped. A sexual fantasy or a flesh-and-blood woman? A real person or a creation of press agentry? A megastar or a vulnerable human being? I would try to help Marilyn to see another course open to her, that she could live as neither the arrested child, forever scarred by her upbringing, nor as the concocted sex symbol. I would try to help her see herself instead as a person with gifts and flaws, like the rest of us. In effect, I would be teaching her to accept herself "as is" and not as a creature of unattainable perfection.

I would try to help her become a loving person rather than a person with a compulsive need to be loved. I would try to get her to know other women as genuine friends. I would want her to establish relationships with females, not as people to look after her but as people to whom she could give as much as she took.

And, as her self-sufficiency grew stronger, I would try to wean her from her dependence on pills.

Marilyn Monroe's ultimate tragedy was that she found no real self, no Column of Authentic Marilyn around which she could revolve. Instead, she bought the role of erotic symbol fastened on her by those greedy souls who exploited her and by a celebrity-crazed public that encouraged the pose. No one can live as a symbol. The main object of all my efforts would have been to make Marilyn accept herself as a person and not a mirror reflecting other people's adolescent and distorted fantasies of "sexiness."

All this advice is admittedly in the abstract. I did not know Marilyn Monroe. Yet, her problems are those of patients I see every day and whose lives are also diminished by their negative emotional obsessions. Yes, she was addicted to—and ultimately the victim of—her negative compulsions. But, above all, she is a flagrant example of shabby cultural clichés destroying a person's life. One poor, lone human being was supposed to represent some sort of twenty-four-hour-a-day, year-round, nonstop flow of irresistible allure. She could not live with that image or for it. Who could? I would like to have been able to help Marilyn Monroe become a real person who could enjoy life and not a "sex goddess" who could no longer bear living.

BECOMING YOUR NOSE

Marilyn Monroe suffered from an ultimately destructive fixation on her physical beauty. She became her body. On the opposite side of the coin are the people fixated on some part of their physical makeup that they consider unattractive. I have patients who *are* their nose (too big or too crooked) or their height (too tall or too short) or their breasts (too small or too big) or their weak chin or bald head. I know whereof I speak, because for years I was—in my obsessed view—nothing but my height. Virtually every emotion I experienced, every thought I expressed, had first been filtered through the fact that I was tall. My mother's efforts to be helpful were a disaster. A sample of what she would say to me when I was a kid: "Penny, I've just been downtown and I saw five women as tall as you are. And they were all wearing wedding rings." My translation? *Even at this height, if I don't land a man, I'm nothing.*

Patients come to me with all sorts of masking complaints: "I'm dissatisfied." "I'm lonely." "I'm anxious." "I'm bored." But, as we peel away the layers, I often find that they are unhappy because of some part of their physical being that has become an obsession. When we have exposed the root cause, I tell them: "Don't make the part of you that you dislike become all of you. Don't become your flaw."

There is a man on my block, and our paths cross from time to time. His mouth is paralyzed on one side. I noticed it the first time we talked, but I never gave it a second thought. Why? Because the man is so confident and charming that you get the impression that he is totally unaware of his flaw. And so, you also bypass it and go directly to the essence of him—which is an admirable human being. My neighbor is not his flaw.

At the other end of the spectrum is the patient who said at our first session: "Do you think I'm a lesbian?" I replied: "How am I supposed to be able to take one look at you and tell if you're a lesbian? Why do you even think you might be?" Her response: "Because I'm fat." Since men weren't pursuing her, she concluded that she was not giving off the right feminine vibes. And since she had allowed herself to get into this fix by getting fat, she must be a lesbian. The woman had become her weight.

Have you ever noticed a beautiful woman on the arm of a man who by Hollywood standards is hardly handsome? He may even be ugly by conventional measure. They both deserve credit. The man has not become his shortness, his hairless head, his broken nose, or his myopia. He is his talent, his wit, his standing in his profession, his character. He has had the confidence to let these qualities shine through, dominate his being, and make him an attractive male. The woman deserves equal credit because she recognized his true worth. She has shown the maturity and discrimination to judge a man by qualities deeper and more enduring than his baby blues.

Unfortunately, the reverse is not true nearly as often. Far less frequently do you find men judging women for their character and inner beauty. I give my sex much higher marks in this department. Women far more often tend to see attractiveness, even sexiness, in a man's whole being, in the things he says, in the way his mind works, in his manner, in his confidence or his reticence, in what he has done or is doing with his life—in short, in his totality. Women recognize more clearly that the ultimate erogenous zones are in the mind, the imagination, and the heart.

What I want my patients and students to say—men and women—is this: "I am Mary Jo Jensen, supersaleswoman, gourmet chef, and a very passionate lady. I am not my admittedly modest breasts." Or: "I am Fred De Franco, sensational ad copy writer, the best squash player at the Y, and a marvel with the ladies. I am not my shiny dome."

That's the way, Mary Jo and Fred! You are not your supposed flaws. Of course, there are people—people you would admittedly like to attract—who are not going to see beyond the physical you. It doesn't matter. Don't allow them to make your flaw become you. And look at it this way: they are exhibiting a very unattractive flaw themselves—a shallow mind. Most people are going to see beyond your nose, your chin, your ears, if you will let them, if you show them a whole human being.

VOICE AND SELF-ESTEEM

Do you know when you are telegraphing your low self-esteem to the world? Your voice is often a dead giveaway. People who speak with the wrong pitch, wrong intensity, or wrong volume are sending an audible message: "Hellooo, Lucille! It's soooo wonnnderful to see you again! You look simply maaaarvelous!" Just beneath the frantic exuberance the low self-esteem shows through. This person is saying, in effect: "If you don't like this voice, obviously it's not the real me. It's the person I am using as a cover because I'm not sure you'd like the real me either. I use this voice as a mask."

The words, along with the pitch and voice, mirror our opinion of ourselves. So watch for these telltale signs in your speech. They will warn you if your insecurity is showing.

- Using too many words, especially heaps of apologetic verbiage before getting to your point: "Gosh, I don't know anything about this subject, so I don't know what business I have saying this, but it seems to me, I guess, I mean . . ."

- At the other extreme, making one-syllable responses that reveal that you are editing your every thought, frightened of what a burst of spontaneous speech might reveal.

- Being repetitious. "Lorenzo's is a nice restaurant." (No response from listener.) "It's a fantastic restaurant!" (Polite "mmmmmm" from listener.) "You mean you've never been to Lorenzo's? You gotta go there!" (Glazed look in eye of listener.)

- Speaking too loudly. This is such a transparent device of the insecure person trying to sound secure that he or she may as well wear a sign saying I'M UNSURE OF MYSELF.

- Not looking people straight in the eye when you speak.

On the other hand, you will know you are becoming self-confident when you do the following:

- Use just enough words—and the right tone.

- Speak clearly and deliberately and not stridently.

- Revolve around your column of confidence as you speak, standing straight, looking poised and relaxed and directly at the person you are speaking to.

SUMMING UP

■

Low self-esteem takes many forms—helplessness, self-abasement, overeagerness, fear of rejection, pessimism, the Impostor Syndrome, getting caught in a marriage or relationship of Mutual Entrapment, becoming your physical flaw. But you can lift your sense of self-worth and break the bad habit of feeling bad about yourself by

- Talking Tenderly To Yourself: "I know that underneath all my fears, I'm a worthwhile human being. I have good qualities. From now on, I'm going to show the world more of that person and less of that whimpering pup with its tail between its legs."

- Giving people predictability about yourself, making yourself unavailable for put-downs, rejection, guilt, or other negative manipulation.

- Recognizing that your actions are not necessarily Stable, Global, and Internal, but dynamic and interrelated to the behavior of others. Your future is not cast in concrete.

- Learning to recognize the clues, the mannerisms, the voice and speech patterns that signal your lack of self-assurance, and replacing them with a confident speech pattern and tone.

- Behaving confidently. It will make you seem confident to others, who will then treat you as if you are confident. Thus, in time, you will genuinely *become* confident.

None of the above is going to happen overnight. You have spent ten, twenty, maybe thirty years telling yourself that everyone else is better than you are. You are not going to reverse that condition in twenty-four hours after reading a book. You have been carrying that behavior for so long that it feels like a part of you. You must practice, practice, practice the techniques I have recommended. And not a dozen times, but more likely hundreds of times, until they become an effortless and natural part of your behavior.

Chapter 12

———————————●———————————

DEPRESSION:
BREAKING THE
BLACK MOOD

Our cave ancestors experienced depression. When famine struck, or bitter cold set in, the clan crawled into the cave and went into what amounted to emotional hibernation—into a depression, in effect—to conserve energy. Depression was genetically encoded into our forebears as an emotion for survival. Like other essentially negative emotions, it could serve a positive purpose in the right circumstances. Behavioral scientists say, for example, that we cope with danger through flight or fight. The fight comes from anger—not ordinarily a desirable state. The flight comes from fear—which is something we usually try to suppress. But, in the face of peril, anger and fear can save us. However, depression has survived beyond its primal usefulness. It is the appendix of the emotions. Still, it is there, capable of causing us serious harm. As the philosopher Bertrand Russell put it: "Gloom is a useless emotion."

Useless or not, depression is depressingly widespread.

At any given moment, 6 percent of the population is suffering from depression severe enough to require clinical treatment. Depression accounts for 60 percent of all suicides. Thirty to forty million of us will probably suffer at least one treatable bout of depression in a lifetime. The condition is on the rise, particularly among young people, evidently quickened by an unraveling of the social fabric in recent years—the weakening of family relationships, a retreat from conventional religious faith, the sexual revolution, and the social upheaval that began in the sixties. And, for reasons not yet clearly understood, depression strikes women twice as often as men.

The clinical symptoms of depression are sadness, insomnia, early waking, suicidal impulses, restlessness, irritability, loss of appetite, fatigue, inability to concentrate, ailments that fail to respond to treatment, and an absence of interest in usually pleasurable pastimes such as sex. I sum up depression as that dread-getting-up-in-the-morning feeling. We would rather pull the covers over our heads and have the world go away.

At one time or another, we will all experience the symptoms of depression. Often for good reason. But we are not concerned so much with the occasional episode of unavoidable depression that strikes even the healthiest personality from time to time. We are concerned with chronic depression. We are concerned with free-floating negative feelings that persist, month after month, even year after year, emotions that cling like emotional Saran Wrap. Depression is one of the most complex negative emotions to deal with because its roots can be both psychological and biological. Body and soul may be involved. Indeed, some of us may be at higher risk of depression than others simply because of our genetic makeup. Like the carrier of a virus, we may be okay until our resistance is lowered by an emotional blow, and then the latent depression surfaces.

One form of biologic depression is caused essentially

by a chemical imbalance in the brain. The most widely recognized condition of this type is the manic-depressive, the person who swings from wild euphoria to black despair and back again without apparent reason. To help these depressed patients, chemical treatments have been developed—lithium, for example. *Psychopharmacology* is the professional term for the treatment with drugs of emotional conditions such as depression.

We call a depression caused by a psychological shock *reactive.* In the reactive depression, we experience a specific, identifiable cause and react to it. The loss of a loved one or a job may trigger such depression. The depressed state follows a fairly fixed cycle. It has a beginning, a middle, and, we hope, an end. For example, the period of psychological recovery from deep grief—say the loss of a spouse or a child—seems to run a more or less fixed course of about two years in a healthy personality. This is the normal time for the heart to heal. Of course, the scar will likely remain forever. But the period during which the soul is unwell tends to continue over a more or less predictable period.

My colleagues and I in clinical psychology try to help people through the inevitable stages of reactive depression. We try to help them keep the depression from slipping from a reactive to a chronic state. But our role in these cases is limited. Nature's healing process essentially has to take its course. Shakespeare seems to have anticipated what we try to do when he wrote: "Canst not thou minister to a mind diseased—pluck from the memory a rooted sorrow?" We try.

There are, however, millions of people who suffer depression not only from chemical imbalances in the body or from shocks in life, but as an emotional attitude that has worked itself into their personalities. The depression may have been triggered initially by a blow, a sorrow, or a crushing disappointment. But it has lingered on well beyond the Statute of Limitations. However it started, the depression has become an emotional bad habit—another habit that can be broken.

Depression is an umbrella condition. It usually encompasses clusters of negative behavior, the most common being combinations of helplessness, pessimism, low self-esteem, anger, and fear.

Consider Larry U., a Vietnam veteran, whom I treated for depression. I first saw Larry several years after his military service. He had come to see me after a succession of failures at several jobs because of his apathy, his bleak outlook on life, his low opinion of himself.

I have to confess that it was hard for me to picture this tall, blond, slightly built, bespectacled, quiet man as a combat infantryman. Larry also had about him the dead spirit of the chronic depressive. He seemed disconnected, as though he had thrown all his life switches to the "off" position. And he had the depressed person's habit of filtering out anything positive in his life while accentuating the negative. He was a master of the Mathematics of Guaranteed Unhappiness.

Larry's depression had started out as the reactive type. Something devastating had indeed happened to him. When it happened, his depressed feelings were only natural. He had earned his depression. But when I saw him, it was many years after the triggering event.

He told me his story. Larry had been married just before he shipped out for Vietnam. His bride, Jerrie, was apparently a great beauty and Larry loved her wildly. He had never quite gotten over the astonishment that Jerrie had chosen him for her husband. As Larry tells the rest:

"I was scared every minute I was in Nam. The only way I held on to my sanity was by thinking about what I was coming back to. I blotted out every ugly thought by thinking of Jerrie. When we loaded the body bags on the chopper, I'd just focus on my wife. If I made it, it was going to be for her. I lived for her letters. And then one day I got a letter telling me she was pregnant. But not by

178

me. She was sorry, she said, but she had fallen for this guy and she wanted out—a divorce. My whole world fell apart. A grenade exploding in my gut couldn't have killed me any quicker. I got careless in the field those last few months. I didn't really care what happened. It was as though I wanted some Cong to end my agony."

The Dear John letter had been the initial blow. When Larry came home, he was steeped in depression. His first reaction had been shock. Then the shock turned to anger. The anger in time transformed itself into low self-esteem. (He could not be much of a man, if a woman could do this to him.) Then followed pessimism. (What else will go wrong in my life?) Then a fear of risking any new close attachments (social suicide). Finally, he sank into an overall disinterest in his work and everything else in life (alienation). As the years passed, he never really pulled out of the depression.

Yes, what happened to Larry while he was off fighting a war was enough to devastate any young man—for a time. But the statute of limitations had long since run out in his case. He had by now simply acquired the emotional bad habit of facing the world depressed.

THE STATUTE OF LIMITATIONS

Let's pursue that idea of the Statute of Limitations for a moment. The Statute of Limitations is a useful device in dealing with depression and several other negative emotional habits. When someone commits a crime, the authorities are required to bring charges within a certain time, or else the statute of limitations runs out. For example, in certain states you cannot charge a suspect with embezzlement five years after his alleged misconduct has been uncovered. In other words, you cannot keep a prospective defendant dangling indefinitely.

We can employ a similar principle in dealing with our emotional problems. Of course we are going to be depressed if we get fired from a job. The Statute of Limitations for depression induced by job loss? A month or two. By then we should have picked ourselves up, dusted ourselves off, and started back on the road to recovery. The pain over the loss of a loved one might well last a lifetime. But the resumption of a normal, healthy outlook on life, as we noted earlier, will probably occur within two years. Again, the Statute of Limitations. A friend disappoints you by ignoring your birthday. Statute of Limitations on depression induced by a friend's thoughtlessness? One day maximum. (Remember how I feel about our "deserving" applause, kudos, praise, gratitude, and so on.)

Larry had long ago exceeded the Statute of Limitations for a reactive depression. Even he no longer associated his depressed state with the faithless Jerrie. But he had allowed himself to slip from a reactive to a chronic depression. He had attached himself to this insecurity blanket for so long that it was like his skin. Depression had become his habit, the gloomy lens through which he looked at life.

I am discussing Larry's case in detail because my treatment of him illustrates a great deal of what we can do to break the habit of depression. I began by helping him to learn a New Math to replace the Mathematics of Guaranteed Unhappiness—at which Larry was such a whiz. Not only did he not count his good fortune; Larry had so conditioned himself that he rarely even recognized it. I wanted him to understand that nobody has a monopoly on bad news. For example, we would take a day on which something happened that reinforced his depression. Say, the day he had had the door of his Nissan Sentra reshaped in a parking lot. I had Larry concentrate on everything else that had happened to him that day. It turned out that he also had received a tax refund from the IRS, a larger check than he had anticipated. He had also finally gotten over a cold that had plagued him for three weeks.

Larry had filtered out all the good news, but he had a vivid recollection of the dented door. I was trying to let some positive light in. I was urging Larry to put a value on the fortunate things that happened to him, rather than blotting them out. I was forcing him to put the good and bad of any particular day on the scales so that he could see that not every day tipped to the negative. He had always ensured that outcome in the past by his habitual attitude, by weighing only the bad, by using the Mathematics of Guaranteed Unhappiness.

NATURE'S HIGH

Larry typifies the dread-getting-up-in-the-morning type of depression. His usual reaction on opening his eyes was: "Oh, my God. Another day." He told me that he often put the pillow over his head to blot out the day and lay in bed until the last minute, until he had to get up.

I persuaded Larry to do one of the hardest things that the depressed person faces—to overcome the inertia of depression. Of course, it is easier to stay put. It is tempting to wallow. It is difficult to start swimming against a tide of despair.

What I recommended to Larry was a task in behavior modification. I had him choose a form of exercise. Then, when he woke up, instead of lying there dreading the day, he was to get out of bed and perform the exercise. He decided on an exercycle because he could pump the machine and watch *The Today Show* at the same time. I was all for that. Any evidence of interest by the depressed personality in virtually anything is always welcome.

But, more important, when we engage in physical exercise, two things happen. First, researchers have found that physical activity generates substances in our bodies called *endorphins*. These endorphins act like nature's own uppers. They work on the brain to produce a tranquilizing, even euphoric effect. When we hear people talk about a "runner's high," they are referring to the desirable state that endorphins produce in runners and joggers. Endorphins act as benign, nonhabit-forming, no-side-effects drugs that give us a natural high.

This high is exactly what Larry started to experience after working out on his exercycle. After showering and dressing, he still felt the positive effects. He faced the day, at least initially, in a mood of tingling well-being. Later, the black cloud might settle over him again, but for now he was off to a fresh start, free of depression.

The way Larry put it to me: "After a half hour of hard pumping on that bike, I'm pooped. I don't have room for depression. I'm too tired. But it's a nice, healthy kind of tired." In part, Larry is indeed describing the endorphin effect. But a second force is also at work.

EMOTIONAL DISPLACEMENT

He is experiencing Emotional Displacement. Do you remember the old rule from freshman physics? Two objects cannot occupy the same space at the same time. That principle applies to the emotions as well, to some degree. It is difficult for us to contain two opposing feelings at the same time. In Larry's case, healthy exhaustion displaced unhealthy depression. There was not room for both in his consciousness simultaneously.

The same phenomenon is at work for someone who is habitually anxious. I say to patients plagued by the anxiety habit: "Go out and do something physical. Swim, jog, play tennis. Work up a sweat. Tire yourself out." It is hard to be both anxious and exhausted—edgy and bushed—at the same time. One feeling displaces the other.

BENIGN DISTRACTION

When I urged Larry to find a morning exercise, I was, in effect, leading him to a form of diversion. When we are depressed, we need to be diverted physically—and mentally and socially as well. We need to find activities that unstick us from twenty-four-hour-a-day concentration on our unhappy selves. This is easier said than done. It's far more tempting to soak in the trough of despair and let waves of apathy wash over us. I asked Larry what he did to distract himself from his depression. I asked him what his hobbies were. "None," he answered. "None whatsoever." Had he ever had any hobbies? Well, yes, he had. But he didn't have the energy for them now. He could not overcome his emotional inertia. The idea of having to deal with people, to put on a happy face, was just too much effort for him.

But, when I learned that Larry had been a good softball pitcher years before, I virtually ordered him to get into one of the leagues that play in Central Park. And he did. When I asked him how the first game went, I heard Larry's habitual dead tone: "I got a sore arm. I gave up a dozen hits. We lost." Yet, he could not suppress a dancing light in his eyes as he added: "Anyway, I homered twice." He stayed with the league. The games lasted a couple of hours. Afterward, the players retired to a pub on Third Avenue and Larry was invited along. Here was one evening a week at least in which Larry did not have time to soak himself in his misery.

The depressed person is constantly chewing on himself. He needs to find something else to chew on. The form of diversion is not important, but the *act* of diversion is. The answer may be softball. It could just as well be needlepoint, chess, amateur theatricals, or skydiving. Part of the cure for depression is simply to distract our way out of it. The hardest part is the first step, overcoming the seductive inertia of depression. And here we get back to something I said earlier. Are we unable to change? Or do we choose not to change? Are we doomed to remain inactive? Or do we choose to be inactive? Once we have made the decision to change, we have made the crucial move against inertia. The rest will come easier. In Larry's case, it involved finding his old glove and trotting out to the park.

I cited earlier the major role that depression plays in suicides. And I have no doubt that one reason for suicidal depression is an absence of purpose. That thought was brought home forcefully to me years ago. I was at the University of Michigan on the eve of World War II. In that final year before the war, more than a dozen students attempted suicide, and nine succeeded. But in the year immediately after Pearl Harbor, no suicides were attempted on the Michigan campus.

I am convinced that far more than coincidence was at work here. A national purpose—inspired by America's marching off to war—had transmitted itself to individuals, especially the young. Suddenly their lives were given a meaning that they might not have found by themselves. Being swept up in a historic time and event *put* purpose into their existence.

We don't need World War III to overcome a personal depression. But we do need to find something that engages us and lends meaning to life. As in the war effort, when we commit ourselves, particularly together with other people, we become part of something larger than ourselves. And we are distracted from the despair—the depression—of a life lived in solitary, obsessive fixation on ourselves. Our headlights, again, are turned outward, illuminating the wonder of the world around us, instead of inward, blinding us to everything but our own unhappiness.

RECORDING THE GOOD TIMES

There is a tool that I predict is going to come into increasing play in treating emotional problems, including depression: the tape recorder. That's right. Let me explain how.

I have often thought that when a dog has a thorn in his paw, part of his unhappiness is due to the fact that a dog knows only the present. He cannot remember what it was like not to hurt. And he cannot envision a painless future. He knows only what he feels now, and he is feeling pain. We humans have the capacity to remember the past and to imagine a future. We can recall bygone happy days and we can conceive of better days ahead—even in our hour of pain. People who suffer from chronic depression particularly need to be reminded of this human capacity. But sometimes they can be like old Spot. They have been down for so long that they forget what up feels like. They cannot remember what it was like to feel good.

When you are feeling good—particularly if you have suffered past bouts of depression—talk your feelings into a tape recorder. Tell the recorder what it is that is making you feel good. Describe your emotions as fully as you can. And then save the tape for a rainy day. I have my patients do this. Then, when they slip back into a depression, I ask them to bring in the tape and we play it. The object is obvious. The depression, when we are suffering it, may appear to be our permanent emotional state. It is not. It is a stage. It is subject to change. It is replaceable. By playing the tape, we recognize this fact. We were happy once. We can be happy again. The depression is a period, not a life sentence. There can be no better proof of this than the sound of our own voices speaking of better times.

I had a patient, Kate S., who was a film editor for an ad agency. I saw Kate on and off whenever she suffered extended bouts of depression. I had told her about the tape therapy. It so happened that one season, Kate won an award for her editing of a very successful television commercial. She was euphoric. That night, she had the presence of mind to record her feelings on tape.

The next time Kate came to me with her heart located somewhere between her knees, I reminded her of that tape. She looked at me with a woebegone expression and told me that she was not in the mood for fun and games. I told her to go home and play the tape. And the next time she came in to see me, she was to bring it with her. We listened to it, and afterward I said: "Who's that speaking?" "Good old Katy," she answered. "And what's good old Katy talking about?" I asked. "She's talking about the fact that she is one hell of a talented film editor. And all the guys know it. So they gave her a plaque that said so." "And does that good old Katy still exist?" I asked. At last I got a smile out of Kate. She grinned and said: "Here and now!" Kate had forced herself to remember what a poor, suffering animal cannot know. She had known happy days in the past, and she could know happy days again. She was not doomed to live forever in the darkness of the moment. Her own voice had told her so.

WHAT ARE FRIENDS FOR?

Inertia is the hand that depression uses to hold us in its grip. In Kate's case, I used a tape to break her out of her inert state. But what usually happens is that we become too emotionally exhausted to want to fight back, too listless to overcome our despondence. We don't have the energy to get on the phone and make social plans. We don't feel like putting on the "Smile Mask" to get through a party. We let our relations with our friends begin to wither. We begin committing social suicide. We deliberately keep ourselves isolated in our splendid misery.

Withdrawing from the world when we are depressed is a terrible mistake. Difficult as it is to do, we *can* reach out to our friends. A real friend—an honest and compassionate friend—can have enormous therapeutic value, if we will only let that friend into our inner life. I am not talking about simply dumping our woes on others. I am recommending that we share our feelings with someone whose friendship we value and whose judgments we respect.

In offering this advice, I confess that I have much greater success with women than with men. Too many men still swallow the cultural party line. To admit an emotional problem to another man is to admit defeat. It represents a loss of pride, a form of weakness. It is downright *embarrassing!* How can you look a guy in the eye after you've confessed to him that you are worried that your wife may be unfaithful? Or that you feel you are in over your head at your job? Or that you are feeling suicidal?

I had this problem with Larry in the beginning. It wasn't "macho" for him to admit his innermost fears to a male friend. Maybe it was fortunate that he had come to a female therapist. With me, his pride was apparently not on the line. I was less threatening to his ego than one of the men in my profession. Yes, I was glad that he had come to me. But friends are an equally valuable resource. And I reminded Larry of what a wise man once said: "No man is a true friend until he has told you his failures."

I finally persuaded Larry to unburden himself to someone whom he felt he could trust. And he did so. He invited an old college pal out for a night on the town. In recent years they had not seen much of each other, because of Larry's social hibernation. But he called his friend and he later told me that they had spent an evening doing a little bar hopping.

They had spent hours together over dinner and drinks. But what I wanted to know was whether they had *talked*. And so Larry told me about the evening: "It was like turning on a faucet. No sooner had I finished telling him what a mess I'd made of my life, than he started to tell me what was bugging him. It was quite a list. Blunders, misjudgments of people, career screw-ups, disastrous love affairs. It seemed to me that he had never leveled with another guy like that before. It was as though he had been corked all this time, and I had pulled out the cork. The serene guy I thought I knew had been wearing a mask."

I said to Larry: "You felt reluctant to bare your feelings to your friend. But when he did it with you, did you think less of him?" "I did not," Larry replied. "I liked him better. He seemed more vulnerable and more human. I felt easier with him. We didn't have to con each other with that stiff-upper-lip, I'm-all-right-Jack stuff. It wasn't that he had any answers for me. And I certainly didn't have any for him. But I saw more clearly some mistakes he'd made. And he did the same for me. Another thing I had not expected—as we traded foul-ups, we started laughing. We started to see the humorous side of our situations. The human comedy. It wasn't all grim. And maybe the best part of the night was finding out that I wasn't the only insecure guy behind all those confident faces I see on the street."

What Larry and his friend were doing for each other was not much different from what a good therapist does. We try to help people see the errors in their thinking, to put matters into perspective, and to make our patients aware that they are hardly alone in their fears and failings. And a good friend is a lot less expensive than a therapist.

Larry and his friend had also cut through a male cultural taboo when they leveled with each other. Women are much better at it, far more comfortable at sharing feelings. Maybe, as the mothering sex, we have a more realistic grasp of life. Women are more forgiving of human fallibility, more aware that we are all vulnerable creatures. We have not made our way through life through raw power, but through accommodation and adaptation to our situations and surroundings. We don't have any illusions about supermen—or superwomen, for that matter.

Still, both men and women hooked on depression need to overcome psychological inertia and reach out to a friend. Hard as it is, it is something we can do. I suggest being fairly direct in the approach. Pick someone you like, trust, and admire and say: "Listen, Laura, I know I haven't called you for ages. But I tend to do that when I'm feeling down. I tend to pull the covers over my head. I want you to help me to stop it. I want you to drag me to a movie, or out to dinner, or for a run around the park. I'm crawling into a shell, and I want you to help pull me out."

Once you have established this kind of rapport, use your friends as sounding boards. Don't hesitate to ask them for constructive criticism: "Let me know when I'm slipping into negativity. Tell me when I'm sinking in self-pity. Tip me off when I begin behaving defensively or hysterically." Whether for advice or a sympathetic ear, or even a shoulder to cry on, most friends will be happy to help, knowing that you would do the same for them.

SUMMING UP

What have we learned about breaking the habit of depression?

- First of all, we are not alone. As many as one person in five suffers a serious episode of depression in a lifetime.

- The most common symptoms of depression are sadness, poor sleeping habits, suicidal impulses, restlessness, irritability, loss of appetite, lingering ailments, and loss of interest even in life's pleasures.

- Depression is usually an umbrella condition embracing several other negative feelings including helplessness, pessimism, anger, and fear.

- Depression generally falls into three categories or a combination of them: depression due to chemical imbalance; reactive depression, brought on by setbacks in our lives; and chronic, free-floating depression, which seems to stick to everything we do.

As we noted, chemical depressions may require medical treatment. Reactive depressions and chronic depressions can be treated by therapists. But in the latter two classes, we can do a great deal ourselves to break out of depression in the following ways:

- Abandon the Mathematics of Guaranteed Unhappiness, and give just as much weight to the good news in our lives as to the bad.

- Put a Statute of Limitations on ourselves; don't let the depressed state drag on beyond what the bad news warrants.

- Engage in physical exercise, which can produce a natural high and which substitutes healthy exhaustion for depressed self-absorption.

- Overcome inertia and occupy our minds with positive interests, by taking up new hobbies or resuming old ones, above all, *doing something* besides chewing on our unhappiness.

- Make a tape of our feelings in the good times, so that we can use it as a reminder when we slip into depression.

- Make therapeutic use of friends to help us crawl out of our depression and to reenlist in life.

Chapter 13

SEX AND EMOTIONAL BAD HABITS

A few years ago I wrote the book *Why Do I Think I Am Nothing Without a Man?* I must have struck a nerve, because the book became a bestseller and sent me on the talk-show circuit—Donahue, Merv Griffin, *The Today Show*. Evidently, the problem is not only an American dilemma, as the book was published in several foreign editions. Literally millions of women, single or married, are emotionally crippled, diminished, defeated in the pursuit of happiness because deep down they are convinced that if they don't have a man, they aren't really living. And if they lose the man they do have, they are finished as worthy human beings. This conviction is a negative emotional habit. Again, the habit is rooted in erroneous thinking. Again, it is wasting these women's lives. And again, the habit can be broken. The belief that "I'm nothing without a man" is not always stated quite so baldly. Instead, what I hear from women in my office is:

"I'm doing beautifully in my career. Still, I feel so empty all the time."

"I live in terror that my husband is going to leave me. And he isn't even much of a husband."

"I go around feeling like there is a big hole in me. Something incomplete."

"I've got loads of friends, a good job, hobbies. Yet, I really feel that I'm just marking time. When I am going to be happy?"

Translation of all of the above? "Why Do I Think I Am Nothing Without a Man?" At least 95 percent of the women I treat, deep down, however revealed or concealed, are asking themselves that question.

Let me put my cards on the table. I am not about to urge some far-out feminist stance that says women should *prefer* life without men. I utterly reject the flaky fringe notion that men are the enemy. Horrible creatures! Shun them! I like men. I like them very much indeed. Furthermore, I am not about to knock the joys of love, the pleasures of sex, the rewards of marriage or of living with a man. I have a happy marriage. And I treasure it.

But not to the exclusion of all else in my life. What I am concerned with is the woman who denies her wholeness as a human being because there is no man in her life. If you go through life on hold—waiting for the magic moment until *he* comes along—you have an emotional bad habit as debilitating as self-flagellation, hystericalizing, or poor self-esteem. You are filtering your life through a lens that leaves out all the happiness that can be found as a single woman. And you are wasting precious life.

Three beliefs apply in breaking this particular bad habit, rules that I have stressed again and again:

First, the "no man" terror has been foisted on women by the culture. It's part of the social conspiracy.

Second, the belief that the society fosters—that you are nothing without a man—is not an unchangeable truth. It is a bad habit that women form.

And third, you can break the habit. You can get over the idea that without a man you are only half a woman.

What has the culture done? It has programmed us to believe in a double standard for judging men and women. A man's worth is validated by other men. If his classmates, his teammates, his co-workers, his comrades-in-arms esteem him, then he is a successful human being. He is judged as a distinct individual on his own merits. It doesn't matter to whom he is married, or even if he is unmarried. His marital status will not affect his reputation much one way or the other. He is confirmed by *his* life.

Yes, women have made important strides since the inception of the women's movement. Nevertheless, things have not changed all that much. A considerable part of the double standard remains intact. *A woman is still largely validated by the man in her life, by the man who loves her, marries her, lives with her—and takes care of her.* If she lands a brain surgeon rather than a truckdriver, she is presumably a success, she is a *better* woman, even though she is the same woman. It's as though her height is measured after she stands on a man's shoulders. In brief, men look to other men for status and approval— and women also look to men for *their* status and approval.

Listen to these voices from my case book:

JOYCE C., a social psychologist: "My mother's dying words to my brother were: 'Take care of Joyce. She can't take care of herself.' I went around believing that for years. I didn't want to be disloyal to my mother's low expectations for a daughter."

DORIS K., a housewife: "I was brought up as a gender, not a person."

FLORENCE M., a physician: "When I'd call home from college to tell my folks I'd made the dean's list, my mother would worry that I wasn't dating enough. She was terrified I wouldn't land a man."

How did women get into this fix? The origins are obscured in the mists of human history. We were shaped in the beginning by sex, both as a gender difference and a physical act. In prehistoric times, Man, the hunter, went out and wrested the necessities of survival from a harsh environment by his strength and cunning. Women stayed near the cave and reared children. Thus, the man's life was active, dynamic, and dominant. The woman's life was relatively passive, stable, and submissive. As for the sex act, the man is again seen as active. He thrusts. The woman receives the thrusting. He gives. She accepts. He fills her and thus presumably fulfills her. The woman is seen as an empty vessel waiting for a man to give the vessel purpose and meaning—*by his actions!* Obviously, a million years ago, and today too, a woman is nothing without a man. That view has a certain anatomical neatness to it, even a simple primal poetry.

But couldn't we just as well turn it all around? The man and his appendage are meaningless until he enters the House of Woman. Only there does life begin and can the species be perpetuated. Modern test-tube experiments have clouded this picture somewhat, but the truth still remains essentially intact. A man, and *mankind* for that matter, is nothing without a woman. The male has no hope of coming into existence apart from the existence of women.

So much for trying to unravel the tangled roots of the past in figuring out how we arrived at our current sex roles. The point is that we followed an evolutionary trail where men almost always came out on top. Listen to Myra A., whose views could represent those of millions of women: "I'm scared. I couldn't make it except as some sort of psychological valet to a man. I'm not competitive enough to do it on my own. So I'll get my rewards by giving my life to someone else. I'll make myself indispensable to him. That way, I'll be viewed as part of his success. I'll be seen as noble and virtuous. I'll have a purpose. And then I can expect that he won't leave me. That he'll always stick by me and take care of me."

As I listen to Myra and so many patients like her, I have before me the image of a mirror. The man is the mirror in which the woman has to look to find herself. If he is not there, no image is reflected back. So, she does not really exist.

As I'm sure you know by now, I am a great believer in using the right words. I like to pose questions that jolt people and make them think about what they really believe and what counts in their scheme of things.

When I work with women who are hooked on the belief that they are nothing without a man, I ask them this: "What if you had to live your whole life without a man?" That one is a show stopper. The reactions range from stunned silence to: "That's not possible. I just couldn't do it. I wouldn't want to live." I have a stock phrase to describe this reaction—Desperate Dependence. Remember our earlier discussion about having a column of confidence? Desperate Dependence means suspending yourself from *a man's* column of confidence and not having one of your own. And, if he's not there? Why, then, you collapse into a heap of helplessness.

Yet, millions of women, for shorter or longer periods, *are* going to live without a man. For one thing, there are simply more women than men of marriageable age in this country. And the deficit grows wider as we move up the age ladder. There are also various periods of unavoidable singlehood—the years prior to marriage or a serious relationship, separations, divorces, and widowhood—when a woman will have to live without a man.

Just as I've used the phrase Desperate Dependence to define the ailment, I've adopted another phrase to define its cure—Undependence. No, not "independence," which is fine, but something else. Many women can be independent in their views and behavior—as long as they have a man in their lives. What I want women to achieve is a state of Undependence: that is, an ability to survive as whole human beings even when living alone. Undependence for a woman means unhooking herself from desperate reliance on having a man in her life before she can begin living. I want to lead women away from the Desperate Dependence I observed in my own growing up. When my father died, my mother said: "I can't go on without him." And, sure enough, she had leukemia a few months later and died not long afterward. It may have been coincidental; there may have been no correlation between my father's death and my mother's. But I can't help thinking that, on some psychosomatic level, she had willed her life away. She had decided that she was nothing without a man.

Women who come from happy homes generally think that they are nothing without a man. They want to duplicate the happiness they saw in Mom and Dad's marriage. Women raised in miserable marriages also think that they are nothing without a man. They are looking for the happiness they missed in childhood. Women from broken homes, where the father deserted and the mother was an alcoholic, still crave a husband. They are going to make it where their parents failed. Women who have failed in one marriage or relationship get involved again and again. They are sure that they have not yet found the right combination. But they will. And in all these cases, God forbid the alternative, that they wind up alone—because they would be nothing without a man.

Terror of life without a man is rooted in a number of widespread misconceptions. These misconceptions involve sex, the nature of living alone, and nonsexual relationships between men and women. Let's take each case in turn.

WHY DO I THINK I AM NOTHING WITHOUT SEX?

When I ask women: "Suppose you had to spend the rest of your life alone? What is your greatest fear?" No sex. At least that is the answer they give most frequently. Elsie P.: "Sex is necessary for a healthy, normal life. It's like eating, isn't it? So I've got to have a man in my life to stay healthy."

Sex is also supposed to prove:

I am desirable.

I am loved.

I am secure.

I have landed a man.

Here again we find women validating themselves through men—in this case, through the sex act with them. Since so many women think that they are nothing without a man, they equate having sex with having a man. And, by having a man, they have proved that they are something.

Let's start with Elsie P.'s nutritional notion of sex. Is sex like food? Is it something that we have to have? Will we wither up and die without it? Men and women—whether because of the absence of available partners, sickness, religious vows, incarceration, or whatever—can go months, years, even a lifetime without sex. Sex has no bearing on our physical health.

If a woman is just feeling a good old healthy need for sexual release or relief, there is always masturbation. It may not be the stuff of love songs or poetry, but it will do the job. Yet, I am amazed at how many women are reluctant to satisfy their sexual needs in this way. They have a feeling that masturbation is a form of defeat, an admission that they could not snag a man, even for a bout of sex. There are even those who still feel a moral inhibition against masturbation.

And so we find women who believe that sex with any man is better than no sex. In a woman of any sensitivity, this attitude leads in time to feelings of self-debasement. She finds hit-and-run sex, without feeling, a cheapening and degrading experience. Sex with a stranger or a mere acquaintance, sex as a contact sport, is not particularly ennobling. It is not necessarily better than nothing. It is often an exercise in nothingness.

Now let's look at a sex life as proof of one's desirability or attractiveness. This reaction may have some short-term validity. But it can be short indeed. Which explains the one-night stand and the guy who never calls back.

As proof of love, or a guarantee that a marriage or a relationship is successful, sex can be a misleading barometer indeed. Look at it from a man's point of view, in the case of Tony C., a real estate developer who was brought to me by his wife to help save their failing marriage. Tony was a darkly handsome Latin-lover type. Women had always expected him to play the hot-blooded lothario. And Tony had felt cultural pressure to deliver. He had played the same role with his wife, Lynn, during their courtship, except that she was the first woman he had really fallen in love with. But Tony confessed in his lone sessions with me that he had a perfectly ordinary sex drive, maybe even on the low-normal side. And so, after Tony and Lynn were married, he had not expected to have to keep on proving himself. Lynn, on the other hand, regarded their lovemaking as proof of his love. When the sheer volume started to fall off, Lynn got scared. Obviously, Tony was falling out of love with her.

They were unknowingly operating at cross purposes. Lynn assumed that sex measured love, and Tony hoped that now he could relax the macho-man pose. Lynn's expectations put him under unrelenting pressure to perform to "prove his love." Consequently, they were living under constant tension and the marriage was crumbling.

Here is a perfect rebuttal of the common misconception that sex is necessarily a measure of love, and that more sex equals more love. Lynn's incessant demands did not produce proof of Tony's love. She only placed a strain on him and hence on their marriage. Sex in this case was not the solution. It had become the problem. My job was to bring Lynn around to a point where she was not measuring her husband's love for her on some sort of orgasmo-ejaculatory meter.

THE BETTER-THAN-NOTHING MARRIAGE

Tony and Lynn's marriage was worth saving and was saved. But must all marriages be saved at all costs? I don't think so. At times a breakup is the best answer to irreconcilable differences. It is never my first recommendation. But in time it becomes clear that certain couples do more damage to each other together than they will apart. The relationship is not worth saving. Yet, so many of my women patients come to me desperate to repair the irreparable. They can twist themselves into a verbal corkscrew explaining why the marriage must be preserved, no matter how miserable it makes them, no matter how appalling a failure it is. Why? Because they would be nothing without a man.

Remember Gertrude? She was married to Roy, the alcoholic stockbroker and wife beater. She came to me not to find out how to rebuild her life. Instead, Gertrude came to find out how to save her marriage. Or take Ellen and Bill, mutually entrapped in a hellish marriage. For years Ellen had been prepared to go through virtually any degradation, swallow any indignity, put up with torrents of abuse—anything to let Bill feel superior to her. Why?

So that this sick man would not leave her. So that she could present herself to the world as "Mrs." It took his suicide to release her from this bondage.

FUSING

———◆———

I recently saw a one-character play entitled *My Gene*, about Carlotta O'Neill, the widow of the playwright Eugene O'Neill. The play opens with Carlotta—played brilliantly by Colleen Dewhurst—confined to the mental ward of a big city hospital. What eventually becomes clear in Carlotta's agonized monologues is that her life was completely swallowed up by her husband's. Carlotta gave up her own career on the stage and devoted her life to anticipating and meeting every desire and whim of the difficult and demanding O'Neill. She maintained his ever-changing homes, fended off his intrusive friends, kept him from drinking, even deciphered his illegibly tiny hand-writing and typed his manuscripts—while O'Neill wrote great dramas. She was an appendage, an extension of the playwright's eyes and ears, his arms and legs. She had no independent existence of her own. Her life became his. Thus, when O'Neill died, there was no Carlotta. The mirror in which she needed to see herself in order to affirm her existence had been buried with her husband. This loss of identity and purpose eventually drove her to mental illness.

Carlotta had entered into an unspoken contract with Eugene. She had colluded with him to allow her life to be sacrificed to his. We call this relationship "fusing." Fusing is a red flag warning to us that we are locked into an unhealthy emotional dependence. When we find that we are living *through* and *for* another person, rather than *with* that person, we have denied our very being. Selfless service to others has a noble ring. And it can be among the highest human acts. But fusing goes beyond service to another. It is total immersion in another. In the case of Ellen and Bill, Ellen existed to provide Bill with an emotional punching bag. But Ellen, unlike Carlotta, ultimately found her individuality after her husband's death. A whole person emerged after the fusion was broken.

Earl and Grace were patients who came to me because their marriage was in deep trouble. I saw them separately at first, and then I saw them together for the first time. Earl wanted out of the marriage. Seeing them together, I understood why. At one point, Grace burst out tearfully: "Earl, just tell me what you want. I can be anything you want. I *know* I can do it." Earl's eyes rolled upward in a "see-what-I-mean?" expression. Grace was guilty of attempted fusion. "Whatever you like, I'll like. Whatever you hate, I'll hate. Whatever you want, I'll want." What Earl wanted was a woman, not a lump of putty.

The marriage, not surprisingly, ended in divorce. And it has been a long and still unfinished journey to help Grace find an authentic *independent* self. We are still working on it. We are told so often that roughly half of all marriages end in divorce that the fact has become a cliché. I tend to view that statistic somewhat neutrally. I hesitate to say whether it represents a good or a bad development. Obviously, tons of marriages are bad bargains. They are not worth patching together, just for appearance's sake. Yet, the fear of winding up alone, the terror of not being a Mrs., along with economic fears, keep countless women caged in what are often little better than two-inmate prison cells.

I had a patient, Bettina K., who was married to a dilly. Karl was so insecure and distrustful of people that he wanted to live on a deserted country road where he and Bettina would not have to deal with people. He pressured her to give up all of her friends (he had none of his own). For a long time he conned Bettina into thinking that he went into town to work every day, when actually he was seeing other women. He had no income. He and his wife were in fact living off Bettina's inheritance. She put up with this malignant marriage for seventeen years, while Karl virtually squandered her estate on crackpot schemes. Throughout all that time, the fear of living alone had reduced Bettina to a state of Desperate Dependence. She is divorced today, and, I am happy to say, an Undependent woman. Poorer, but wiser.

A PRISON CALLED SECURITY

In Bettina's case, money had not bound her to Karl. Quite the reverse. The money had bound Karl to her. But all too often economics are a major factor in a woman's Desperate Dependence. Women feel economically trapped in a marriage. Often these are women who were raised to believe that helplessness is a seductive pose and that their helplessness would compel men to take care of them. Which the men did, for a while. But some men leave and some men die. And the prospect of finding herself alone is a terrifying thing for the Desperately Dependent woman. I have known women who were widowed or divorced in middle age and who still didn't know how a checking account worked. I know formerly married women in their forties and fifties who had never worked a day in their lives, who were suddenly thrown into the job market. The experience can be traumatic. But it need not be fatal.

I am all for women working, whenever they can. The working woman enjoys these benefits:

- If she is single and earning a good living, she is not going to be stampeded into the wrong marriage just to have somebody "take care of her."

203

- If she is married, she will not have to feel that she is entirely dependent on her husband. She does not have to look to him for an "allowance," like an eleven-year-old. She can know a degree of independence within marriage.

- Work builds up our feelings of self-worth. A job or profession gives life shape and purpose. The work that one loves, if we are lucky enough to find it, can be as rewarding an experience as any we can have in life. It is harder to believe that you are nothing without a man when you know that you can earn your own keep, perform a valued service, and make your own way in the world.

STICKY MARRIAGES

I had a patient, Norma D., a school nurse, married to Clint, a successful thoracic surgeon. Norma had come to me feeling vaguely dissatisfied with her life. In our first session, Norma told me that she valued her time with her husband above everything else in her life. What did they do together? I asked. They went deep sea fishing. They played bridge. They collected coins. Were these her interests? I wanted to know. No, they were Clint's interests. Norma had merely gone along with them. What were her interests? Amateur dramatics had once been her passion. Was she involved in any little theater groups now? No, she told me; she had given all that up when she married Clint. He hated the theater. Did she enjoy the deep sea fishing? Norma gave me a wan smile and said: "Clint loves it, but I get a little seasick." What about bridge? "I'm a dreadful player. But Clint's very patient with me—most of the time." And the coin collecting? "I kind of sit and watch Clint work at it."

After this discussion of their—or should I say Clint's—outside interests, I began to understand why Norma was dissatisfied with her life. We were getting to the root of her problem. Norma had submerged herself in another person. Clint was her mirror. And if he was not there to look into, she did not exist. Norma D. was nothing without her man.

I told Norma that I wanted her to start finding herself. I told her to get involved. I virtually ordered her to join a local amateur theatrical group. I told her that it is far better to do things with friends who share our interests than with a spouse who doesn't. Yet, too many couples fear that if they don't stick like glue, they will fall apart. Not so. I like to go snorkeling in exotic places. My husband doesn't even like to travel. Does that make us hopelessly incompatible? Not at all. It makes us two individuals who share important parts but not the totality of our lives. And after we have gone our separate ways, we come back to each other enriched and refreshed, because we have fulfilled ourselves. As Leon puts it: "I won't tell you how to snorkel if you don't tell me how to play Mozart's *Concerto for Clarinet in A.*"

ALONE, NOT LONELY

There is a world of difference between being alone and being lonely. Women, particularly as they get older, need to learn to make that distinction—since, biologically, they outlast men. Confronted with the prospect of living alone—due to divorce, the death of a spouse, or the breakup of a relationship—women will often say: "No, I couldn't face that. I couldn't go on living." On the surface, that sounds like a touchingly romantic tribute to the man. But to say: "I couldn't stand to live without Harry," is like saying: "I couldn't stand living with myself." Circumstances may force us to live alone. And, given a choice between an unhealthy relationship and living alone, I'll recommend the half-empty bed every time. (Again, I speak from experience.) The dead-end relationship is another form of social suicide. Hopeless marriages and unsalvageable relationships are not worth enduring—just to have a man. Released from this dead weight, we can learn to live again as complete individuals.

Think of the women you know who live alone. Are all of them sex-starved, desperate, pathetic creatures? I am sure they are not. In fact, behavioral researchers have reached a fascinating conclusion: married men *and single women*, especially those with a good support system of friends, appear to fare best in life psychologically.

I am reminded of my friend Nadine W., an interior decorator. Nadine escaped from a disastrous marriage twenty-six years ago. During the intervening years, she has had several serious relationships with men. But she has lived alone. Today, she is still alone—*but not lonely.* As for those relationships with men, she values them, but, as she put it: "None of the guys was so great that I wanted to give up my independence for marriage."

Nadine is a popular woman who often ends up as a friend of the clients whose homes she decorates. Many of them are famous and fascinating people. And she has loads of women friends, among whom I am happy to be numbered. She takes two vacations abroad a year. She is a violinist with a rather good amateur string quartet. She is committed, involved, engaged.

I have often thought about Nadine's attractiveness as a human being. And I have come to the conclusion that it lies in a certain completeness about her. She gives off no sense that she is somehow only part of a person because she happens to be a single woman. You never have the sense that Nadine is marking time until Mr. Right comes along. She gives a clear impression that she is enjoying life to the hilt *now*, that she is exactly who she wants to be. She is single, not solitary. She is alone, not lonely. This woman would be something with or without a man. The negative emotional habit that I find in so many women—thinking of themselves as half a person because they are not half of a couple—appears never to have crossed Nadine's mind.

Another message that I get from Nadine—and that I have experienced in my own periods of living alone—is that we all need interludes of solitude. Married or single, we need time to be by ourselves. The frantic compulsion to surround ourselves with people every minute of the day suggests that we are not happy with the person called "me." Face to face, alone with ourselves, we should not feel terror, we should not experience an irresistible compulsion to reach for the phone. There can be enormous satisfaction at times in doing nothing—absolutely nothing— except what we want to do, with no responsibility to anyone else. Whether it is soaking in a hot tub or curling up with a spy thriller, we can learn to be a friend to ourselves. We are never really alone, if we see ourselves as worthwhile companions, if we can learn to be like my friend Nadine, alone but not lonely.

We can practice learning to live alone successfully just as we can practice every other life skill. If a person has always lived with parents, siblings, a spouse, or children, and then suddenly finds him- or herself alone, the change can be traumatic. But the trauma need not be, indeed should not be, permanent.

We begin to condition ourselves to aloneness little by little. Like everything else, it takes trying. At first, the impulse may be irresistible—the moment the door closes behind us in an empty house—to reach for the phone or for our walking shoes, or to grab our purse and head for the supermarket, even if there is not a thing that we need. This is the moment to apply our own homemade behavior modification. Start out the first time by promis-

207

ing yourself that you will wait a half hour before calling anybody or fleeing the house on a pointless mission. And don't stare at the clock. Find something useful to fill those minutes, something diverting, like practicing your Spanish for that trip you have been talking about, or baking cookies for a sick neighbor's kids.

The next time, increase the period of solitude to an hour, always having something enjoyable or useful to do to pass the time. Don't let the empty minutes hang over you like a terrifying void. Keep raising the ante until you have spent a comfortable evening or a Saturday afternoon alone—but not lonely. Productive solitude, like anything else, is a learned habit. It is a good habit. You can acquire it, just as you can break the habit of dreading your own company. You can learn to make a good companion of yourself, by working at it, by practicing.

Another effective cure for loneliness is a pet. Yes, a pet. I do not have to prove this to my fellow animal lovers. But many people who have never owned a pet do not know the pleasurable company that a pet can provide. Social researchers have found that pets have a wonderful therapeutic value, especially for older people who live alone. Warm-blooded pets whose heartbeats we can feel make us feel connected to real life. Television is not quite the same thing.

THE SISTERHOOD OF FRIENDS

Women alone who feel that they are nothing without a man are underestimating the friendship of other women. Living alone and having a dependable circle of female friends can give a woman the best of both worlds. And it beats imprisoning ourselves in a failed, miserable relationship with a husband or lover. The woman who lives alone and has friends has enviable control over her life. She can experience the pleasures of solitude when she wants to. And she can forestall loneliness by turning to the companionship of her friends. Yet, I am surprised at how many of my women students and patients suffer from a cultural hangover about female friendships. They simply do not value them. They are seen as a poor substitute for the company of a husband, a boyfriend, a lover. That old demon culture is again doing its dirty work. Listen to Virginia C., a patent attorney: "A bunch of guys together are fine. They're out having a good time. But a bunch of women? That's a hen party. I always have the self-conscious feeling when I'm out with other women that people are looking at us with pity. We couldn't get a man. That's why we're together." On goes the flaw detector, finding something wrong even with a group of women enjoying themselves together.

My fellow feminist friends know better. They don't look for flaws in female-to-female friendships. And I'm not talking about the radical fringe who see men as "the enemy." I am talking about feminists who can enjoy the company of women without thinking they have settled for second best. What we have learned is that there are special rewards to friendships between women. Look at some of these advantages:

- You can more easily be yourself with other women. You are not playing the sexually assigned role. With a man it is difficult to shed the sex poses. He acts a certain way, because he is *supposed to* as a man. You act a certain way, because you are *supposed to* as a woman. You are likely to be thinking about how you look. Is your hair all right? Why did you wear this ridiculous blouse? With another woman, you can literally let your hair down. You relate person-to-person rather than role-to-role.

- You and other women can discuss family, children, and marriage problems more easily. You are like soldiers who have fought on the same side. You have worn the same biological and anatomical uniform. You speak from shared experiences that no man can understand as well.

- You can discuss sexual problems with another woman in explicit detail without embarrassment. And you can learn about sex from other women—while such a conversation might be uncomfortable or misinterpreted if you had it with a man. With a man, such a conversation would be like tiptoeing through a mine field. Discussing a love affair, trying to sort out its meaning in your life, is something that you can do more comfortably with another woman.

- And let's be quite candid, there *are* subjects that interest women and that do not interest many men. That is not to say that women's interests are more trivial. We are capable of holding our own on art, literature, or politics. But women do like to discuss child-rearing more than men do. And why not, when we wind up with a disproportionate share of the job? We do like to discuss fashion and makeup and compare recipes. And we can indulge these occasional interests comfortably with women friends.

- Finally—and here women are fortunate—we are not afraid to "mother" each other. Our maternal impulses carry over from motherhood to other relationships. We can be more patient and sympathetic, less coldly analytical than men think they have to be. We are willing to work our way around a problem rather than power our way through it. Listen to Alice L.: "Sometimes I don't need that let's-get-to-the-heart-of-the-problem approach that my husband always uses. Sometimes I just need someone who'll let me 'emote.' I need a 'mom' who'll put her arm around my shoulder and say: 'There, there, I understand. I know how you feel. You just have yourself a good cry and then I'll fix us a nice cup of tea.' I can get that kind of understanding from my women friends. I couldn't get it from many men. And certainly not from *my* husband."

When I meet women who have disenfranchised themselves—women who think "I'm nothing without a man"—I urge them to open themselves up to other women. Make friends with them. These are not second-class substitutes for the real thing. They are rich and rewarding relationships that can stand on their own merits—and that can yield benefits possible only with other women. So don't disparage them, avoid them, or lose out on them. Make friends with your sisters.

NEVER LOVERS, EVER FRIENDS

My clinical practice convinces me that under the carefree bachelor facade, the single man's problems are strikingly like those of the single woman. My single male patients are often seeing me because of bad or no relationships with women. Adult males feel the pangs of loneliness as much as if not more than women. Men plunge back into marriage after a divorce much more quickly and more often than women. The male "Swinging Single" is more likely a "Lonesome-Onesome." I remember discussing with one patient in his early thirties the desire of women for someone to take care of them. He laughed and said: "I understand perfectly. That's what I want too, someone to take care of *me*."

Women are just as wrong to swallow the stereotyped ideas about men as men are when they accept a cookie-cutter vision of women. My profession allows me to see men with their macho guard down. And I know that:

- Men are often as insecure and vulnerable as women. Stoicism is the mask our culture has taught men to wear to hide their feelings, the mask of approved masculinity.

- Rejection hurts a man every bit as painfully as it does a woman.

- Men are often trying to please, tailoring their behavior to what they think will impress a woman, just as women try to please men.

- A man is not an appendage to his penis. All men are not always thinking of all women solely in terms of sexual conquest.

- Most men—though perhaps not to the same degree as women—tend to feel incomplete if they are not half of a couple.

One way for *both* men and women to lessen their loneliness is through friendships with both sexes. I have numerous friendships with men that have lasted over thirty years. And I continually urge both my male and female patients to form nonsexual friendships with members of the opposite sex. After all, why rule out roughly half of the human race as a potential source of friendship just because of anatomical differences?

There are several pluses to nonsexual friendships between men and women:

- Nonsexual friendships—when they are accepted by both parties as such—can be comfortable and nonthreatening. They place less role-playing pressure on us.

- Having several friends of the opposite sex reduces Desperate Dependence on one member of that sex (a husband or lover).

- Just as you can get a special point of view from a woman friend, you can get insights from a man that you will not get from other women. And vice versa. Both insights have their value.

- It is particularly useful for career women to learn how to make friends with men, since males still dominate virtually every career field.

"Nonsense," says one of my women patients. "I've never met a man yet where sex didn't rear its ugly head or at least keep peeking around the corner. It's always there, spoken or unspoken."

True to a point. True of some men more than others. But the presence of sexual chemistry does not always have to result in sex—or rejection and hard feelings. We do not have to act on every impulse we feel, sexual or otherwise. If, for example, we acted out every murderous rage we ever felt, there would be more people behind bars than on the streets.

On this subject, let me quote Stephanie, an extremely attractive and happily married friend of mine: "I met Alan at three or four cocktail parties. We suddenly seemed to be moving in the same set. I always came with my husband, and he always came with his wife. I had stimulating conversations with Alan from the start. We just hit it off. Alan was a college drama prof and I'd been a drama major. So there was plenty of common ground. That's what we talked about mostly. Nothing else at first. Then, one night at a party, we were chatting and Alan suddenly blurted out: 'Stephanie, I'm wildly attracted to you.' I was so stunned—even scared—that I wanted to run away! I thought, Oh my God there goes a nice friendship and here comes a threat to my happy home. You see, I found Alan attractive too, which scared me all the more. But everything was safe as long as nobody had said anything. Now here it was out in the open. And I just wanted to flee. I mumbled something about being 'a happily married woman' and started to back away. And then Alan said with a wonderful smile: 'Stephanie! I know that you love your husband. And I'm happy with my marriage too. But I wouldn't want to die without your ever knowing that to me you are a marvelously attractive woman. What I said was intended as a compliment. That's all.'

"The smile on his face was so warm that I stopped backing off. I swallowed nervously and said: 'Well then, it is a lovely compliment, Alan. I accept it as such.' Then Alan said: 'I'm glad you didn't run away just now. It would have been terribly embarrassing to me. And it would have made it difficult for us to be friends afterward. And that is what I really want for us.'

"Alan never brought up anything romantic again. And we have stayed friends for years. But let's be frank, that subliminal tingle is still there. It's like an unspoken link between us that makes the friendship special. And I'll confess that it has started an occasional harmless fantasy on my part about Alan. Which I don't think is all bad. Even if you're married. In fact, especially if you're married, because the daydreaming acts as a kind of safety valve when marriage gets a little heavy-going or boring, as they all do at one time or another."

I fully endorse Stephanie's and Alan's handling of this situation. They rose above stereotyped role-playing and responses, and each kept a good friend in the bargain.

Because men and women face similar problems in singlehood, maybe we ought to rephrase the original question to: "Why do I think I'm nothing without a mate?" Yet, the attitude is admittedly far more deeply ingrained in women.

SUMMING UP

Let's now summarize what we have learned about sex and the negative emotions:

- The culture teaches women to think that they are nothing without a man. A man is validated by himself and other men. A woman is validated largely by the men in her life.

- Consequently, many women slip into Desperate Dependence. They are nothing alone. Their existence, their survival, depends on a man to take care of them.

- The cure for Desperate Dependence is Undependence, unhooking ourselves from the obsessive need for a man. Undependence means starting to live *now* instead of waiting for a man to signal the start of real living.

- Sex is the umbrella answer that women often give as to why they think they must have a man. The real reasons are deeper. They want to feel wanted, taken care of, secure. And sex creates the impression—or illusion—that it fulfills all these wants.

- Aloneness need not mean loneliness. Better a rich single life than a poor relationship just to hold on to a man. There are underestimated rewards of living alone.

- The way to successful singlehood for many women is to develop job skills and thus escape economic entrapment in a failed relationship.

- Single people—men and women—can enrich their lives through nonsexual or not necessarily sexual friendships with both sexes.

Chapter 14

FANTASIES: USE YOUR IMAGINATION

We all fantasize at times. Is it a waste of time? Is it unhealthy? Is fantasizing itself an emotional bad habit? Or do fantasies have a role in dealing with our negative emotions?

Someone who goes around with his or her head in the clouds, who lives in a world of make-believe, is probably in or headed for emotional trouble—or else may be a budding artist. But my experience also tells me that fantasy, indulged in consciously and deliberately and used sparingly, can be therapeutic. The important thing is to have our hand on the fantasy "on-off" switch, to know when we are imagining—and when we are behaving as though illusion is reality.

THE REVENGE FANTASY

Few human emotions are less attractive than the desire for revenge. Or more common. Several negative emotional habits tend to provoke the desire for revenge—

anger, rejection, and low self-esteem among them. When we believe that someone has done us wrong, it is natural to want to strike back. Turning the other cheek is a saintly reaction in a world with few saints. But vengeance is another of those poisons that we pump into our systems at our own peril. When we fill ourselves with rancor and hate, we debase ourselves. We begin to become the thing we despise.

Nevertheless, contemporary psychology is finding a useful place for revenge when it is confined to the imagination. There is likely value in the revenge fantasy—vengeance imagined, but not carried out.

I had a patient, Marsha K., a teacher at a swank private girls' school. Marsha had been having an affair with Steve, a fellow member of the faculty, who was married and had two children. And then Steve dropped her. When she came to me, Marsha was seething with hostility. She wanted revenge for the pain that Steve had inflicted on her. She wanted to *destroy* the man who had hurt her. And she believed that she had just the weapon. In the course of their affair, Steve had confided to Marsha that he had previously been involved with two other women. Steve's wife did not know about any of these *amours*. If she did find out, it would likely ruin the marriage. The headmaster of the school was also a straitlaced gentleman. Thus, if Steve's behavior became known at school, it would have finished Steve professionally as well. Marsha had her scheme all worked out. She knew that she had it in her power to wreck the man who had *wronged* her. She confessed to me that she had written two anonymous letters, one to the man's wife and another to the headmaster, telling about Steve's extramarital adventures. She was just waiting to mail them.

I asked Marsha two questions. First, was Steve a good teacher? And, as far as she knew, was he a good husband and father? She looked daggers at me. But in the end, she admitted that he was an outstanding teacher. And, as far as she could tell, his dalliances had not damaged his home life. He was apparently a good husband and father. Then I asked her what she expected to gain by depriving his school, his wife, and his children of this man. "Revenge," Marsha said. "He deserves it, the rotten bastard!"

I told Marsha to go ahead, to indulge her wildest fantasies. "Imagine the letters have been mailed. Steve is called before the headmaster. He is confronted with the charges and is reduced to a quivering blob. He pleads for mercy, but the headmaster fires him on the spot." Marsha's eyes by now were ablaze with sadistic glee. "Imagine that Steve goes home," I continued. "He finds the house empty, his wife and kids gone. And on the empty living room floor is your letter to his wife. Go ahead, Marsha, revel in the poor man's agony—his career destroyed, his marriage in ruins. Then go home, tear up those letters, and get on with your life."

If she had actually carried out the fantasy—had wrecked Steve's career and home life—Marsha might have felt a vengeful satisfaction for a few days, maybe even weeks. But ultimately she would have had to live with herself and the damage she had done. None of it would have bettered her life one iota. And she would most likely not like the person she had to live with. It was almost as good just imagining Steve caught in her coils. And the fantasy did no harm to anyone. Revenge is something better fantasized than realized.

Marsha's therapy meanwhile progressed to issues of her own. Why was she drawn to Steve? What did she need in relation to herself? She was able to really focus on her own life now that her desire for revenge against Steve was out of the way.

Helen G. was a patient of mine who underwent a messy divorce. One clause of the divorce agreement required Helen to sell the couple's sailboat and split the proceeds with her ex-husband. Helen told me, triumphantly, that she had sold the boat for fifty dollars—and mailed her ex a check for twenty-five. I suggested to her that it would have been smarter to fantasize this act of vengeance. She could have conjured up in her imagination the horrified look on her former husband's face when he got a check for twenty-five dollars for his precious sailboat. But, having enjoyed that fantasy, she could have sold the boat for its actual worth and put her share of something like eight thousand dollars into her money-market fund.

LEAVE REVENGE ON THE CUTTING-ROOM FLOOR

I had a student in my New School class on negative emotions who told us how she dealt with her anger habit. Maggie W. had destroyed friendships. She had lost jobs. She had provoked bitter family feuds by her angry outbursts. She had gotten the idea into her head that anger was a "clean, honest emotion." It was, she thought, dishonest and unhealthy to suppress her "pure" angry feelings. To give people who had presumably wronged her a "piece of my mind" meant that she was not putting on "a phony front." Except that it did not work. Witness the lost friends, lost jobs, and family feuds.

One day as Maggie was driving to work, she was rehearsing in her mind how she was going to tell off a co-worker who had left her in the lurch on a crash project. Maggie tells what happened next:

"I practiced calling her every name in the book. Since I was alone in the car, I really let her have it out loud. Then a strange thing happened. When I finished ranting and raving, I suddenly felt exhausted. And a few minutes later I felt calm. Suddenly it dawned on me! I didn't have to spew that poison all over the office. I'd already gotten it out of my system, all alone in the car. When I got there, instead of laying into the girl who'd let me down, I was just cool toward her. And later she actually apologized! That experience taught me something. Now I just get things off my chest in privacy. In the car or in my room. I'm like an actress who gets all the bad lines, the over-acting, out of the way in rehearsal and saves her best performance for opening night."

Maggie had taught herself the beneficial uses of fan-tasy. She had stumbled onto it on her own. But the principle is exactly what I believe: leave the poison-pen letters in the waste basket. Leave your worst lines at the dress rehearsal. Leave the murder scenes on the cutting-room floor.

FANTASY AS A PATH TO OUR GOALS

There is another use of fantasy that I find positive and healthy. Remember Millie, who parlayed her pleasure in baking into a first-class bakery? Fantasizing can be a way of figuring out our goals. Imagining what we would like to be doing can focus otherwise vague ambitions. We can fantasize—*plan* is perhaps a more respectable word—what we want and how we are to get there. I had steered Millie around to fantasizing what she could do with her talent for baking. She imagined which recipes she might use. She pictured the layout of the shop. She calculated the employees she might need. She envisioned opening day, a ribbon stretched across the doorway, a crowd eager to get in.

All of this was healthy. Millie had moved from total apathy to caring about *something*—and how to get there. Call it fantasizing. Call it daydreaming. The point is that she was glimpsing what she might be. With Millie, fanta-sizing was healthy—because she eventually acted on her dreams. But fantasy employed only to escape from reality is dangerous. Being able to distinguish between the two is crucial. If you become so hooked on a soap opera that the characters seem like friends, like members of your own family, fine. No harm done. But if these characters begin to substitute for real relationships in your life, this is unhealthy. You are filling your life with characters who have no reality beyond your TV. You are killing off a part of yourself.

The important point is that we not confuse fantasy with fact. Take Millie's case again. For her to fantasize about the bake shop simply as an escape from her humdrum life—while continuing to lead the humdrum life—would have been futile, even unhealthy, because it would have continued her immobility. To dream about the bake shop, not as escapism but as a plan for escaping from her dreary life, was positive.

WHO IS YOUR MODEL?

When I talk to patients who are hooked on guilt, or anxiety, catastrophizing, or any of another half-dozen negative habits, I often ask: "Who are you modeling yourself after?" The question often catches them off guard. They had not looked for an explanation of their behavior in someone else. They had not seen their actions as something handed down. But, on reflection, they will often say: "My mother always got hysterical." Or: "My father was always tearing himself down." Or: "My grandmother always expected the worst." They had found a life model. Unfortunately, in these cases, it was a negative model.

But models—the right models or even bad models used in the right way—can be invaluable. Thinking of models is another way of using our imaginations to deal with our negative emotional habits. There may be no quicker way to break a bad habit than to observe its unattractiveness in someone else. It is even better to observe the person who handles a problem in a way that we admire. In one case, we have an example of how not to behave. The other shows us how to behave. One we dislike and avoid. The other we can admire and emulate.

Observing others also makes clear to us that there are alternative ways to handle the same situation. There is not only one approach. There are people who rarely feel guilty. And yet they are not necessarily selfish, thoughtless people. We know people who are no smarter or abler than we are. Yet, they do not go through life with a low opinion of themselves. There are people who make worse mistakes than we do. But they do not flagellate themselves to a frazzle. These people can all be positive models for us.

When I was a school psychologist, I came to understand that there was always more than one teacher in a classroom. There were twenty or thirty teachers, depending on how many kids were in the room. Children are deeply influenced by their peers. And it soon became clear to me that the children I saw were learning as much from the behavior of the other children as from the teacher. As far as everyday morals and mores, they were probably learning far more from their peers.

I put this perception to work in my school counseling. I would tell troubled youngsters to watch the children they liked and admired. Watch how they handle themselves, how they play with the other children and talk to the teacher. And I would say: "Try to model your behavior on what you like in them. Don't try to *be* them. You are still you. Just borrow their good traits. In the same way, watch the children whom you do not like or admire. What is it about them that bothers you? Do you see some of that behavior in yourself? If so, then decide to change it."

It is much the same throughout life. Our friends and colleagues provide models for us of how and how not to deal with life. Pick out people you admire and borrow from them. Again, slavish copycatting is not the answer. Your tennis teacher can show you a better serve. But it will come out slightly different even when you do it right—because you are you and not him or her. Look at behavior that turns you off, and say: "Do I ever look or sound like that? If I do, I'm cutting it out."

We do not have to limit our models to real people. They can be fictional characters we have admired. They can be composites of qualities we admire or may be drawn from several different people. I have modeled my own conception of mature love in part on a character from the opera *Der Rosenkavalier*. The Marschallin is willing to let go of the man she loves because she knows that he is in love with another woman. As she puts it, she loves everything about this man, including his love for the other woman. I found in the character of The Marschallin a mature, unsuffocating kind of love that is closer to the divine than selfish, possessive love. And I have tried, not always successfully, to model my feelings of love on hers.

CASTING

Here is another use of the imagination that I often recommend to my patients. I call it "casting." Choose somebody whose behavior you admire, and cast that person in the particular problem that you are currently facing. How do you think he or she would act in the same circumstances? How would that person play the role? Since you admire the person, there may well be a clue for you in his or her likely behavior.

Jessica R. was a thirty-four-year-old patient of mine

who was emotionally paralyzed by her obsessive attachment to a man who had abandoned her. Jessica had lived with this man for five years. They had started a business together—a market polling service. And then the man had run off with the secretary whom Jessica had hired for their firm. Rubbing salt into Jessica's wounded heart, her former lover and the secretary moved to the West Coast and launched a similar business.

A year and a half later, when Jessica came to me, she was still obsessed with this man. She thought of him and talked about him constantly. Everything that happened to her was filtered through her fantasies about him. In one of her daydreams, her ex-lover opens *The Wall Street Journal* to read that Jessica has sold their old firm for seven figures to a giant conglomerate. In another fantasy, her old lover turns on the television to see Barbara Walters interviewing Jessica as the Woman of the Year. The poor guy is, of course, eating his heart out as he watches.

Jessica had turned her runaway lover into her mirror. She existed only as a reflection of what this man saw or thought about her. And since he was no longer around to reflect any image of her, it was as though Jessica no longer existed. Her fantasies were unhealthy and all-consuming substitutes.

I talked to Jessica about models. I asked her to try to conjure up as a model someone whom she admired and to imagine how this admirable person might handle a similar breakup.

I did not make much headway until Jessica came in one day for a session after she had spent a weekend in the country. As she tells it:

"My friend Paula had about eight people out. Some married and some single. I hit it off right away with a woman named Bernice who had a quiet, confident way about her. Bernice was a good listener and when she spoke she was self-effacing and could kid herself. I guess what impressed me most was her composure. She didn't seem self-conscious or wrapped up in herself, which is how I always feel. She seemed to be at peace with the world. Consequently, she had something to give others.

"I mentioned to Paula how much I liked Bernice. 'Yes,' Paula said, 'she is wonderful, isn't she, especially considering what she's just gone through with that heel of a husband.' What was that all about? I wanted to know. And Paula told me that Bernice's husband had left her the month before for a nineteen-year-old cocktail waitress. I was absolutely stunned that this could have happened to such a refined, attractive woman. Yet, from Bernice's behavior, I would never have guessed what she was going through.

"After that, I met Bernice in town two or three times for lunch. And she was always the same. She showed great interest in me. And I only managed to learn about her situation slowly. And even then, she did so with such pride and dignity that I was envious. So I started 'casting' Bernice in my situation. When I found myself mooning over this guy who'd left me a year and a half ago, I'd say to myself: How would Bernice react in this situation? Would she be pining away, night after night, all alone, concocting those silly daydreams for spiting him? Would Bernice be working like a dog, not for herself, but to 'show him up'? You can bet she wouldn't! Would she still be living for a guy who obviously didn't care if she lived or died? By now Bernice would have gotten on with her own life. Well, I'm not Bernice. I can't behave exactly like her. But I could learn from her. I could try to model myself on somebody I admired—her—instead of somebody I'm sick of—the old whining me."

Jessica had cast Bernice into her drama. She had learned what I had learned in those classrooms years ago. There are teachers all around us, models for good and bad behavior. And, by using our imaginations, we can learn from both.

225

SUMMING UP

————■————

What have we learned about the positive uses of fantasy and imagination?

- When we feel vengeful, it is psychologically healthier to work off the feeling through a "revenge fantasy" rather than actually try to "get back" at our adversary. The revenge fantasy acts as a safety valve, letting us blow off steam, without doing something rash that we may later regret.

- Fantasies—when used consciously—can help us find out what we really want out of life. The fantasy can serve as a goal-setting tool.

- The harm is not in fantasizing, but in confusing fact with fantasy. We are better off using fantasy to motivate ourselves, but not to fool ourselves.

- Modeling our behavior on that of others whom we admire can help us break negative emotional habits.

Chapter 15

ANGER AND ANXIETY

ANGER AND ANXIETY: CUTTING THE BARBED WIRE

"**I**'m mad all the time. I'm mad at everybody."

The patient who said this to me was Helen S., a thirty-six-year-old actuary with an insurance company. Helen looked angry, too. There was a hard edge to her voice and hostility in her eyes. Her mouth was always set, her lips tightly pursed.

Among the emotional bad habits, anger is a crippler. When we give vent to our anger, it robs us of good judgment. We behave inefficiently. We tend to make rash decisions. We err. On the other hand, if we suppress chronic anger, it is like a volcano waiting to erupt. And, as we noted back in chapter 1, anger is one of the emotions that can make us physically sick. It smolders, causing headaches, insomnia, ulcers, and a host of other ills.

A searing description of what anger does to us was penned by Karen Wood, a favorite writer of mine for

Provincetown's *The Advocate.* "Of all the emotions," she wrote, "my anger is the hardest for me to deal with. It comes as blind rage, tearing through me like an out-of-control fire, scorching and searing and sending hot, cruel words to my lips. I scream out with ugly contortions, and feel my throat gasp and catch at the words as they pass. I see my own spittle fly from my mouth and even as I am tossed in this tempest, part of me stands back and watches and is disgusted. Is that me literally frothing at the mouth? I ask in amazement from some very far detached place." *That* is hot anger.

There is also cold anger. This is the brand often dispensed by passive-aggressive people. The "silent treatment" is the most common form. Almost invariably, anger represents a breakdown in communication. We are not communicating effectively when we are sputtering in rage. But the worst breakdown of all occurs during the silent treatment. Here, communication is totally blocked, as dead as a cut telephone line.

Whether hot or cold, we all get angry from time to time. And let's be honest, like Karen Wood—we are both exhilarated and disgusted by our angry explosions; or we take a secret pleasure in freezing somebody out with the silent treatment. There is even a place for beneficial, therapeutic anger, which we will get to in a moment. But for now we are concerned with people who are chronically mad at the world, people caught in the barbed wire of habitual anger. Let's consider how the angry man or woman got that way. What are the roots of habitual anger?

Very many of my patients, I find, have picked up the anger habit by observing a parent. Children who see a parent as frightening and forbidding are apt to copy this behavior when they become parents. Why? Frankly, because it appears to work. They were cowed into submission or obedience by a fear of this angry giant looming over them and shouting at them, so they employ it on their kids. Thus, the habit of anger is passed from generation to generation. The same people may adopt anger as a control technique when they attain positions of authority. They rule by anger and by instilling fear in their subordinates. Sometimes they use anger to compensate, in a perverse way, for the anger directed against them in childhood.

Another factor in chronic anger is that our culture conditions us to react angrily to certain situations and provocations. There are times when we are *supposed to* get angry. We see this with little boys in the schoolyard. Certain taunts are supposed to produce an angry, fighting response, or else the kid is seen as not "manly." ("Your mother's a . . .") Whatever the taunt, the culturally conditioned response is to lash back.

The angry personality is often one who sees him- or herself as a victim. It is a way of rationalizing low self-esteem and lack of achievement. The angry person has wound up a loser again because somebody has done him wrong—again. In effect, these people go around waiting to be stepped on. They expect it. That is their fate. They are victims. And each time they feel victimized, it sets their anger loose all over again. They get mad at themselves. They get mad at their supposed victimizers. They get mad at the world.

Finally, there is anger produced by chemical imbalance. People thus afflicted become terrified by their own anger. They may become homicidal or suicidal. They feel such uncontrollable rage that they are capable of doing violence to themselves or others. A chemical imbalance is like a defect in the machinery. Most of us, when we get angry, have a valve that knows when to shut off the anger before we do damage to ourselves or others. But in the person suffering a chemical imbalance, the valve is stuck. It does not shut off the anger, and rage continues to pour out like lava from a volcano. Obviously, people suffering from such chemical imbalances have serious emotional problems. They need professional help. Often, they can be helped by psychopharmacology, by mood-controlling drugs.

By the time she came to see me, Helen, the angry actuary, had been in and out of more psychiatrists' offices than a couch salesman. She explained her chronic anger by her unhappy childhood. She was, she said, starved for attention from an irascible, impatient, stormy father. Now, as an adult, she can barely remember when she did not feel angry. She suffers from the chronic, free-floating variety. Instead of getting angry at a particular situation, Helen carries her anger around like a tattered insecurity blanket—and flings it over whatever is happening to her at the moment.

I was interested in Helen's explanation for her habitual behavior—the childhood neglect and exposure to anger—but I was more concerned with the here and now. How would we disentangle her from the barbed wire of perpetual hostility in which I found her caught?

In one early session, Helen told me of an experience she had had at work. Her boss had treated her well, up to this point. As Helen put it: "But I was waiting to see how long it would be before he'd pull something."

Not long, apparently. One day the boss told Helen that he was moving her to a smaller office. Her response? "I got so mad. I let him have it. I knew it wasn't a space problem, which was his excuse. I knew that they were putting me in the deep freeze. I fixed him. I filed a grievance against this guy with management. And if that doesn't work, I'll go to the State Commission on Human Rights. I think he's guilty of sexism."

I asked Helen if she had given her boss a chance to explain the reason for the move before she gave vent to her rage. Her answer: "I'm not about to be sweet-talked into putting up with second-class treatment. I don't let people walk all over me."

Helen's response is typical of people hooked on habitual anger. Anger is a powerful emotion. Therefore, those addicted to it often take a perverse pride in their chin-out defiance: "I don't put up with anybody's guff. I stand up for myself. Don't try to push *me* around." They see themselves as the exact opposite of The Pleaser, the compliant, doormat personality. Their forthright behavior has a superficial appeal. Getting mad seems preferable to getting stepped on. Anger creates the illusion of dealing with a problem from strength. We all loved the character Peter Finch played in the movie *Network*, who threw open the window and shouted: "I'm mad as hell and I'm not going to take it anymore!" Finch was expressing the anger that we all feel at one time or another. That is how the angry Helen saw herself, a woman who was not about to take it anymore. Unfortunately, her habitual anger was doing her more harm than good.

Because anger is so strong, and in the short term so satisfying, it is not an easy habit to break. Look at Helen. She was afraid that if she lost her anger, she would lose her strength, like Samson getting his locks clipped. I told Helen: "Think carefully. What is it that you really want?" When I first put that question to her, I got angry defiance: "I want people to stop stepping on me. I want people to stop mistreating me."

"You're not really answering my question, Helen," I said. "You're telling me what you don't want. And I am asking you what you *do* want." I was trying to get her off the emotional low road and up onto the positive expressway. "What good things would you like to have happen in your life?" I asked. The question caught Helen off guard. She wasn't used to thinking in terms of what she was for, but, rather, what she was against. After a long pause, she replied: "I guess I'd like to get a promotion. And I'd like people to like me." The latter wish was not surprising and fitted in with Helen's conviction that she had never won the love of her father. "All right," I said. "If that's what you want, you are going to have to change.

And you can. What you are doing now is reveling in your self-righteous wrath. You are enjoying your anger, luxuri-ating in it. But you are paying a high price for it. It is defeating the positive things you want for yourself. The Helen that people see is unlikely to win friends, or affec-tion, much less get a promotion."

SENDING IT TO THE FRONT OFFICE

What I explain to patients like Helen, whose negative habit is anger, is a little elementary anatomy and physiol-ogy. Elementary, but crucial. Just below the brain's cere-brum is an egg-sized bunch of nerve cells called the *thalamus*. Think of the thalamus as a routing station for most of our incoming feelings. Its job is to relay these feelings to the frontal lobe of the brain for a response. In effect, the thalamus is the seat of our emotions and the cerebrum is the seat of reason.

Let's examine what happens when we experience an emotion such as anger. Let's say that we think someone has insulted us. The message reaches the thalamus first. If we deal with the anger at that instant, our response will be emotional, even violent: "How dare you!" (Bared nails lunging at the accuser's eyes; or a fist swung at his chin.) However, if we will just delay for a few seconds, the thalamus can relay the message up to the cerebrum, the seat of reason. If we deal with the perceived insult there, our powers of reason can take over and determine our response. In other words, the thinking part of the brain, rather than the emotional part, will be processing the problem. I call this delay "Sending It to the Front Office." As you have probably guessed by now, this delay-ing tactic is the biological basis for the sound old advice about counting to ten before we blow up at somebody. The ten-count is just long enough to relay the message from the hip-shooting part of the brain up to the thinking part—to Send It to the Front Office.

We can learn to control that relay switch located at the thalamus. It is all a matter of practice and habit. The anger-prone person is doing just the opposite—letting the thalamus rather than the cerebrum handle problems, acting in haste, and often repenting at leisure.

Let's again compare how two different personalities deal with the same set of facts. The situation: an apparent case of a subordinate going behind the boss's back. The boss learns that his subordinate has sent a sensitive auditor's report on their division directly to the president of the company.

BOSS A *(a hothead):* [His face the color of a tomato, he bursts into the subordinate's office shaking a copy of the report clutched in his fist.] You scheming son of a bitch! Did you think you would get away with this? Did you think I wouldn't find out? I trusted you and now I find out you're a disloyal snake in the grass—going behind my back. You've had it! (An emotional response backed up by irrational thinking.)

SUBORDINATE *(too stunned to answer):* But . . . but . . . but . . .

BOSS B *(a cool customer)*: [On learning that the subordinate has sent the report directly to the president of the company, his face turns the color of a tomato. But he forces himself to sit calmly for two full minutes. The crimson drains from his face. He rises and walks casually into the subordinate's office.] Morning, Bob. I see that Mrs. Throckmorton has the auditor's report.

SUBORDINATE: Yes, she called last night, just after you left, and told me to get it up to her pronto. I'm not sure how she even knew we already had it.

BOSS B: You did the right thing. As usual. [Smiles.] She's not a lady to trifle with.

Boss A reacted with his thalamus. His emotions drove his behavior. He didn't give the problem time to get up to the front office, the cerebrum, the thinking part of his brain. Consequently, he made unfair accusations, made an ass of himself, and possibly drove an able employee from the company. Boss B was as upset as Boss A. But he waited that critical interval. He gave himself time to hit the button that relayed the message from the thalamus to the cerebrum. He sent the problem to the front office. Consequently, he reacted on the basis of reason. He used information instead of inflammation to guide his behavior.

In our cave ancestors, the thalamic reaction had its place. When the saber-tooth tiger swooped down on Og, he had to react before he had time to think. Even today, we occasionally find ourselves in situations where split-second reflexes are more vital than quiet reflection. But in sophisticated modern society, the shot from the hip is almost always off target. We have a choice of two behaviors, if only we have the patience to wait for the cool-headed part of the brain to take over from the hotheaded part. Think about it first. Send It to the Front Office.

MORE TAPE RECORDER THERAPY

Earlier I said that there is a great future for the tape recorder in dealing with our negative emotions. The tape recorder can be helpful in our switching from angry outbursts to real communication. Do you remember Marge and Stanley A.? Marge used Broken Record to try to break Stan of the habit of coming home at all hours. They were also chronic arguers. I told Marge that the next time she and Stan launched into a battle royal, she ought to turn on their tape recorder. Afterward, they each ought to listen to what they had said. Not to prove what a louse Stanley was or what a scold Marge was. Not to prove that the other guy was wrong. But to listen to themselves, to see whether they were really communicating or just trying to score anger points off each other. We don't know what we sound like most of the time. And we certainly don't when we are blowing our top. The tape recorder says: Now listen to yourself. Is this what you really wanted to say? Is this really what you want to be?

BREATHE EASIER

There are other useful anger-control techniques that I recommend to my patients and students like Helen S. One that is related to Send It to the Front Office is deep breathing.

When something or someone makes you mad, start breathing slowly and deeply. This action will help you in two ways. First, the deep breathing gives you the stall time—the count-to-ten effect—that will get the anger processed at the cool cerebrum, instead of at the hot thalamus. Next, the deep inhalation of oxygen has a tranquilizing effect on us. It acts something like the endorphins we discussed earlier, which are produced by physical activity. The effect of deep breathing is almost instantaneous. We immediately start to feel calmer. And this "drug" is nonhabit-forming, not dangerous—and it is as free as the air.

Or take a brisk walk. Again, walking will give you the

stall time to think through the cerebrum rather than explode through the thalamus. And it will oxygenate the body and soothe the mind too.

REVENGE FANTASIES AND ANGER

Another anger-control technique: remember the revenge fantasy that we discussed in chapter 14? When someone makes you angry, don't say: "I'm going to figure out how to get back at that guy. I'll fix his wagon. I'm going to blow him away!" All you are doing is pouring poison into your system and beginning to blow yourself away. Say instead: "I think I'll indulge in a little fantasy about that SOB." The more improbable the fantasy, the less likely you are to act on it. And the more likely that you will see the humor in it and steer yourself from a self-destructive overreaction. I suggested to Helen, our ever-angry actuary, that she come up with a revenge fantasy for her boss. Here was Helen's concoction: "Move me into a small office, eh? Well, I'd like to see him in *his* office. The ceiling starts to move down. The floor starts to come up. The walls start closing in on him. He's screaming: 'Helen! Helen! Please! Stop it! I'm sorry. Forgive me. You can have your old office back. You can have the Astrodome for your office if you want it. Just stop crushing me!' "

Interestingly, the next time Helen came in, I questioned her further on this business of the small office, and it turned out that the boss intended the move to put Helen *closer* to him. It was a positive sign. But in her addiction to anger she had forced herself to see good news in a bad light. She had let her habitual anger blot out her good fortune.

Helen has made a start, but she is still far from breaking her anger habit. After all, she has been perversely enjoying her anger for years. She is not about to abandon that familiar, raggedy insecurity blanket overnight. But I do have other patients, just as addicted to anger as Helen, who finally saw the self-defeating effect of their behavior. One of these was Luis R., an export-importer originally from Spain. He was married to an old-line WASP named Allison. Actually, Allison was my patient first. She brought Luis to me because she recognized something in her husband that he could not admit to himself—Luis was addicted to anger. Getting him to come to me was no mean feat in itself, since seeing a therapist went completely against Luis's cultural conditioning.

As a Spanish male, Luis was full of his own imported *Supposed-tos*. He was *supposed to* have a strict code of honor. He was *supposed to* be hotheaded. He was *supposed to* be ready to defend his honor at the drop of an insult. As a result, Luis had often embarrassed himself and Allison by blowing up in public at the slightest provocation. They had lost friends and, thanks to Luis, were getting a reputation as a couple to avoid.

One of the first things that I discussed with Luis was the thalamus and the cerebrum. I turned his own cultural clichés back on him. I explained that the thalamus reacts like a bull. It is easily provoked, becomes enraged, and blindly attacks. The cerebrum is like the matador, cool and calculating, thinking before taking action. I also pointed out that the bull rarely wins. Which did he choose to be?

I saw Luis for several sessions. I asked him if he liked the angry person that he was. No, he said. Did it make him feel more masculine to be regarded as a hothead and a troublemaker? No, he told me. After each ugly incident, he felt like a caricature, a cartoon Latino. What he really envied, he told me, was Allison's patrician coolness. But she was from a completely different background. He couldn't change, he said. Wrong, I told him. His being Spanish was a cultural influence, not an unbreakable genetic code. "The problem, Luis, is not that you cannot change. You do not choose to change," I said during one session. But I did not rush him. "Let me know when you decide that you want to change," I told him, "and I'll help you." Months went by. I knew that Luis was indeed trying, and I saw small signs of progress. But I knew that he was probably out of the woods when he told me about a party that he and Allison had gone to one night. The host and hostess were old friends of Allison whom Luis had not met before. He had been looking forward to the party because several people were going to be there who could be helpful business contacts.

When he arrived and was introduced to his host, Luis was insulted by the man! Even I have to admit it. The host seemed to have had a head start at the bar, and he greeted Luis with: "Oh yes, Allison's Latin lapdog."

"I wanted to tear him to pieces," Luis told me. "But I could see he was drunk. I remembered all the things we had talked about. About my thalamus and my cerebrum. The bull and the matador. And I saw all the interesting people. It looked like a nice party. So instead of punching this rude fellow and marching out, I threw the switch so his insult went to the high part of my brain. I forced myself to count to ten. I took deep breaths. I walked away and introduced myself to the other guests. So every time this fellow walks by, I am having a conversation, making one of his friends my friend. It felt very good, like he is doing me a favor that he does not want to do. Every time I am eating his caviar, I give him a big smile, and it tastes even better. I was, as you say, winning with myself. And this fellow was losing. I think this is the first time in my life I have controlled my anger so well. And I did not feel less of a man. I felt like more of a gentleman.

"Then comes the best. After we go home, Allison told me this fellow didn't have a dime when he married his wife. And he is known by everybody as a gigolo. Now I understand his insult to me. He is ashamed of himself and he wanted to paint me with the same brush. And I felt even better that I have controlled myself. It was a wonderful party, and I did make good business contacts that night too."

Luis had learned a difficult lesson for angry people to grasp. They are more often bent on proving a point than on solving a problem. They are so blinded by anger that they lose sight of any positive goal. They twist themselves into a tightly coiled spring of self-righteousness and explode. They would rather crush their adversary than sign a peace treaty with him. Short-sighted, short-term emotional satisfaction had been Luis's way for years. He had been ruled by his thalamus instead of his thinking brain. And he had paid dearly. But he had changed.

Ted C., a foreclosure officer with a bank, may have been an even harder case than Luis. As Ted sat in my office, he reminded me of one of those bombs with a fuse burning that you see in cartoons. I expected him to go off at any moment. Ted lived in a suburb that was directly in the flight path of an airport. The noise was driving him crazy. So Ted had decided to draw up a petition to present to the airport officials to have the path changed. He wanted all of his neighbors to sign it. But first he brought the petition to me to get my "psychological" opinion. I will spare you the full text. But I think you will get the idea of Ted's mentality from the first line: "Anybody who refuses to sign this petition has got to be stupid, scared of city hall, or deaf."

Ted's habitual anger had gotten in the way of his thinking. The petition seemed to have been written by his thalamus instead of his cerebrum. "Ted," I said, "let's look at your objective. What are you after? Is it to get some peace and quiet in your neighborhood? Or is it to find out which of your neighbors is stupid, cowardly, or deaf?" Ted looked at me as though he did not know what I was talking about. "Stop shaking your fist at the universe," I told him. "And let's try to figure out where you are trying to go—and how we get from here to there."

With that, I helped him draft a petition enlisting his neighbors in his cause, rather than insulting them. Sometimes a therapist gets involved in strange matters.

Ted's chronic belligerence is standard behavior among anger addicts. "I'm right. You're wrong. And I don't just want to win my point. I want you to admit how bad you are. I want to *crush* you!" I try to show the Teds among my patients that they have locked themselves into a self-defeating posture. Yes, *you think* that you want to "get him, fix her, show them a thing or two." But, after that, what? Do you want to go through life with a chip nailed to your shoulder, with your intestines twisted into a knot, with bile pumping through your system? Or do you really want to break the anger habit and start living a serene, healthy life? Do you want to stop being overlooked for promotion, stop fighting with your in-laws, and stop losing friends? Then, let's start.

One effective technique for breaking the anger habit is a modified version of Broken Record. In this case, you use the technique not on somebody else but on yourself. I tell my anger-ridden patients: "When you find yourself going into a situation that may anger you, try to know where you want to come out. Have a positive goal clearly established in your head." Not: "I'm going to show the boss that he is a miserable tightwad." But rather: "I want the boss to agree to give me a raise." Keep saying it to yourself: "I want the boss to agree to give me a raise." Have that thought firmly fixed in your mind when you are talking to him, so that you do not allow yourself to be provoked into anger and thus distracted from your goal. You want a raise. This time, you are going to win the peace, not just the war. When you go to your ex-girlfriend's apartment, what is it that you really want? To prove what a terrible woman she turned out to be? Or to get back your stereo? One message is very likely to defeat the other. Venting your anger is only going to arouse hers. Again, use the Broken Record on yourself. On the drive over, keep repeating to yourself: "I want her to give me back my stereo. I want her to give me back my stereo." And keep that thought foremost in your mind while you are talking to her. As they used to say in my youth: "Keep your eye upon the doughnut, and not upon the hole." Anger is the hole, an empty reward and a lot of hot air. You want your stereo. You want the doughnut.

DOES ANGER HAVE A PLACE?

Are there no times when honest anger has a place in our lives? Of course it does, occasionally. Great art and literature have been forged in the crucible of anger. Moral outrage against injustice has fueled noble human crusades. Anger is also a clear way of letting people know that they have displeased us, disappointed us, or deceived us. Anger can put steel in our spine when we face our fears. But anger that we wear like a hair shirt, anger as a habitual response to life, will destroy us quicker than it will the objects of our anger. When we give way to our furies, we dehumanize ourselves. We diminish our dignity. We ignore the reasoning part of our brain in favor of the rash, unthinking part. And we make regrettable mistakes. Think of it this way: Do you admire many short-tempered people? Is there a permanent grouch whom you like?

ANXIETY: THE JANGLED HEART

Anxiety is an emotion that is produced by several negative feelings—rejection, helplessness, catastrophizing, and guilt among them. At the heart of anxiety is fear, a nameless, formless dread. Anxiety is a particularly debilitating negative habit, since the anxious heart can know no peace.

Anxiety is as much a physical as an emotional state. We feel jittery. Our stomachs are tied in knots. Our mouths are dry and our appetites nil one minute and insatiable the next. We feel as though our nerve endings have been pulled out, rubbed raw, and left naked and exposed. One of my patients described anxiety as "being in a constant state of electric shock."

David D., a librarian, was a patient of mine whom I liked very much. David was a handsome young man, with large, sad eyes and the sensitive features we expect in a poet. David offers a vivid illustration of the anxiety-plagued personality: "I wake up in the morning and glance at the clock. It's always too early, before the alarm even goes off. Almost immediately a sense of dread comes over me. I want to crawl under the covers and disappear. I want to fall back asleep, but I can't. I feel jangled and groggy at the same time. My stomach is churning. The hardest part is just getting out of bed. I hate facing the day. I'm a little less anxious once I'm on my feet. Still, the anxiety follows me all day long like a vulture. I'm nervous about what's going to happen. Will I have a run-in with this woman I hate at the library? Should I apply for the opening in the next higher grade? Do I really have to visit my folks over the weekend and listen to my father's unsubtle hints that he doesn't think much of a male librarian? I'm brushing my teeth, and all these unpleasant thoughts are spinning through my head."

David is a classic example of free-floating, chronic anxiety. The anxiety follows him wherever he goes and attaches itself to whatever he is doing. But—and this was hard for David to believe—his anxiety was a formed habit, a learned reflex that could be broken. It was not the way that he had to go through life. It is the way that he *thought* he had to go through life. My role was to show

David how someone carrying the crushing weight of habitual anxiety can free himself.

First, let's look at his behavior when he woke up in the morning. All parts of the body and senses do not wake up at the same pace. David's eyes open with a snap and he feels instantly alert—and anxious. You have probably experienced this sensation yourself. You wake up feeling fully conscious. Then you swing your legs over the side of the bed, start to stand up, and are a little shaky. That is because the rest of your body is not yet as awake as your brain.

As with depression, physical action is the best early-morning medicine for anxiety. The instant you feel the urge to pull the covers over your head, force yourself out of bed. Energize your eyes by gazing out the window and fixing on outdoor objects. Energize your ears by turning on some music that you like. And then exercise. Have a regular program of physical activity. Run in place; do calisthenics; go jogging. However you do it, get your body in motion. Again, it is the displacement idea. It is hard to contain anxiety and healthy exhaustion in the same body at the same time. Of course, for hard-core anxiety cases, the jitters will move in again after a time. But exercise at least helps us to get the day off to a reasonably tranquil start.

WHAT TRIGGERS YOUR ANXIETY?

What I next suggest to people like David is that they try to separate out the various components that make up their anxiety. Anxiety is another of those vague sensations. We feel it, but we don't know quite what we are feeling—or why. So, once again the first step is to pinpoint the cause or causes, so that we can begin work on the cure. And, once again, I find the notebook technique enormously helpful as we try to become detectives of our own souls. What we are looking for are the trigger points. Why, when one minute we feel perfectly cool, do we suddenly feel, the next minute, like that cat on a hot tin roof? Why are we nervous, on edge, jumpy? And how does our anxiety express itself physically? In sweaty palms? A fluttery heart? In tongue-tied speech? And where are we when the anxiety begins? Visiting the old hometown? Arriving at the office? And who is involved when we get anxious? A boss? An older brother? An ex-husband? By keeping a notebook and jotting down the Where, When, How, and Who of our anxiety attacks, we have put ourselves on the path of the Why. We will likely see a pattern begin to emerge. We will have identified the anxiety trigger.

Let's say that your notebook reveals that you start feeling anxious whenever your mother-in-law is coming to visit. You feel jangled. You get headaches and tend to drop things. Now we can begin dealing with your anxiety trigger. Why do you suppose your mother-in-law's visits make you so anxious? You say it's because she finds fault with everything you do. The way you feed the baby; the way you do your hair; the prices you pay for your groceries. Everything. No matter what you do or say, she criticizes. Now we're getting somewhere. We've got something tangible to work with.

Some of the anxiety may be triggered because you feel guilty. You are troubled by a suspicion that maybe your mother-in-law is right. Maybe you are doing things wrong. After all, she's older and has had a lot more experience than you. And she raised five children who all adore her.

You are also likely feeling anger. You can't be doing *everything* wrong, though she seems to think you are. Actually, everyone else—your husband, your friends, *your mother*—thinks you are doing a terrific job as a wife and mother. They tell you that you are well organized, good with the kids, an excellent cook and hostess. So why should you have to put up with this nonstop criticism from a woman who simply cannot be pleased?

With this knowledge of what may underlie your anxiety, we can apply some of our other tested techniques. Your anxiety is no longer a formless mass. It has clearer outlines. We have already identified two of its components, guilt and anger.

As for the guilt, you might begin by asking yourself: "What's going on here? Whom is this criticism coming from? Why is my mother-in-law saying all these things to me? Is her constant carping the real message? Or is it cloaking a hidden message?" More likely the latter. And your mother-in-law's unconscious message no doubt runs something like this: "For years I raised my family. It was my greatest joy. It filled my life. I never needed anything else. Now I am a widow. My children are grown up and gone. I'm old. I feel useless and empty. I'm trying to relive my life, to feel that I am a part of something, through my children and their families. And I am doing this by telling them everything I know. Take my daughter-in-law. She's a good girl. But she doesn't realize how much I can teach her, though I am constantly trying to help her."

By understanding where your mother-in-law is coming from, you can begin to answer the question: "What's going on here?" You see your mother-in-law's true agenda. It is not that she is so dissatisfied with you, but with her own life. And it makes you a little more sympathetic toward her—even if she does drive you crazy. And it explains why there is no reason to let her make you feel guilty. She can't help herself.

We have an effective technique for dealing with this situation: To You-ness To Me-ness. For example, one of your mother-in-law's pet peeves might be handled in this way: "*To you,* Mom, I know you think I should iron Howard's shorts. I know that you always ironed your husband's shorts. But *to me,* we have these perma-press fabrics these days. And I can put my time to better use—

like baking a cake for your birthday tomorrow." Or, take another example: *"To you,* Mom, I know you would like us to spend Christmas with you again this year. But *to me,* all of us will get along better if I don't slight my mom and dad and spend an occasional holiday with them."

Broken Record can be helpful too: "I know, Mom, you sent all your kids to parochial school. *But Howard and I want ours to be exposed to kids from all kinds of backgrounds.* Yes, Mom, I know that the nuns taught strict discipline. *But Howard and I want our kids to be exposed to kids ..."* And so on.

There is a place for the Three Windows of Perception to help put your feelings of guilt and anger into perspective. Window One: we see an older woman criticizing a younger woman. Window Two: an older woman is criticizing a younger woman *who fears that she may indeed be doing everything wrong.* Window Three: we see an older woman criticizing a younger woman perhaps because she is trying to recapture her own young motherhood; or who is irritable because her rheumatism is acting up; or who talks constantly to cover up the fact that she is growing deaf and can't hear others well. Whatever the truth, Window Three helps you get the burden of blame off your back. It allows you to stop feeling guilty. And it makes you less angry, because you realize that your mother-in-law's behavior is not necessarily—and not even likely—your fault.

And finally, Talk Tenderly To Yourself: "There. She's gone. That was a tough five days. She complained about virtually everything. But that's her way, and she can't seem to change. Anyway, I know I'm a good wife and mother. I do a terrific job. And I didn't let her talk me out of my self-esteem. I also was sympathetic toward her because I know she is getting on and is basically unhappy." It won't hurt to say all this out loud to yourself, so that these tender words can sink into your brain.

When we start to analyze our generalized anxiety, we

can start to see the component parts that it is made of—in the above example, guilt and anger. Once we can be specific, we can begin to apply the appropriate remedies we have learned—and the anxiety should start to dissolve.

RELAXATION TECHNIQUES

Since anxiety is a physical as well as an emotional state, it also yields to physical remedies. Relaxation techniques can be very effective in relieving anxiety. So are meditation or chanting a mantra, for the more spiritually inclined. I have had good results personally and with my patients by using Dr. Edmund Jacobson's relaxation techniques described in his book with the unfortunately unrelaxing title: *You Must Relax.*

Let me describe a typical Jacobson exercise to give you the idea. This one is a progressive exercise. You can do it in a chair, in bed, practically anywhere, anytime. Start by letting your body sink into a chair or mattress. If you are doing the exercise in bed, put a small pillow under your knees. Uncurl your toes. Unclench your fists. Now, breathe deeply. Concentrate first on your right foot. Tell it to relax. When you feel the tension go out of your right foot, move to your left foot and tell it to relax. Keep moving up your body, relaxing your thighs, pelvis, chest, and arms in sequence. Think of yourself as a half-filled sack of flour, and sink into a soft chair. Imagine your body taking on the contours of the chair. Give your body up to the pull of gravity as the relaxation progresses. Let all harsh thoughts slip from your mind and replace them with pleasant musings. Keep practicing this technique. In time, the anxiety, along with the tension, will lift from your body and drift off.

Most progressive relaxation exercises are based on

Jacobson's techniques. Arnold Lazarus has developed a useful relaxation tape. There are several more approaches, and I find them all effective to some degree. Relaxation techniques are also useful in the treatment of phobias, about which I will have more to say.

Jacobson's techniques work for me. But there is no single way to relax. Studies have shown that an hour of Jacobson, or meditation, or chanting a mantra, or walking, or even napping may have the same anxiety-relieving effect for different people. You may find one method better suited to you than another.

ANXIETY CAN MAKE YOU ILL

Just as the other negative emotions can help trigger a host of illnesses, untreated anxiety also takes its toll on our bodies. To cite just one example: anxiety produces tension, and bursitis, a terribly painful condition, is often triggered by tension.

Migraine headaches are so excruciating that just the fear of one is enough to induce anxiety. As a veteran migraine sufferer, let me tell you about a technique that I have found helpful. When you feel a migraine headache coming on, imagine that your hands are hot. Imagine how they would feel getting hotter and hotter. For many people, this kind of auto-suggestion can actually redirect the blood flow from the brain to your extremities and thus reduce the pressure inside your head and give you some relief from the headache. Just knowing that a relief tool like this is available can also stave off your anxiety that a migraine may be about to strike.

SUMMING UP

Summing up the two big *A*s—anger and anxiety—handle them in these ways:

- When you are provoked, relay the provocation from the thalamus up to the cerebrum. Send It to the Front Office.

- Practice relaxation techniques. Oxygenate your system. Breathe deeply. Take a walk. Exercise.

- Work off your rage in harmless, even humorous fantasies about what you would like to do to your tormentors.

- Try to change the situation that is making you angry instead of attempting to "get back at" the person who angers you. Don't win the war while losing the peace.

- Don't be distracted by your anger into a short-sighted, short-term victory for your spleen.

- Use Broken Record on yourself to keep your eye on your positive goal. Keep repeating to yourself *what* you are trying to accomplish, not *whom* you are trying to destroy.

- To deal with anxiety, break the anxious mood in the morning by getting out of bed immediately and doing something physical.

- Since anxiety is usually compounded of several underlying feelings, keep a notebook to help pinpoint the sources. Record the When, Where, Who, How, and Why of your anxiety. When you know the cause, you will know better which therapies can help.

- Practice relaxation techniques to dispel your anxiety.

- Be aware that anxiety is not only robbing you of happiness; left untreated, it can trigger medical problems.

Chapter 16

---•---

PHOBIAS AND OBSESSIONS: PRISONS OF THE MIND

Phobias are prisons constructed of unreasoning fear. I have had patients who were:

- Terrified of going to a doctor
- Too frightened to get on an airplane
- Incapable of driving over a bridge
- Panicked by the idea of taking a test

Phobias paralyze us. They seal us off from the normal activities of life. They can be among the most crippling negative emotional habits.

Jerry K. provides a case in point. When Jerry first came to see me, he had what is known as a "back room" job on Wall Street. He did clerical tasks, taking care of the paperwork generated by millions of stock market transactions daily. Jerry knew that he was working well below his capacity, and the thought depressed him. What he really wanted was to be a stockbroker, not a paper pusher. But first he would have to pass the broker's examination. And Jerry had a phobia about taking tests. He broke into a cold sweat at the thought of an examination. Jerry's phobia was costing him dearly in self-respect, self-realization, earning power, and hence his standard of living.

Of course, Jerry's fear was unreasonable. He was intelligent, a college graduate. But it does no good to tell the phobic that his fears are unfounded. It only annoys these people to be told that their phobias are foolish. If you do so, they will begin to look at you not as a friend but as the enemy, part of an uncomprehending and unsympathetic world. If the problem yielded to reason, it would not be a phobia. For example, I had a patient with a worrisome growth on her shoulder. She refused to do anything about it for months and months—because she had a phobia about scars! You and I might find it preposterous that a woman would risk her life for such a foolish reason. But I did not belittle her fears, because they were real to her. Instead, I tried to help her overcome them.

In Jerry's case, he had had it wasting his life in the back room while others, no abler than he, went onward and upward on Wall Street. It was his professional frustration that finally brought him to me.

Jerry's phobia was overwhelming to him. When he thought of taking a test, he fell apart. In a way, my approach was similar to my treatment of Leonard G., the unemployed geologist, and his can of worms, back in chapter 3. What we had to do was break Jerry's phobia down into pieces that he could manage.

Jerry and I started by analyzing his terror of taking tests. When did the fear set in? "I start to sweat even when I hear the word *exam*," Jerry told me. His hands began to feel clammy. His legs went rubbery. We went on, tracing each step in the process of taking a test, from the announcement of it to actually sitting down with the questions in front of him.

This breakdown of test-taking into its component parts led us to the next step. I call it Building A Stairway. We took the thing that Jerry dreaded doing, and then we restructured it as a series of separate steps to be performed in sequence. The last step in this stairway was to have Jerry actually "do the thing that couldn't be done," in his case, taking the broker's test. You cannot leap from ground zero to the rooftop in a single bound, unless you are Superman. But you can make it to the top one step at a time. That is how we conquer phobias—by Building A Stairway.

In Jerry's case, we broke down his test phobia into about twenty steps. Some were easier, some harder, but they were all part of the staircase leading to his goal. As his first task, I had Jerry lie down at home and practice Jacobson's relaxation techniques while he softly repeated the word *exam, exam, exam*. He did this until those two syllables no longer sent shivers down his spine. Then we moved on to the next phase. I had him say: "I want to pass that exam." Notice, I had him say that he "wanted to pass" the exam, rather than that he "wanted to take" the exam. The former was what he desired, and the latter was what he feared. And we were accentuating the positive.

When Jerry was comfortable talking about the exam, we moved on to the next step. He put on his coat and walked to the subway that he would have to take to get to the exam. All the while, he was to imagine that he was actually on his way to the real thing. The first time he took this trip, he told me that he thought he was going to vomit. But he kept repeating the trip until it began to feel natural. He was practicing. He was gaining a skill as we do by repeating anything long enough. It is difficult to feel stark terror the tenth time that we have done something we feared—and realize that no dreadful consequences ensue.

In the meantime, I had Jerry buy a manual of practice tests from a bookstore and take these samples, night after night, again imagining that he was doing the real thing. As Jerry practiced these various tasks, he was, in effect, traveling the same paths, over and over again, through the forest of his fears until the forest no longer held any terror for him. As I say, Jerry was intelligent— and highly motivated. Over several months, he climbed that stairway of tasks until he was comfortable at each succeeding step. As you might have guessed, he took the test and passed with colors flying. Today he is a success- ful stockbroker—and works in the front office of the same firm where not long ago he was a clerk in the back room.

What I did with Jerry is standard treatment for pho- bias. Take the phobia and break it down into its subfears; then Build A Stairway of ascending tasks leading to ulti- mate conquest of the phobia. Have the patient begin that climb gradually, slowly, not moving on to the next step until he or she is completely comfortable with the pre- ceding step. Up and up the person moves until familiarity has banished all fear and he or she can do the thing once dreaded.

Phobia treatment, along with everything else, seems to have entered the age of specialization. For a common phobia, such as fear of flying, I refer my patients to a program called Travel and Fly Without Fear, conducted at La Guardia Airport. With some of my phobia patients, however, I have to start the stairway of tasks even earlier. As one patient put it: "I start to get nervous about flying when I call the travel agency." Another one told me: "I break out in a cold sweat just telling a cabdriver to take me to JFK." But once we are over these hurdles—through the step-by-step stairway technique— then the clinic takes over.

At a flying-phobia clinic, fearful flyers may spend one session just walking aboard the airplane, sitting down, and buckling up. They do these things until they no longer seem like death-defying acts. Next, a pilot may take them up to the cockpit and explain the instrument panel and just what flying is all about. Frightened flyers learn about the relative safety of air travel compared to other forms of transportation. They learn, for example, that when they drive home from the airport in a car, they are statistically in far more danger than they are on an airplane.

In another session, the pilot may actually start the engines; and in another, taxi down the runway several times, without taking off. Step by step, our white-knuckled flyers climb the stairway. The small steps lead up, finally, to the big one—one day they are airborne. And more often than not, they are flying without fear, since flying-phobia clinics have been shown to work. The program at La Guardia reports a success rate of 90 percent.

Of course, it is best to overcome a phobia in a professional setting like the flying-phobia clinic. Having dealt with a problem in thousands of other cases, the professionals have the cure down to a science. Also, there is psychological comfort in numbers. We feel better when we know that we are not alone in our terror, that we are not some sort of freak. Other quite normal people share the same unreasoning fears as we do.

Besides clinics, therapists can help. We can help you break down the phobia into its parts and help build that stairway leading to the conquest of your bugaboo. As I did with Lenore T., who was driving herself crazy with her phobia. Lenore made countless useless trips back to her house and had ruined whole vacations because of her particular fear. Lenore was always afraid that she had left her door unlocked, or had forgotten to unplug the iron, or had not turned on the answering machine. No sooner would she be out of sight of her house—to go to the supermarket or on a European vacation—than the anxiety would set in. She was always driving back home to check her gas jets or lock the windows. She was forever calling neighbors from London or Rome to make sure her front door was locked.

It emerged in the course of our conversations that Lenore had led an overprotected childhood. She had been the pampered darling of parents who convinced her that they would always smooth out the bumps in the road of life for her. All that Lenore had to do was sit there and be their beautiful little doll. The unspoken message was that a pretty little doll did not have the sense to take care of herself. And Lenore grew up believing that. I worked with Lenore on two levels. First, I had her Replay The Tape of remembered conversations with her parents. I also had her apply To You-ness To Me-ness to these replays. Here is one conversation that she remembered:

LENORE (age 12): I don't want a baby-sitter anymore. I'm embarrassed. Betty's only two years older than me anyway.

MOTHER: How would Mommy and Daddy feel if anything happened to our precious angel? Besides, we're just going out to dinner with the Frenches. It's only for a couple of hours. Just look at it as though Betty's a friend coming over to visit you.

LENORE: Then how come you're paying her?

Replayed Tape Version:

MOTHER: Betty is coming over to sit with you while Dad and I go out to dinner with the Frenches.

LENORE: Mom, *to you* I'm not old enough to spend three hours by myself. But *to me*, I've got to begin growing up. Someday I will have to look after myself and it would be useful if you could help me to start learning how.

255

In rethinking her past experiences with her mother through these new words, Lenore was making herself aware of the dependence that had been bred into her as a child. And this awareness of past dependence now motivated her to want to become more independent, more responsible for herself as an adult.

Besides Replaying The Tape, I taught Lenore a behavior modification technique for dealing with her particular phobia. I told her to draw up a check-off list whenever she was going away. The list would contain items like: "Gas jets off; Burglar alarm set; Doors locked." As she performed each task, she was to check it off. I told her to bring the list with her. Then, whenever she started getting panicky, she could look at those check marks and feel reassured that she had done what needed to be done. I also had Lenore imprint each task on her memory as she was doing it, saying aloud: "There, I am unplugging the iron. I feel the plug in my hand. I am locking the front door. I just heard the lock click." After a while, between the checklist and the mental training, Lenore lost her fear of forgetfulness that had plagued so many of her short trips and longer journeys away from home.

For my patient with the growth on her shoulder and the phobia about scars, I again proceeded on the stairway principle. I set up an ascending order of tasks that culminated in a preliminary talk with a surgeon who could perform the operation. During this visit, he showed her a number of "before and after" photographs of operations that he had performed. And, I must say, the man was an artist. The scars were virtually invisible. I was particularly pleased with our success in overcoming this patient's phobia because the growth that the doctor removed proved to be malignant, and it was removed in time.

Frankly, phobias are usually so deeply embedded that they may be difficult to root out by yourself. But, if your particular phobia is not too serious and causes you more inconvenience than paralysis, you may want to try to overcome it yourself, before seeking professional help. Try, as I said, to see the thing you fear as a series of steps. Build your own stairway of tasks. And then start the climb. Leave step one when it no longer stirs up butterflies in your stomach. Then repeat step two until you are comfortable doing it, and so on, until you are doing the thing that couldn't be done.

But if the phobia is serious and beyond your handling, ask your local mental-health service to help you find a phobia clinic or a therapist who specializes in these problems.

LESS THAN MAGNIFICENT OBSESSIONS

Othello was destroyed by an obsession. He allowed Iago to plant the seed of doubt in his mind about Desdemona's faithfulness. The seed grew into an all-consuming obsession. Othello was driven to murder his innocent wife, the thing he loved above all else on earth.

Obsessing is a harmful emotional habit. It magnifies a person, a thing, an experience out of all proportion and destroys our judgment in the process. I have patients who obsess over someone who "done 'em wrong"— a friend, a co-worker, a boss. The obsession occupies a ridiculous part of their waking hours. It grows like a giant hogweed, taking over the brain and driving out healthy thoughts. People become obsessed with guilt. Night and day, they chew on some wrong—real or imaginary— that they committed against someone else. In extreme cases, people will give over their entire lives to a failed love affair, as in the song describing the insane obsession of Delta Dawn. Listen to these patients from my "obsession" file:

257

FRED R., an insurance executive: "I know somebody stabbed me in the back at the home office. I know that's why I missed out on the vice presidency. I go to bed at night thinking about who did it. I wake up in the morning and start all over again. I haven't thought about anything else for a year."

AUDREY S., a housewife: "I've relived the accident a thousand times. That little boy just ran out from between those parked cars. Everybody says it wasn't my fault. But I can never erase that horrible picture from my mind. It seems I spend my whole life dwelling on it."

MARIAN A., a market researcher: "He betrayed me. He exploited me. I went to this psychiatrist for help—and instead he abused me sexually. I finally had a nervous breakdown. It was two years ago, and I still can't stop thinking about it."

I have treated patients with every sort of fixation. But Marian A.'s case is typical of a large share of women whose emotional bad habit is an obsession with a man. So, let's consider this problem.

Often, the obsession starts off healthy enough. A woman falls in love with a man. She thinks about him constantly. She fantasizes about him. Her daydreams make her happy. But then, as time passes, a dark shadow starts to invade her thoughts. The romantic daydreams begin to turn into an all-consuming obsession. Instead of, "Won't it be lovely, Hal and I honeymooning in Ischia," it becomes, "What if Hal leaves me! I would die without him!" A married patient tells me that she calls her husband's office four and five times a day. She cannot stop herself. She knows that the calls infuriate him. And she knows that she has made a fool of herself before his secretary. And she knows why she really keeps making these calls, no matter what flimsy excuses she gives. She is "checking up on him." When he is gone for a two-hour lunch or comes home late, she is terrified. She becomes obsessed, torturing herself with suspicions. He must be having an orgy with that nubile receptionist, or carrying on a torrid affair with that brazen woman in public relations. She went into a panic the day her husband slipped a comb into his breast pocket. He had never done that before! What was going to happen that day to muss up his hair? Here was a grown woman driving herself crazy for an entire day over a comb in her husband's pocket. What real evidence does she have to justify her obsession? Her overreaction.

Another problem with obsessions relating to matters of the heart is that they are usually one-sided. Let's take the woman who daydreams obsessively about romantic flights of fancy with a particular man. Her obsession becomes more real to her than her daily life. But, often, she is living out a script, without ever giving a copy to the man. He has no idea of her fantasies. If he knew, one of two things might happen. He might start to enter into the script if he shared her feelings, and help make her fantasies come real. Or he might warn her that she had picked the wrong leading man. He may not share her feelings. And she is setting herself up for hurt and disappointment. This truth—hard as it may be to accept—may mark the beginning of a cure of her obsession.

Now let's get back to Marian A.'s obsession. Marian is the woman who believed that she had been sexually exploited by her psychiatrist. Marian was a smart, outwardly confident woman of thirty-five, and a success in her field, market research. She was also tall, dark-haired, and striking. You would more likely imagine men obsessing about Marian than the other way around.

But Marian had serious problems in her sexual relationships with men. She had gone to see a psychiatrist for that reason. Unfortunately, the man took advantage of her: "He'd ask me to sit on his lap! He'd fondle my breasts. He ran his hand up my skirt!" she told me.

259

Nevertheless, she did not stop seeing this man. Instead, Marian became his willing pawn. She was so wrapped up in her psychiatrist that she brought him a present every time she went in for a session. She became virtually an unpaid volunteer, going to the library and getting books for him, catching up on his filing, running office errands. And, in the meantime, he was billing her regularly for her "therapy." Finally he tired of her obsessive attachment to him and tried to fob Marian off on another psychiatrist. His rejection of her triggered Marian's nervous breakdown. Shortly afterward, she came to see me.

She was still obsessing about her psychiatrist night and day. She would work herself into a fit in my office telling me about him, about sitting on his lap, the fondled breasts, the hand up the skirt.

In time, I understood the root of Marian's unhappiness. Nothing had happened! Her slavish devotion, the man's fumbling sexual advances, had all led to nothing. She realized that she was not going to become his wife. She never even became his mistress, and, most shattering of all, in the end he got rid of her. And so Marian had her breakdown. She continued to dwell on this man and his abuse of her throughout almost all her waking hours. The quality of her work at the market research firm was suffering. If Marian had to answer a question on a form asking "occupation," the most honest answer would have been: "Thinking about Dr. M."

Erroneous thinking lies at the heart of virtually every emotional bad habit we have. When we become obsessive about a person or a situation, we are engaged in erroneous thinking. In obsessions, the error is one of distortion. We magnify the object of our obsession out of all proportion. The emotional tail starts wagging the dog. And the first step toward breaking this emotional bad habit is to get the object of our obsession back to normal size.

Let's take Marian's case. Whenever we talked, it was

always, "Dr. M. said this . . . Dr. M. said that." The very word *doctor* gave this person a certain undeserved power and authority in her mind. Certain words—particularly titles—do carry psychological weight: Doctor, Mother, Father, Reverend, General. And sometimes the title gets in the way of our judging the individual clearly as a human being.

I told Marian: "Your Dr. M. is a very foolish man. He certainly behaved stupidly for a practicing psychiatrist. What he did was both unethical and unprofessional. It could cost him his license, if you want to pursue it. But let's get our charges straight. The man may have been a fool. But I doubt if he consciously set out to torment you and drive you to a nervous collapse. He was just a stupid and short-sighted person who abused a relationship of professional trust. So let's not get too carried away by this 'doctor' business." I asked Marian what the psychiatrist's first name was. "William," she told me. "All right," I said, "here we have a psychiatrist who risked his professional standing and who hurt a patient by his mistakes. So from now on, when we talk about him, he won't be Dr. M. He is henceforth 'Little Willie.' "

Marian brightened immediately. "Little Willie," she kept saying with a sly smile. "Yes, I like that. Little Willie—the little worm!" Already Dr. M. seemed less worthy of her twenty-four-hour-a-day obsessions. It is not so easy to become obsessive about someone whom we have knocked off a pedestal and who is standing in front of us with his dandruff showing.

The business of first names and nicknames is interesting. Very often I have found that when grown children have to look after their aging parents, they will almost unconsciously start using the parent's first name ("Come on, Mildred, it's time for bed." "No, you don't, Earl. No more cigars for you today.") What has happened is that the reversal of roles has broken the old lines of authority. There may be some benefit to this approach. Using first names (or thinking of a person in terms of his or her first name) is a way to fix our attention on the individual rather than on his or her stereotyped role. And there are times when we have to judge and deal with individuals, not their "position." Titles—Mother, Doctor, Professor, Reverend—all carry a certain authority and can influence our perceptions. We may find ourselves intimidated by the title rather than perceiving the actual person. And thinking of them in terms of their first names can help to put them into perspective. Marian's psychiatrist had certainly forfeited his right to the reverence in which she held him. And "Little Willie" helped her cut him down to size.

I had Marian do something else that I recommend for patients whose ball and chain is an obsession with a member of the opposite sex. Draw up a balance sheet. On one side, write down all of the person's virtues. Assign the virtue a grade from 1 to 10 (Honesty, plus 9; Good Lover, plus 7; Sense of Humor, plus 5; and so on). Then on the other side, list and grade their failings (Liar, minus 10; Whiner, minus 6; Bad Dresser, minus 1). When the evaluation is complete, come up with a final grade. Obviously, what I am doing is helping my obsessed patients to dethrone the objects of their obsession, to cut them down to human scale and restore them to realistic proportions. It is an exercise in making molehills out of molehills.

There are other techniques useful for breaking the bad habit of obsessing.

DISPLACEMENT

Do something that puts demands on your mind, something that requires thought. In other words, force your brain to switch its power from the subject of your obsession to another task. Start those guitar lessons that you've been talking about. Write to all those friends to whom you owe letters. Immerse yourself in a good book. I remember once visiting a friend and admiring a beautiful bookcase. He told me that he had made it himself to get a disastrous love affair off his mind. All this had happened over thirty years before. And I couldn't help thinking that here was this beautiful object, born out of my friend's pain, and still giving use and pleasure three decades later. He had turned his negative obsession around and rechanneled the energy to a positive, creative end.

A FRIENDLY EAR

If you are lying in bed, unable to sleep because you are chewing on your obsessional cud, you might call a friend—assuming it is not too late. Talk about what is bothering you. Your friend will not necessarily have an answer. But just talking the matter out—hearing yourself say the words—may show you how you've magnified the issue. The talking can put it all into perspective. And talking to a friend dispels the idea that you are all alone in wrestling with your demons.

I find that the above advice is far easier for women to follow than men. Women are less reluctant to bare their feelings, fears, and failures to each other. They take it all as a natural part of the pain of life. To men, however, such confessions smack of weakness. That is too bad. For no one is our friend until we can reveal ourselves to them as we genuinely are.

THE STATUTE OF LIMITATIONS

By imposing the Statute of Limitations, we can also help break the habit of obsession. Let's say you find yourself starting to obsess about *him* again. Or you are drifting into that angry obsession over the way the boss treats you. Or you start to feel that obsessive old guilt again about what you said to your sister two years ago. Put a time limit on the obsession. Impose the Statute of Limitations. Say to yourself: "All right, today the obsession gets fifteen uninterrupted minutes. No phone calls, no distractions. I am allowing fifteen minutes for pure unadulterated obsessing. Then, I'll ring down the curtain. Time's up. Time to move on—to the tennis club, to catch up on my work, or to get the car washed. The Statute of Limitations has run out."

We can look at an obsession as a balloon inside of our mind. We have blown it up to ridiculous proportions, and as a result, it is taking up far more space than it deserves. It is crowding out other matters that we should be thinking about. What do we do? We have to let the air out of the obsession and get it down to proper size.

SUMMING UP

What do we know about and how do we deal with phobias and obsessions?

- Phobias do not yield to reason. They may be foolish fears to others, but to the phobic, they are all too real.

- To deal with a phobia, we need to break it down into its components and then set up those components as tasks to be mastered, one at a time—Building a Stairway. We move to step two only after we are completely comfortable performing step one, and so on.

- If the phobia is serious enough, we will probably need professional help from a phobia clinic or a therapist who works with phobic patients.

- Obsessions give things and people unwarranted importance in our lives and thus warp our judgment. One way to cut authority figures who obsess us down to size is to think of them in terms of their first names, or nicknames—the "Little Willie" treatment.

- Let the obsession wither of neglect. Find positive distractions to occupy the mind and crowd out the obsession.

- Call on or call up friends when you are being obsessive over something or someone. Friends can help you put the obsession into better perspective—or at least distract you from it for a time.

- Place a Statute of Limitations on the time that you will allow yourself to obsess.

Chapter 17

THE LAST WORD

Often when I am working with my patients to help them overcome their negative emotional habits, I find myself thinking of Yvette. Remember her, the dancer in chapter 1? Yvette was virtually destroying her career because of her addiction to rejection, her low self-esteem, her Impostor Syndrome. I had told Yvette that she was trying to dance with an albatross slung around her neck. And it couldn't be done. Her negative emotional habits were her albatross. My job is to help my patients and students to see their emotional habits as hindrances to living, and then to show them how to go about casting off these hindrances, how to free themselves from their addictions.

I may have risked my standing in the therapists' union by freely confessing that we have no black magic, no trade secrets for arriving at this objective. Our best therapy is a patient who has made up his or her mind to change. That attitude is half the battle. As I have said repeatedly, emotional bad habits are rooted in incorrect thinking, misperceptions, and distorted attitudes. What the therapist does is to help *you* straighten out *your* thinking. We try to lead you to find your solution, since it is not in our power to hand you one. When you correct the errors in your thinking, you will likely throw off the albatross.

I have also stated my deep conviction that our negative emotional habits are not entirely of our own making. We are born and raised in an environment that virtually teaches us guilt, fear of rejection, self-flagellation, helplessness (for women), and other negative responses to life. We have been *conditioned* to feel bad. Our culture's deeply embedded *do*s and *don't*s, the *supposed-to*s and *must-not*s were there long before we arrived. They rob us of independent thought. And they are like a virus passed on from generation to generation, perpetuating negative thinking and behavior.

But all this is by way of explanation of—and not an excuse for—the persistence of negative emotional habits in our lives. While we cannot singlehandedly change the culture we inherited, we *can* change our attitudes toward it. We do not have to accept the dictatorship of outworn, useless, irrelevant cultural claptrap. We can create our own social environment—one that is not ruled by pernicious and clichéd thinking. Our ability to change ourselves and our environment is the real message of this book. Summing up that message in a nutshell:

- We are not locked into or doomed forever by our chronic negative behavior.

- Our negative responses, more often than not, are *habits* that we have come to look upon as inevitable parts of our personalities.

- Much of our negative behavior is the result of our bowing to cultural clichés.

- *We can change.* We can break our negative emotional habits. We are not stuck with them for life.

As I said in the introduction, there are obviously people whose emotional disorders are too deep to be dealt with

267

by reading this book. They require treatment by mental-health professionals. But the vast majority of us, plagued by negative emotional habits, can do a great deal to break those habits ourselves.

In these chapters you have met my patients and students who did change. I hope that you will come to look at them as old friends who have traveled down the same rough road as you may be traveling now. They suffered from the same emotional bad habits that may be crippling your life.

Remember Ellen, sunk in low self-esteem, afraid to break out of a marriage of mutual entrapment with the pathological and suicidal Bill? Remember Claude W., whose promising acting career was stagnating because he was suffering from Perfection Paralysis? Remember Estelle P., a classic victim of social clichés? Estelle gave over her entire life to being a wife to her husband, a mother to her children, and a baby-sitter to her mother-in-law—because her husband convinced her that that was all she was *supposed to* be. (But where was it written?) There was Leonard, the unemployed geologist with his can of worms, afraid to get close to people for fear "they might die." There was Denise C., who had branded herself a "reject," committing social suicide rather than risk rejection. Remember Ed Z., the author, still flagellating himself mercilessly for everything that went wrong in his life? There was Vicki, overcoming a lifelong inferiority complex foisted on her by a jealous older sister. And remember the people we met suffering from the Impostor Syndrome? From the famous—Marilyn Monroe and Richard Burton—to the guy next door, Abe T., a workaholic who was destroying his marriage because he thought he had to keep proving himself on the job.

You now know the techniques that these and others used to change their negative habits. You know how they shed their insecurity blankets and stopped playing those losing games. You learned about The Three Windows of

Perception that helped Mary Ann McC. understand that there were many possible reasons—besides her being "a reject"—why the man at the party may have gone off with that other woman; and Broken Record, which Leonard mastered to make himself more assertive, and which first worked for him at the camera shop; and To You-ness To Me-ness, which Inez G. used to get her boss to stop harassing her—and that Loretta used to end the guilt that her crippled father was dumping on her; and Talk Tenderly To Yourself, through which I myself broke the rejectee habit and stopped making myself miserable for being "too tall"; and Replaying The Tape, which helped Ruth B. to understand that her mother was unfairly ignoring Ruth's career successes while gushing over her other daughter's marriage; and Keeping a Notebook, which helped the ex-cover girl, Dolores R., figure out that her chronic anxiety stemmed from her fear of aging; and Casting, through which Jessica R., still obsessed by a man who had left her long ago, imagined how the admirable Bernice would deal with such a situation; and Building The Stairway of tasks, which enabled Jerry K. to overcome his phobia about taking tests; and Giving Predictability about ourselves, through which my friend Doris G. cued her husband, Russell, that she was not available for his attention-getting suicide threats; and Send It to the Front Office, which taught hotheaded Luis to deal with his anger at the cerebrum (the front office) instead of at the thalamus (the seat of the emotions); and the Statute of Limitations, which helped Larry, the Vietnam vet, recognize that it was time to get out of his chronic depression and get on with his life; and Undependence, which has helped so many of my women patients to free themselves from the bad habit of believing, "I am nothing without a man."

You learned about Emotional Displacement for crowding out anxiety and depression through plain old physical exercise and mental diversions. And the Emotional Re-

hearsal, which teaches us to anticipate all potential outcomes of a situation, so that we are not knocked flat by
an unexpected outcome. We learned how to start forming
our Column of Confidence, the right posture with which
to face the world. We learned that revenge fantasies are
harmless, while real revenge can be a two-edged sword.

Remember the symptoms of the negative-prone personality we described back in chapter 1? The Center of
the Universe Syndrome? We learned not to assume that a
seeming rejection, a hasty word, a frown from someone
else is always our fault. Everybody is not always reacting
to us. People have their own problems. We are not the
center of everyone else's emotional solar system. The
flaw detector? We learned to turn it off so that we are not
obsessed with finding what's wrong with our relationships, our reactions, our experiences, and thus miss
what is right. And the tribulations of Job? We learned to
abandon the unreasonable conviction that of 6 billion
mortals on earth, the deities have somehow conspired to
get "me." And the Mathematics of Guaranteed Unhappiness? We learned to drop it for the saner math of putting
the good and bad of our lives into sensible proportion.
Remember the feeling of being trapped in the wrong
lane? We learned that we are not doomed forever to stay
on that road. Our life is not a one-way street. We can
change direction. And finally, Unanswerable Questions.
We learned that it is futile to torture ourselves asking
Why? Why? Why? about matters that are in the past and,
indeed, cannot be changed, or for which a cause cannot
be found.

These, and all the other techniques we covered, are the
keys to the shackles—the emotional bad habits that may be
hobbling our lives. Guilt? We learned that you can exchange it for a clear conscience. Rejection? You can
learn to risk rejection instead of run away from it and
thus commit social suicide. Anxiety? You can trade it in
for peace of mind. Anger? You can abandon it for inner

calm. Depression? You can switch it to a hopeful outlook. Low self-esteem? You can supplant it with self-confidence. Hysteria? You can replace it with cool-headedness. The Impostor Syndrome? You can drop it in favor of genuine pride in your achievements. And so on, down through the whole catalog of negative emotional habits.

Will you succeed overnight? Because you tried once? Because you read a book? And even if you do succeed for a time, will you never slide back? The truth is that breaking our emotional bad habits is often a game of two steps forward, one step back. You will experience setbacks. There are plenty of repeat customers in my business, believe me. Larry U. came to me after being depression-free for eighteen months and said: "I'm down in the black hole again. I failed." "No, Larry," I said, "you did not fail. You conquered your depression for a year and a half. And you will do it again, because you proved you can do it. When do you want to start?" He was not perfect. None of us are. Larry tried, succeeded, suffered reverses, and tried again. But the inspiring part is that the overwhelming majority of people who have come to me suffering from negative emotional habits have managed to break them by using the techniques I have described here.

Our negative emotions. Albatrosses? Without a doubt. Insecurity blankets? They certainly are. Losing games? Indeed. But these are burdens that we don't have to lug around for life. We can cast them off. These are insecurity blankets we don't have to carry. We can shed them. These are losing games that we do not have to play. We can end them. My fervent hope in writing this book has been that while your reading it may not mark the end of your negative emotional habit, it will mark the beginning of the end. My hope is that somewhere in these pages you will have found the way to break your emotional bad habits and will have learned how to be happier.

ANNOTATED BIBLIOGRAPHY

The following books are helpful in learning to appreciate yourself and to treat yourself with tender loving care. In various ways, they all foster an awareness of cultural edicts that result in learned emotional habits. These books also give suggestions and exercises designed to free you from unwanted emotional habits.

Burns, David D., M.D. *Feeling Good.* New York: Signet, 1981. One of the best books on understanding depression and what to do about it.

Citrenbaum, Charles, Mark King, and William Cohen. *Modern Clinical Hypnosis for Habit Control.* New York: W. W. Norton, 1985.

Clance, Pauline Rose, M.D. *The Imposter Phenomenon: When Success Makes You Feel Like a Fake.* New York: Bantam, 1985. This book deals with the feeling of inferiority that prevents the enjoyment of success because "me as a success just isn't credible. It must be a mistake."

Clanton, Gordon, and Lynn Smith. *Jealousy.* New York: Prentice-Hall, 1977.

Ellis, Albert, M.D., and Irving Becker, M.D. *A Guide to Personal Happiness.* New York: Wilshire, 1982.

Fagan, Joen, and Irma Lee Shepherd, editors. *Gestalt Therapy Now.* Palo Alto: Science and Behavior Books, 1970.

Halpern, Howard M., Ph.D. *Cutting Loose.* New York: Bantam, 1978. This insightful book helps you free yourself from guilt feelings in one of the tightest bondings.

Hodge, Marshall Bryant. *Your Fear of Love.* New York: Doubleday, 1967. A hard book to find, but one of the best books on understanding the fear of love.

Jeffers, Susan, Ph.D. *Feel the Fear and Do It Anyway.* New York: Harcourt Brace Jovanovich, 1987. Although I do not agree with some of the suggestions in the book, the title is brilliant and in keeping with the concept that fear is often a breakable habit.

Knaus, William J., M.D. *How to Get Out of a Rut.* New York: Prentice-Hall, 1982.

Lerner, Harriet Goldhor, Ph.D. *The Dance of Anger.* New York: Harper and Row, 1985. Written primarily for women, this book makes women aware of the causes of their frustration and offers suggestions on what to do about the anger. Men, too, can learn a great deal from this book.

Naifeh, Steven, and Gregory W. Smith. *Why Can't Men Open Up?* New York: Clarkson N. Potter, 1984. This book is a masterpiece in understanding men's fear of intimacy and what can be done to help.

Novak, William. *The Great American Man Shortage and Other Roadblocks to Romance.* New York: Rawson Associates, 1983. This helps women relax their desperate search for a man and offers some tips on dealing with the painful situation.

Russianoff, Penelope, Ph.D. *Why Do I Think I Am Nothing Without a Man?* New York: Bantam, 1982. This book helps women see that they do not need to be validated by a man in order to be an acceptable person. It is designed to help women free themselves from culturally imposed gender roles and to learn how to develop inner security.

Seligman, Martin E.P. *Helplessness: On Depression, Development and Death.* San Francisco: W. H. Freeman, 1979.

Shostrom, Everett L. *Man the Manipulator.* New York: Bantam, 1978. This book helps you identify your own manipulations and to become aware when you are the target of others' manipulations.

Smith, Manuel J., Ph.D. *Kicking the Fear Habit: Using Your Automatic Orienting Reflex to Unlearn Your Anxieties, Fears and Phobias.* New York: Dial Press, 1977.

————. *When I Say No I Feel Guilty.* New York: Dial Press, 1975. This book is one of the best on assertiveness training, a discipline that is fairly easy to learn, and gives you language to use in situations where you are bound to guilt and other negative emotions by the culture.

Viorst, Judith. *Necessary Losses.* New York: Simon and Schuster, 1986. Written with compassion, this book helps you understand that you have to let go of guilt and mourning, when it is time to "give up in order to grow," and so on.

DEVELOPING SELF-ACCEPTANCE AND SELF-CONFIDENCE

Bolles, Richard Nelson. *What Color Is Your Parachute?: A Practical Manual For Job Hunters and Career Changers.* New York: Ten Speed Press, reprinted yearly.

Coudert, Jo. *Advice From a Failure.* New York: Stein

and Day, 1965. This book tells how to deal with yourself and others.

Freedman, Jonathan. *Happy People, What Happiness Is, Who Has It, and Why.* New York: Harcourt Brace Jovanovich, 1978.

Freedman, Rita. *Beauty Bound: Why We Pursue the Myth in the Mirror.* New York: Lexington, 1985. This helps you to enhance who you are, without getting obsessed with looks and feeling inferior about flaws.

Friedman, Sonya. *Men Are Just Desserts.* New York: Warner, 1983.

————. *Smart Cookies Don't Crumble: A Modern Woman's Guide to Living & Loving Her Own Life.* New York: Putnam, 1985.

Gallwey, Timothy W. *The Inner Game of Tennis.* New York: Random House, 1974. Substitute whatever you want for "tennis." Application of Zen to a skill like sex, courtship, friendship, and so on.

Lazarus, Arnold, Ph.D. *In the Mind's Eye.* New York: Guilford Press, 1984. This book suggests having a trial run of future dialogues and experiences before they occur, so that you can imagine and deal with them in fantasy, and be somewhat prepared for the real event.

Pogrebin, Letty Cottin. *Among Friends.* New York: McGraw-Hill, 1987. Learning to have strong, loving, caring platonic relationships with friends who mutually help each other in emotional crises, in addition to mutual enjoyment of life; a valuable part of growing and feeling good.

————. *Growing Up Free.* New York: Bantam, 1981. I use this book with students and patients to diagnose their own childhood, in terms of gender roles and other culturally prescribed behavior. Once aware of the indoctrination, it is easier to become free of its personality-stifling consequences.

Sanford, Linda Tschirhart, and Mary Ellen Donovan. *Women and Self-Esteem.* New York: Penguin, 1984.

Zilbergeld, Bernie Ph.D., and Arnold A. Lazarus, Ph.D. *Mind Power.* Boston: Little, Brown, 1987.

OVERCOMING MALE/FEMALE RELATIONSHIP ANXIETY

Bessell, Harold, Ph.D. *The Love Test.* New York: William Morrow, 1984. This book has a diagnostic questionnaire for lovers that is thought-provoking and helps in self-understanding.

Cowan, Connell, M.D., and Melvyn Kinder, M.D. *Smart Women, Foolish Choices: Finding the Right Men, Avoiding the Wrong Ones.* New York: Clarkson N. Potter, 1985. This book has some good insights into attitudes women have toward themselves, men, and relationships. A tape that goes with the book is also available. It is an audio program titled *Smart Women, Smart Choices* and is designed to help the reader move from negative feelings about self toward self-confidence.

Halpern, Howard. *How to Break Your Addiction to Another Person.* New York: Bantam, 1983.

Hite, Shere. *Women and Love: A Cultural Revolution in Progress.* New York: Knopf, 1987. Overlook the statistical controversy of her survey, and turn to the Table of Contents, which is extremely thought-provoking. Many of the direct quotes from women respondents will interest you.

Sills, Judith, Ph.D. *A Fine Romance: The Psychology of Successful Courtship, Making It Work for You.* New York: St. Martin's Press, 1987. This is the best book I've read on the analysis of courtship procedure, from both the male and female viewpoints. Many people find the courtship procedure a situation in which the "right" moves are unfamiliar. Judith Sills gives you your bearings, is understanding, and pilots you along. Her observations and wisdom are comforting to the jangled, anxious participant in courtship.

Tannen, Deborah, Ph.D. *That's Not What I Meant!: How Conversational Styles Make or Break Relationships.* New York: Ballantine, 1986. This book develops an awareness of the values and pitfalls of communication.

OVERCOMING SEXUAL ANXIETY

Barbach, Lonnie, and Linda Levure. *Shared Intimacies.* New York: Doubleday, 1980. This is an excellent book about lovemaking.

Barbach, Lonnie. *For Yourself.* New York: Doubleday, 1975. This book is about the fulfillment of female sexuality, including the case for masturbation and sexual fulfillment for women.

Comfort, Alex, M.D., Ph.D. *The Joy of Sex.* New York: Crown, 1972. A delightful classic; try to get the illustrated edition.

Hajcak, Frank, Ph.D., and Patricia M. S. Garwood. *Hidden Bedroom Partners.* New York: Libra, 1987. This book examines the needs and motives that destroy sexual pleasure.

Meshorer, Judith and Mark. *Ultimate Pleasure.* New York: St. Martin's Press, 1986. This book reveals the secrets of women who achieve orgasms easily.

Silbergeld, Bernard. *Male Sexuality.* New York: Bantam, 1981. A great book for men and women on a little-understood topic.

UNDERSTANDING MALE
PERSONALITY SYNDROMES

There are several books that identify male personality syndromes that, once diagnosed properly, help a woman cope differently with a man. These same syndromes can be present in women also.

Carter, Steven, and Julia Sokol. *Men Who Can't Love: When a Man's Fear Makes Him Run from Commitment.* New York: M. Evans, 1987.

Forward, Susan, and Joan Torres. *Men Who Hate Women and the Women Who Love Them.* New York: Bantam, 1986. This book explores "misogyny," or the hatred of women.

Norwood, Robin. *Women Who Love Too Much: When You Keep Wishing and Hoping He'll Change.* New York: Pocket Books, 1986.

Index

—■—

Other CEDAR titles . . .

*For further information on how to obtain Cedar books,
please contact the publisher:*

William Heinemann Ltd
Michelin House
81 Fulham Road
London SW3 6RB